RULES

Powerful Policy Wording
to Maximize Engagement

International Edition

Lewis Eisen

pixley
press

COPYRIGHT INFORMATION

H2

CATALOGUING IN PUBLICATION DATA

Eisen, Lewis S., 1957-
        RULES

978-1-988749-13-6 Hardcover
978-1-988749-14-3 Softcover
978-1-9887749-12-9 e-book

1. Business and Economics — Business Communications — General. 2. Business and Economics — Business Writing. 3. Business and Economics — Leadership. 4. Reference — Writing Skills.

DEDICATION

To my mother and father.

RULES: Powerful Policy Wording to Maximize Engagement

"The reason for our success is no secret. It comes down to one single principle that transcends time and geography, religion and culture. It's the Golden Rule – the simple idea that if you treat people well, the way you would like to be treated, they will do the same."

~ Isadore Sharp
Founder, Four Seasons Hotels and Resorts

RULES: Powerful Policy Wording to Maximize Engagement

CONTENTS

Detailed Table of Contents

Part I — Rules in Context

1. The Traditional Approach

Executive Summary   23

2. Evolving Trends

Executive Summary   39

3. The Basics

4. Corporate Culture

5. Stakeholders

6. The Documentation Landscape

7. Policy Governance

8. Enforcement

Part II — Internal Authorities

9. Primary vs Secondary Sources

10. Policies

11. Standards

12. Procedures

13 Breaking Down Silos

Part III — Drafting

14. Drafting Principles

15. Drafting Techniques

16 Must, May, and Should

17. Packaging

18. Terminology Management

Part IV — Values-based Policy

FOREWORD TO THE INTERNATIONAL EDITION

by Bill Morey
Global Information Management, Oracle

My parents should have made "Change" my middle name.

As a toddler I loved climbing inside our kitchen cabinets and rearranging pots and pans in new and imaginative configurations, always pushing my mother's patience to higher limits. In high school, feeding dad raw organic wheat germ as a new power breakfast before his closing arguments in an important murder case had disastrous (and embarrassing) consequences. But I've put my learnings from these experiences, and from my early days as an English composition teacher, to good use in the corporate world, driving change in behavior and culture through projects large and small. It is my life-long passion.

In my 30 years of building peak performance teams that drive world class Information Governance programs at Oracle and other large corporations, the key ingredient for success has been the use of respectful, clear, and positive language in policies, business cases, team interactions, and written communications. It is the magic ingredient that drives this success. Meeting Lewis Eisen in person and reading *RULES* pushes these lessons learned to the next level.

The Covid-19 pandemic, mass-migrations, climate, and other disasters continue to teach us the necessity, as individuals and organizations, for calming, clear directives and positive human interactions to support rapid change. Standing up

Oracle databases in days versus months around the world to pinpoint outbreaks and their epidemiology was but one example of real-life demand for rapid, positive, and effective response. Today's workers, like never before, demand such behaviors, which align their daily tasks with core values focused on making the world a better, safer place for current and future generations.

RULES provides us with the concepts and practical tools for creating positive policies and directives that speak to and amplify our better nature. As world conflicts increase, the demand for these skills and alignment of values will continue to expand. Their use will serve as essential lubricant for enabling positive and rapid human interactions to meet these accelerating demands.

May 2024

FOREWORD

by Carol Ring, FCPA
CEO, Culture Connection

www.carolring.ca
Recognized as one of Canada's
Top 100 Most Powerful Women

For more than 35 years I've been passionate about building high performing teams. I see these teams as a way not only for our businesses to succeed, but also as a path to releasing the full potential of each person in our organization.

As a specialist in company culture transformation, I am always on the lookout for experts whose work can support and complement the creation of workplaces that allow people to do their very best work. And that's how Lewis Eisen came into my life.

We met over coffee at a local Starbucks. I was curious about Lewis's work in the written rule world. Many people believe that culture is all about the behaviors of the leaders and how that sets the tone for the organization. However, tone can also be set by our physical surroundings at work, our reward and recognition programs, and most definitely by internal written communications.

I remember being in Sudbury for a keynote speech presentation. I arrived the night before, checked in at the front desk of my hotel and quickly dropped off my luggage in the room. I was starving, and was looking forward to heading across the street for a bite to eat and a glass of wine.

As I trotted down the stairs, I came across an interesting sign:

> # DO NOT LEAVE ANYTHING
> # IN THIS HALL EVER!
> # INCLUDING GARBAGE –
> # IT IS AN EMERGENCY EXIT ONLY!

Yes, it was written in all caps.

This "rule" made me wonder if it was for staff or for hotel guests? What were people leaving in the stairwell that would cause such a reaction? What type of hotel was I in?

I instantly thought of Lewis and how this business could really use his help.

RULES is not merely a technical guide of how to structure your policies, procedures, or guidelines. It's much deeper than that. In this book you'll learn to dig into the real purpose of the rule you're trying to create and how best to achieve that outcome. After all, there's no point in having a rule if no one follows it.

The command-and-control management style has almost completely disappeared. It's no longer an effective way to lead. But has your written communication evolved as well? As Lewis says, "rules that sound like they were written by angry parents scolding naughty children are no longer appropriate."

I love that phrase! It's no badge of honor to have a thick book of policies. One of my previous employers had a Policy manual that was three binders! No wonder we didn't know what we were supposed to do. Who had time to read and internalize all this information?

Lewis's genius is that he sees the tight correlation between rules and engagement. His *Ladder of Engagement* lens is a critical one to consider if you want to have a high-performing business.

I regularly recommend this book to my clients as part of our work to align the many aspects of their organizations. It is only with alignment that a culture can become great. Your purpose, strategy, brand promise, and culture must all be congruent. And so must your rules.

This book is about writing better rules. But it's really about creating better workplaces so people can do their very best work. Get ready to create a meaningful difference for the people in your organization!

April, 2024

PREFACE

This book is a major revision, hence the formal change of title.

Whereas the first three editions focused on formal Policies, Standards, and Procedures, this edition pulls the lens back to look at the broader landscape. It expands the scope of inquiry to encompass other instances of written rules, such as warnings posted on signs and instructions printed on forms. A number of new topics have been introduced, including some relating to high level management issues, such as the effect of policy wording on corporate culture and the role that organizational values play in maximizing engagement.

Over the years, people have often commented about how my respectful approach to policy drafting is applicable to situations beyond regulatory ones. They point out that the concepts I promote are transferable to specialty fields such as customer service, communications, corporate culture, human resources management, and leadership, to name just a few. Indeed, I can see the overlap and am convinced of the usefulness of this information generally. I recognize the potential for broader impact and I'm grateful for the opportunity to explore these connections further with specialists in those fields.

Readers of previous editions will notice some changes in terminology. For the most part, these changes were prompted by the confusion created by other specialized uses of the original term in some circles.

Approver

In previous editions, the term *policy owner* was used to describe the body accountable for putting the contents of a policy into effect. A number of readers found the term problematic, however, because in their organizations, once the approving body had finished its work, it passed total accountability for the contents down to a lower level. From this perspective, the approval body was no more the **owner** of a policy they had approved than they were of a contract they had signed. To rectify this mis-match, in this edition the term for the person or group approving the rule has been simplified to *approver*.

Toolkit

The term *Toolkit* has replaced the term *Guidance* to refer to the set of documents produced internally by the organization below the Authorities level. The change was made because it was apparent that too many individuals equate the *authorities* vs *guidance* distinction with a *mandatory* vs non-*mandatory* distinction. For those organizations, calling a statement *guidance* is enough in itself to indicate that it is elective.

Those two distinctions are worlds apart, so conflating them is problematic; for example, it leaves no way to describe mandatory rules that are not created by formal policy. To avoid the confusion, however, *Toolkit* is used in the documentation framework in place of *Guidance*.

The examples

As before, you'll note that I collect real-life samples for illustrative purposes. I'm always on the lookout for poorly-drafted rules documents and rudely-worded signs; they make great examples for teaching purposes. If you come across something that's particularly egregious, feel free to send it to me at <leisen@pfx.ca>.

Successes make great stories, too, and I love hearing about them. If what you read in this book leads you to revise any of your current rules documents, feel free to send me "before" and "after" copies.

Most of the examples included in this book are pulled from real instances that have come across my desk. Though I normally like to give credit where credit is due, in this case details that could be used to identify the source organizations have all been hidden to avoid embarrassing anyone. Still, I would like to express my deepest appreciation to those organizations for unknowingly contributing their bad policy statements as shining examples of what not to do. Without them, this book would not have been possible.

Acknowledgments

My appreciation to Murray Whitby of Edmonton, Canada for graciously permitting me to reprint one of his Procedures. While Murray's expertise extends to Policies and Standards, his methodical approach to structuring Procedures is invitingly practical, and complements the principles outlined in this book.

I also extend my appreciation both to Carol Ring, for updating the Foreword she wrote for the previous edition, and to Bill Morey for providing the Foreword to the International Edition. Both colleagues are dedicated to keeping culture at the forefront of their efforts to improve the workplace.

As with all my previous publications, I rely on other people to let me know when my own writing is unclear. Many thanks to my policy colleagues Brenda Platt and Isabelle Bélanger-Brown for helping me refine the sequence of the concepts and for identifying gaps. Thanks also to Joyce Eisen for reviewing the content to keep the overall tone on track. Shari (proofreading.by.shari@gmail.com) did an outstanding job demonstrating her precision with grammar, in addition to applying a keen eye for typographic consistency. Thanks also to Jeanne Martinson of Wood Dragon Books, whose extensive knowledge of book publishing logistics has been invaluable.

Finally, my heartfelt thanks go to everyone who has encouraged me to persevere in advocating for this important topic. Despite the considerable work ahead, your supportive posts on social media and your active promotion of my workshops strengthen my conviction that we are on the right track.

INTRODUCTION

Executive Summary

Aggressive policy language not only casts a negative light on the organization but often fails to achieve its intended effect. Adopting a respectful language approach can improve the effectiveness of our rules. Levels of buy-in are explored by reference to a *Ladder of Engagement* model, extending from *disengagement* at the bottom to *champion* at the top. The chapter concludes with a look at the book's structure and terminology conventions.

The Sign at the Clinic

The straw that broke the camel's back for me one day was posted on the wall of the waiting room in a medical clinic. I've reproduced it in Figure 1.

The approach is startling — perhaps more for its irony than its content.

RUDE AND AGGRESSIVE BEHAVIOR WILL NOT BE TOLERATED

You will be asked to leave. If you do not leave the authorities will be called.

No exceptions.

Figure 1

The clinic, in a bid to deter aggressiveness, uses language that is itself aggressive. More than aggressive, actually: the wording is threatening and dictatorial. It's a stark example of how the tone of our rules can contradict their intended purpose. True, it provides information, but it slaps us sharply across the face while doing it. Even the use of a bright red background is no accident; they want it to jump out at us when we come in the door.

If the sign's tone of voice doesn't seem out of place to you, it's only because those types of declarations are still the norm in many environments. We hear rules that sound like authoritarian commands so frequently that we often don't give the tone a second thought.

Maybe we should.

Shortcomings

This sign, proudly displayed on the wall next to the receptionists, has obviously been placed there in response to a number of past incidents. While the desire to avoid future incidents is understandable, the methodology is problematic.

The wording of this sign suffers from four major shortcomings.

1. It creates a confrontational atmosphere

The wording puts visitors on the defensive from the get-go. Typically, people coming to a medical clinic arrive with a mix of emotions, including anxiety, fear, and apprehension about test results and diagnoses. Instead of being reassuring or having a calming effect, this sign can serve only to aggravate their anxiety. If an individual wasn't feeling apprehensive before walking into the clinic, this sign has the potential to change that quickly. Before we arrive, we may not be aware of a confrontational atmosphere in the clinic, but upon reading this sign we can feel the tension in the air.

2. It airs dirty laundry

The clinic is not doing itself any favors by revealing its history of disorderly conduct. What would have been an internal issue, known only to a select few, is now broadcast publicly. Any negative emotions a patient may be experiencing due to medical issues are now compounded by anxiety around the possibility of being an unwilling witness to an altercation.

Announcing disturbances that the clinic experienced in the past is negative advertising. When I first saw that sign, I wondered if I'd be better off looking for a different clinic, perhaps one where I wouldn't be at risk of becoming an innocent bystander caught in the fray.

3. It is likely ineffective

The instructions are clear as a bell, but will they fall on receptive ears? Consider the patient at the front desk who's about to lose their temper. We can see steam coming out of their ears. Does anyone seriously expect an individual in that condition to stop, read the sign, and then calm down? People in an agitated state tend not to be open to attempts to control their actions through threats.

4. It can damage your brand

Finally—and most serious of all—is the tarnish it needlessly paints on the entire clinic. This sign conveys the impression that everyone working at that location is on high alert, walking around with clenched fists and ready to handle a brawl at the first sign of trouble.

The effect on the organization's branding is palpable. The aggressive wording may have been the choice of a single individual, but everybody at the clinic wears it. Its confrontational tone positions the entire staff — from doctors and nurses to the technicians and office support — under a cloud of animosity. It casts a dark shadow on the kindness, professionalism, and empathy of the people working there by imposing a narrative that may not have involved any of them.

Whether for better or for worse, the tone of our organization's rules reflects directly on each of us individually, even if we personally didn't hold the pen or have any influence on the drafting process.

The toll

It seems paradoxical that someone expects a brusque, antagonistic sign to be able to have a positive influence on anyone's behavior. Instead of accomplishing its objective, the sign

- sets and promotes a confrontational atmosphere
- reveals the clinic's dirty laundry to everyone, and
- paints a disparaging portrait of the people who work there.

At worst, we'll see a set of patients sitting uncomfortably in the waiting room, silently praying that the altercations predicted by the sign will not happen while they are present. At best, the sign will not leave too much of a bad taste in anyone's mouth, and visitors will forget about it quickly enough and eventually ignore it.

Did you catch that? I'll repeat it: **at best, people will forget about the sign and begin to ignore it**. Is that truly what the clinic wants?

Frankly, few people benefit from the sign's wording, outside perhaps of the person who chose it. That individual might have experienced some psychological payoff, along with whoever hung the sign. Maybe that payoff was a sense of smug satisfaction, feeling that they successfully got the upper hand on potential troublemakers.

Typically, policy drafters come to my workshop with a request along these lines: "I'd like you to teach me how to draft my policies so that others **have** to follow them." They are clearly tired of experiencing a low level of engagement, and understandably their impulse is often to try to find a bigger stick.

My response is, "Better than that, I'm going to teach you how to draft your policies so that others **want** to follow them."

Scope of this Book

This book is about how we word *rules*. Whether we write them one at a time to post on a sign or compile them into documents and call them *policies*, *standards*, or *terms and conditions*, at their core they are all simply rules. This book looks at how we express those rules, as well as how we organize, classify, arrange, and convey them.

A *rule*, for the purpose of this book, is any statement intended to govern the behavior of others. By "others" I'm including anyone the rule-maker wants to address. We look at rules directed to all kinds of audiences: employees, customers, members of an association, and the public in general. The concepts apply to all industries, in both the for-profit and not-for-profit sectors. They apply to all operations, both the primary functions of an organization and its corporate support services, including Finance, Human Resources (HR), Information Management (IM), Information Technology (IT), Security, and Facilities.

I take no position on the substantive content of your rules. If you believe a specific rule is required to bring you closer to your objectives, that belief is good enough for me. If you decide that your organization should be eastbound instead of westbound, then I'll head east with you. Discussing the merits of a rule takes us down too many rabbit holes, and since I don't profess to have any subject matter expertise in your field, I'm prepared to defer to your decisions on the content in all cases.

My focus is how we communicate those decisions. Once we decide that everybody is going to head east, how do we turn that into a rule? Poor communications means that we end up dragging some people kicking and screaming, making it an unpleasant or even fractious journey. Even when others have no legal right to refuse, emphasizing that point doesn't build any loyalty points. The goal is to communicate our plans in a way that makes people **want** to come along with us.

The Ladder of Engagement

What exactly is the *maximum engagement* proposed in the subtitle of this book? We don't want to set unrealistically high expectations about what is achievable, but we don't want to set the bar too low, either. The whole purpose of the book is to encourage rule makers to elevate their targets, so what does that look like?

As one might expect, engagement is not a binary *on* or *off* state; instead, it is a spectrum with a wide range of possibilities. The *Ladder of Engagement* can be described as having six rungs, which — going from lowest to highest — can be broadly grouped into *passive engagement* and *active engagement* (see Figure 2).

We'll go through the rungs one at a time.

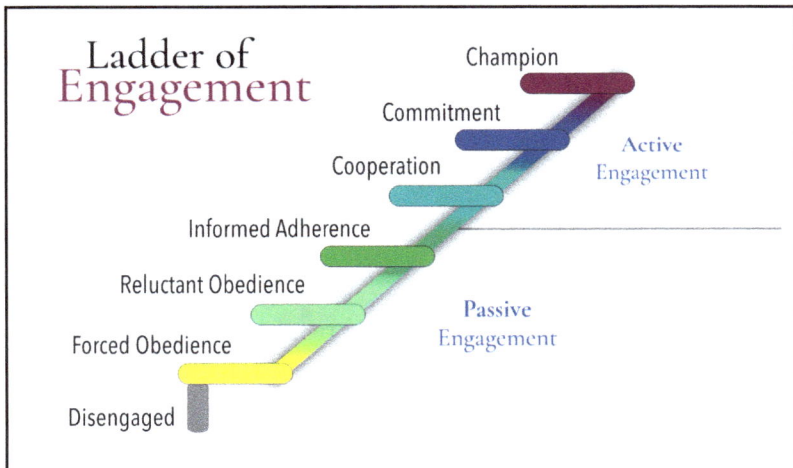

Figure 2

Disengagement

Before we step on up the ladder, we're still standing on the ground. The ground level represents people who are *totally disengaged*. The actions of those individuals are characterized by *overt, intentional non-compliance*.

Totally disengaged individuals make their views known through *deliberate rule-breaking*. While not eager to experience the punishment for that behavior, they're usually not particularly frightened by it, either. Tending to be distrustful of and antagonistic toward authority, these are the people who provoke the most serious disciplinary measures.

If their attitude could be expressed by a slogan on a sweatshirt, it might say *I don't care about your rule and I won't follow it.*

Disengaged employees and customers are uncooperative, sometimes even making life miserable for the rest of us. One could be forgiven for thinking that they cause more trouble than they're worth. If you've wanted to get rid of them for a while, and for some reason you've been holding off until you get my approval, then for whatever it's worth you have it now. Go for it.

Passive engagement

Now that I've taken that group of troublemakers out of the picture, let's start climbing the ladder. The first three rungs are all manifestations of passive engagement in some form. People land on one of these rungs typically in response to a rule-making approach that relies on the threat of punishment as the primary incentive for rule compliance.

In one of the government offices I worked in, a program was under development. Someone asked a senior executive what the plans were for stakeholder consultation around the new policies being proposed to support it. The executive's response was shocking.

"Why should we care whether people support the policies?" she asked. "Don't they have to follow them anyway?"

That executive was clearly content with setting the bar for engagement down at the lowest rung: *forced obedience*. It numbers sixth from the top.

6. Forced obedience

Individuals engaged at a level of forced obedience display clear signs of *active resistance*. People on this rung differ from the disengaged group on the ground by being at least partially compliant. They will follow a rule when it suits their purposes, yet they have no compunction about skirting it whenever they get a chance. Their sweatshirt would say *I don't like your rule and I'm going to try to get around it*.

Employees and customers at this level of engagement generate an undercurrent of toxicity and opposition, which can be detrimental to healthy interpersonal relationships. Forced obedience is only one rung above the disengaged group, and it's not a good place to be stuck.

5. Reluctant Obedience

The individuals on the next rung up are more engaged than the previous group. They tend to be compliant but unhappy. Their conduct can be characterized as *passive resistance*.

This group does follow rules, but they do so in reaction to negative drivers like authority or obligation. Though they may not vocalize their true feelings, their compliance is characterized by minimal effort and subtle deviation from expected norms. Their sweatshirt says *I don't like your rule but I'll follow it if I have to.*

Some organizations believe that this level of engagement is the maximum achievable from their employees and customers. In years past, that was possibly the case. Today, however, it's not a desirable end state and should be the **minimum** acceptable.

4. Informed Adherence

Perched here, on the highest rung of the passive engagement group, we find the individuals who are stoically motivated by duty. They are functional and productive members of the organization, contributing to the assembly line of processes and procedures that mark the daily activities of the enterprise.

These individuals follow the rules but are *not invested* in them. Their sweatshirt slogan says *I may or may not like that rule but it's part of my job.*

Their attitude cannot accurately be characterized as toxic to the workplace, but it's not particularly inspirational, either. Note the change in the slogan from *your rule* to *that rule*, signaling a drop in their personal defenses.

Not surprisingly, many organizations are content to settle for this level. They believe it to be either the best possible or most realistic target, and for them that might be true. In an ironic twist, believing that this is the highest achievable level can be a self-fulfilling prophesy. Certainly, if their rules are worded in the traditional Parent–Child paradigm, they will have a difficult time climbing above the rungs of passive engagement.[1]

I know we can do better.

Active engagement

The next three rungs are manifestations of *active engagement*. At this point, we cross over from a predominantly negative outlook to a predominantly positive one.

3. Cooperation

At the *cooperation* level employees are *moderately invested* in the rules, at least in a professional sense. As a group, they strive to support the organization and its goals. Individually, they are motivated by being a team player, and though at times they might simply be succumbing to peer pressure, in the end they produce positive results.

The slogan on this sweatshirt would be *I follow this rule because I support the organization*. What the lower rung called *that rule* — using distancing language — has become *this rule*, showing the speaker's willingness to be connected. Employees engaged at this level may express an interest in improving the status quo, and they welcome being a part of that process.

---

[1] The terms *Parent–Child* and *Adult–Adult* come from the theory of Transactional Analysis, originally developed by Eric Berne, M.D. Although the science behind his theories has been challenged, these terms are useful descriptors for the dynamics behind the language of policies.

2. Commitment

Moving further up the ladder is the second highest rung, *commitment*. At this level, individuals are firmly supportive of the rules and instances of non-compliance are rare. The rules are consistent with the individual's own strategic approach to how things should be handled, leading to a feeling of personal connection and validation.

Their sweatshirt says *I like our rule because I think it's the right way to do it*. By carrying around this level of engagement, they both contribute to peer motivation and actively encourage others to follow the rule. It's a great level to be at.

But it's not the top rung.

1. Champion

The highest level of engagement describes people who not only adhere to the rules but also *champion* them. They advocate for buy-in on a broad scale, and may believe so strongly in the rules that they promote them both internally and externally.

Their sweatshirt says *I love our rule; every organization should have that same rule*.

Individuals will advocate rules that channel a corporate value when it aligns closely with their personal values. If they've reached this point, their attachment is strong.

The top of the ladder is the best place to be, for both the rule maker and the rule follower.

A Note on Terminology

Policy is a frustratingly ambiguous word in English. At one end of the spectrum, it can be used in the broadest sense possible to refer to an entire political strategy, such as a country's fiscal policy or foreign policy. At the other end, it can be used to refer to one specific rule, such as when a store has a *cash purchases only* policy. In addition, it frequently tends to be the generic term used to describe any formal rules document created by an organization.

To add to the confusion, some industries have adopted the term *policy* for a completely different situation. *Policy* in the insurance world is both a product one can purchase and the contractual document that describes it. The IT industry uses the term to mean the set of business rules controlling the decision-making logic of the computer system, for example, the set of routing parameters that configure a network. No doubt other examples exist.

Even when we confine ourselves to the regulatory environment, a number of rule-related terms in fact do double duty in many speakers' vocabularies. Most confusingly, words like *policy* and *standard* are used to refer to both

- an individual statement, and
- a document full of statements.

That duality creates ambiguity when someone says, "I know we have a policy on bringing animals to the office." On the one hand, the speaker could be referring to a specific document titled *Policy on Animals in the Office*, and that would be a legitimate use of the term. On the other hand, the speaker could be referring to one or two statements on that issue actually located inside a more general document, perhaps one titled *Policy on Office Security*. That, too, would be a legitimate use of the term.

Policy versus *policy*

To clarify the distinction throughout this text, when words refer to titles of documents, they will appear with an initial uppercase letter, for example, *Policy*, *Standard*, and *Rules*. Words that refer broadly to one or more statements will begin with a lowercase letter, for example, *policy*, *standard*, and *rules*. Under this convention, a *Standard on document naming* is a reference specifically to some document with the word *Standard* in the title, while *a standard on document naming* points us to specific statements containing naming restrictions, wherever they are located. In an ideal world, once everything is organized properly, policies would always be found in Policies, standards in Standards, and procedures in Procedures.

To make matters worse, the lexical ambiguity is compounded by a factual one: putting the word *Policy* in the title of a document doesn't turn its contents into policies. Many documents titled *Policy* contain a multitude of statements that are not rules of any kind, much less the specific type of rule that can be correctly characterized as a policy statement. My hope is that by the end of this book you will want to separate them all properly.

Discipline vs generic

The convention of using letter case to mark lexical distinctions has been extended to disciplines and general topics. An uppercase first letter — *Facilities*, *Finance*, *Security* — indicates that we are talking about a professional discipline, or the people trained in that discipline, or even the branch/section/unit of the organization where they work. In contrast, a lowercase initial character indicates a generic use of the term; thus, Security personnel and others working in a Security Office might develop security measures to protect the premises.

Job roles vs job titles

Letter case also distinguishes jobs from roles. *Secretary* with an uppercase *S* is the title of a job position in the organization, and the individual in that job may or may not act as secretary — lowercase *s* — at next week's meeting. In this way, it will be clear that the company's Policy Developers are individuals with that job title, who may or may not be the only policy developers at the organization.

Transactional roles vs identities

Terms taken from the vocabulary of Transactional Analysis use uppercase letters to distinguish roles from identities, consistent with the practice in that field. A Parent–Child relationship is a social construct describing how two parties interact; a parent-child relationship is a familial one.

Subject matter expert

The term *subject matter expert(s)*, used often in this text, is abbreviated to *SME*.

A Book in Four Parts

This book is divided into four parts, with topics evolving from broad to narrow and then back again. For convenience, each chapter opens with an executive summary intended to help readers assess its relevance to their situations.

Part I looks at big picture issues like context, drivers, and goals. It's important to see the effects that both external and internal social influences have on our approach to writing rules. We will explore the interplay between the language of rules and corporate culture, as well as the structures around governance and enforcement.

Part II gets more technical, looking at document structures and relationships. We look at how the various types of rules documents differ from one another, and how to organize rules inside them. In corporate contexts, where these documents tend to use titles like *Policy* and *Directive*, rules documents may be generically referred to as *policy instruments* and collectively called a *policy suite*.

If your main concern pertains to writing one-off rules, for example, to put warnings on a sign or create rules around an event, then the material applicable to full-blown policy suites may be overkill for your purposes. If that's the case, then after finishing Part I feel free to jump directly to Part III.

Part III begins our deep dive into the intricacies of crafting different kinds of rules, so we can examine what makes them sound courteous or appear disrespectful. We look at the problems of the traditionally-used modal verbs *must*, *may*, and *should* and explore a variety of alternative wordings to replace them.

Part III also looks at packaging: the sections of text that bracket the rules, such as scope statements, objectives, roles and responsibilities, and so on. We finish up by spending some time on definitions and terminology management.

Part IV brings everything together, as we discuss how connecting rules to organizational values can cement the buy-in and engagement of others.

Parts II and IV and the latter half of Part III are most applicable to full-scale policy suites, where clearly differentiating policy from standard and procedure is a crucial element in organizing policy architecture. The chapters in those parts use the language of corporate and regulatory environments: *policies*, *standards*, *governance*, and so on.

In the first half of Part III, the emphasis is more on the wording of individual statements rather than how statements interact with each other. For ease of understanding, there the term *rule* is used in a generic sense. If in your context the concept applies to a policy, standard, or procedure, then interpret it accordingly.

Issues related to enforcement

Policy enforcement issues are understandably one of a rule-maker's main concerns. Though the enforcement process itself is not a policy drafting matter, a number of issues related to that process are inexorably intertwined with the wording of the rules we want enforced. Those issues belong to one of two categories: issues related to the mechanics of enforcement and issues related to peoples' attitudes.

The mechanics are dealt with in chapters 7 and 8, where we discuss governance and enforcement mechanisms. A totally separate — and more important — set of factors is related to the corporate attitude on the role of enforcement: Is the threat of discipline wielded as a sword or a shield? Are decisions interpreting the rules inflexible or accommodating? Those factors are strongly influenced by corporate culture and are covered in chapter 4.

Social Change

Policy drafting involves (1) organizing the documents that hold the rules and (2) generating the statements that assert them.

This book asks rule makers to rethink how they approach both those activities. We have the opportunity to reappraise the way we address people in our rules. What will become clear is how the wording we choose reveals the amount of respect we have for those people — or, sadly, betrays the lack of it.

Ultimately, though, this book is about making social change. Like any change, it inevitably comes up against a certain amount of resistance.

The opposition insists that a softer approach doesn't work. That argument is not evidence based, but one they support with confirmation bias: what they've been doing up until now is more than satisfactory, thank you very much. One attorney went so far as to tell me that the more respectful approach was dangerous. She claimed that eliminating the dictatorial language from policies would only encourage disobedience, lulling employees into the false belief that they aren't subject to the master/servant relationship. That attitude is typical of people who highly value the pecking order and are resistant to change.

Courtesy is simply unfamiliar to many as a rule-writing style.

Fortunately, most people are open to looking at the possibilities. But even for those with best intentions, some drafting habits are deeply ingrained. Change comes slowly, but it does come.

Let's work on that together. Let's identify the fossils in our writing styles, gently remove them from the stone, and put them into museums where they belong. We can then replace them with phrasing that's more suitable for the modern workplace.

RULES: Powerful Policy Wording to Maximize Engagement

PART I — RULES IN CONTEXT

Chapters in this part

Notes

1. THE TRADITIONAL APPROACH

Executive Summary

The most common drafting errors in corporate policies are a lack of clarity, of succinctness, and of respect. The unavailability of good training for policy drafters has contributed to the perpetuation of traditional methods, while the undervaluing of policy drafting skills within the organization has dampened professional networking. The heavy-handed language traditionally found in policies is a result of two factors: (1) parental influences on our perceptions of what rules should sound like, and (2) a long history normalizing the acceptability of aggression directed at the workforce. The latter has changed only in recent decades, and the old approach is simply an historical remnant of a past era.

Discovering the Problem

Years ago I led a records management support team in a large government agency. The team members were constantly frustrated with the lack of engagement by others in the organization. They had previously published a series of Policies and Directives containing all the rules they wanted everyone to follow, but no one appeared to be listening, and compliance rates were low.

At first, the team speculated that non-compliance was the result of poor communications. That conclusion guided them to respond with more of the same: memoranda, posted announcements on the corporate intranet, and e-mail reminders. But nothing changed; increased communications didn't inspire anyone to be more compliant.

So the team tried beefing up the language to sound scarier and more official. They replaced the familiar *Employees should* opening gambit with the tougher-sounding *All employees must* or *All users are required to*.

They also increased the amount of **boldface**, *italics*, <u>underline</u>, UPPERCASE LETTERS, and even multiple exclamation marks(!!!!) to ***<u>make sure EVERYONE obeyed the rules!!!!</u>***

As one might suspect, the formatting changes did nothing to improve the situation. Nor did the threatening wording; if anything, it engendered resentment in some corners and caused friction between the policy writers and the rest of the office.

In fact, almost no one at the organization actually ever read the records management Policies. Those who did read them were

- unsure or confused about what they meant
- reluctant to wade through numerous and unnecessarily lengthy paragraphs, and
- disinclined to be receptive to the instructions, given the confrontational tone.

When it became clear that the new policy instruments were no more successful than the old ones, things went from bad to worse. The policy developers grew disillusioned.

"Why should we bother writing Policies if nobody's going to follow them?" the team members would ask. "We're just wasting our time."

The team's morale sank, its frustration level increased, and its productivity decreased. Low morale can take a heavy toll.

The turning point

It was at this point that I had my *aha* moment. Rules, it would seem, are part of a conversation. That conversation tends to go well when both sides are talking to each other; on the other hand, it tends to go poorly when it's one-sided. Too often we shout our rules at people, in some cases even hitting them on the head — figuratively speaking, of course. It's no wonder that people are resistant to rules that come in that form.

It wasn't that the written Policies had been haphazardly thrown together; in fact, just the opposite: the drafters seemed to agonize endlessly over what should and what shouldn't be included in the documents. But updated Policies were almost always rebuilt in the style of older Policies, despite the fact that the older ones might not have been written properly in the first place.

Most significantly, the underlying issue seemed to be that the **purpose of policy instruments was generally misunderstood.** Instead of being written to help people do their work, they were intended to keep people in check.

Looking around me, it was clear that what I observed wasn't just an office workplace phenomenon. I found aggressive-sounding policies, rules, and signs everywhere, in all kinds of industries and at all kinds of locations. The aggressive tone was just the beginning, though.

Policy bloat

The all-too-common complaint about corporate Policies being too lengthy is not unfounded. A quick glance at the rules documents of many organizations reveals a series of swollen, highly repetitive treatises. They are bloated with procedures, standards, principles, explanatory statements, examples, and advice, all of which belong in other documents. Unsure of the different functions of each of those types of statements, writers seemed to default to throwing them all into a single document. Like a disorganized kitchen drawer entangling forks, knives, and spoons together with other cooking utensils, the document ends up being a potpourri of rules, facts, and interpretation.

The bloat of the final product was consistent with the disorganization of the entire approval process. Typically, the whole kit and caboodle — rules, explanations, examples, advice, and commentary — is made to run through the full length of the development process, from drafting to consultation and eventually submission to an approver for sign-off. As a result, an enormous amount of valuable time is wasted editing, explaining, discussing, rewording, re-discussing, and — if all goes well — finally approving many pages of statements that don't belong in Policies in the first place.

Three Common Gremlins

From what I could tell, three shortcomings seemed to appear consistently in these written rules.

1. Lack of clarity

Too many statements are ambiguous, using both poorly-chosen wording permitting multiple interpretations and the inconsistent use of vocabulary within and across instruments.

2. Lack of conciseness

Documents contain irrelevant matter, adding unnecessary length and complexity, consuming time and resources. In addition, the extra length acts as a deterrent to readers.

3. Lack of respect

The policy statements sound like a sergeant barking orders. They admonish instead of inform, generating resistance instead of support.

The Solution

Having practiced law early in my career, I could see an obvious connection between regulating corporate behavior inside the workplace and regulating public behavior outside. After all, organizational Policies are not at the top of the food chain when it comes to guiding people's behavior; that honor belongs to statutes. Since policies and legislation have some similarities in their functions, I started to wonder what lessons the crafting of legislation could offer the world of policy drafting.

One thing was clear to me: we had a **serious training gap**. Without the skills to distinguish good from bad policy wording, writers were unwittingly perpetuating the very problems they were trying to overcome.

Rule-drafting as a skill

In the world of drafting legislation, writers are trained properly. To disrupt their acquiring bad habits by being self-taught, the training offered to them is highly controlled. It seems generally acknowledged in the world of legislation that crafting good rules requires formal instruction.

In contrast, we find little equivalent recognition in the policy world. That gap, combined with the scarcity of good quality training available, means that drafters are learning the craft in a variety of ways, if they are learning at all.

Most policy drafters — especially novices — prefer to take an existing policy and update it than to draft one from scratch. As a result, many of these documents are worded exactly the same way they were 20, 30, or 40 years ago, so that neither the structure nor the language reflect the changing times. Until someone breaks that cycle, poorly-worded rules will be perpetuated throughout many iterations.

Coincident with that bit of clarity was my realization that rule-making skills are **significantly undervalued** by many organizations. Rule-making is most definitely a skill, and a complex one at that, if our goal is engagement and compliance rather than resistance. One might think that fact to be common knowledge, but too many organizations seem to task their SME with writing policies, standards, and procedures without investing in training them for that activity. Drafting rules may not be rocket science, but it's not child's play, either; it requires combining a knowledge of drafting techniques with a number of related skills.

Rule-drafting as a professional competency

The lack of recognition of the value of policy drafting skills in the corporate world is, in part, influenced by the way those skills are regarded by the various associations that support domains of professional specialization, such as HR, Security, IT, and so on. Currently, "policy drafting" is conspicuously absent from the inventory of competencies accredited by many of those associations. As a result, we see gaps in the range of education programs they offer, leaving those professionals to fend for themselves.

One of the repercussions of those gaps is that rule makers from one field of specialization — say, Finance — do not perceive that they share anything in common with those from other fields — for example, Security. As a result of that disconnect, little exchange of knowledge occurs among the various SME. A technique with a proven success rate in the Finance branch is unlikely to be shared with the Security branch, thereby reinforcing the policy silos that are such an impediment to a cohesive policy suite. In reality, though, all policy writers experience many of the same challenges, especially when it comes to negotiating an organization's governance and enforcement challenges, and could benefit from coordinating their efforts.

Typical Traditional Wording

The majority of operational and administrative policies in place today still use distinctly **antiquated wording**. The authoritarian style is representative of the way that management spoke to employees up until about 20 years ago. That style might have been commonplace at the time, but it's inconsistent with modern corporate values. Today, no one talks disrespectfully to their employees in the corporate world and gets away with it; yet, many still write that way.

Even organizations that claim to hold *respect for others* as a core value can fall prey to the traps posed by old wording. Let's look at an example. Compare the statements from Company A and Company B in Panel 1.

Panel 1

A. Employees must submit vacation requests at least one week in advance. Any request not submitted on time may be refused.

B. Requests for vacation are processed when submitted at least one week in advance.

Both organizations require seven days' notice of vacation requests. But the similarity stops there.

It's not hard to read between the lines in statement A of panel 1. Just as with the sign in the medical clinic discussed in the Introduction, this policy statement reveals some dirty laundry that it perhaps shouldn't.

I think it's safe to infer that Company A has had some rocky experiences related to people failing to meet the notice period. But there's more. Look back at their statement and see if you can detect the emotional undertones of the wording. How are HR staff **feeling** about the situation? The undertones are subtle, but they are definitely perceptible. If you can't detect them easily, try to imagine someone speaking those words aloud and listen carefully to the tone of voice.

Can you hear it? Not only is the HR office experiencing a compliance problem, but that problem seems to have taken a toll on the psyches of those who work there. They are not happy campers. The statement conveys pronounced notes of frustration, both about the problem itself and about having to constantly remind others about the rule. In addition, we can detect hints that those workers are feeling **disrespected** by others, perhaps even **unappreciated** or completely **ignored**.

Under the circumstances, those feelings are completely understandable. For the sake of argument, let's go so far as to concede that those feelings are even reasonable and justified. I think we've all been there at one time or another, and we can relate to the experience of administering a policy that too many people don't follow. We get frustrated. It happens.

But the rest of the world doesn't need to know that.

Using this kind of wording in a policy statement, combined with the overt threat, effectively discloses an organization's internal operational problems to everyone, exposing both the compliance issues and the staff frustrations about them.

Moreover, the impact of Company A's policy wording is long-lasting. If the statement were merely posted on a wall sign, it would continue to deliver its dysfunctional message until the sign is taken down, which can be done easily. But by including the text in a formal policy, the organization has

memorialized the disclosure in such a way that it will persist even if the situation improves. In all my years working in this field, I've never seen a case where an organization that resorted to harsh wording in an attempt to increase engagement later decides to adjust the wording after compliance improves. If anything, management tends to commit the logical fallacy *post hoc ergo propter hoc*, in other words, they conclude that since the situation improved after the harsh wording was invoked, the improvement was the result of that wording.

It seems inappropriate that anyone — insider or outsider to an organization — can read its policies and figure out all the problems it's experienced, past and present.

Too many rules in this world are worded deliberately to sound authoritarian, combative, or condescending. Take the examples in panel 2.

Panel 2

Visitors are prohibited from entering the service area.

Returns are strictly forbidden. Customers must check all merchandise carefully before leaving the store.

Aggressiveness is not tolerated.

If you want to speak at our conference, you must submit a proposal. You must meet all our deadlines and not sell services during your presentation.

But why? Why the need to put others on the defensive?

After all, these rules are written for adults, not children. We're at the workplace, not the playground. Why doesn't the wording of these rules take that into account? **Why do rules end up sounding like parents and teachers scolding naughty children when they could sound like one adult respectfully and courteously talking to another?**

Sadly, the most common reason offered is, "because it's always been done that way." This explanation can be heard from people in all types of organizations: for-profit and not-for-profit; public and private; large and small.

Origin of Traditional Wording

Indeed, that explanation is correct: it **has** always been done that way. And while that reason may explain its longevity, it doesn't serve to add validity.

The origin of the wording is actually not much of a mystery.

Our first exposure to rules was in interactions with our parents, teachers, and other caregivers. Consistent with the Parent–Child dynamic intrinsic to those relationships, the rules most of us grew up hearing were intentionally worded in uncompromising language. Rules were calculated not merely to convey information around acceptable behavior, but also to reaffirm the relationship hierarchy, just in case we had any doubts on that issue.

Traditional rules were typically expressed with a formula along the lines of that shown in panel 3.

Panel 3

If you do x, then expect y.

---

where x represents an undesirable act and y represents the threatened punishment. Bad actions beget bad consequences; avoid the bad action and you avoid the bad consequence.

My parents had a dinnertime rule using that formula: if we didn't eat our vegetables, then we didn't get dessert. My school's rule was that if we didn't do what the teacher said, we were sent to the principal's office. And I suspect that those of us who grew up exposed to a strongly religious background don't need any reminder of what the consequences of disobeying those rules were!

To set the record straight, I'm not criticizing that approach for those circumstances. I'm going to remain totally non-partisan about whether dictating rules in an *I-am-in-charge-and-you-will-obey-me* tone of voice is appropriate for children.

But let's put it into proper perspective. Though we may not have been able to understand it at the time, now that we've grown up we can entertain a more nuanced analysis of what we experienced. The rule-makers were, for the most part, well-intentioned and not motivated by malice. They were trying to instill values into children. They felt confident in the correctness of the approach because they were acting in a way that was consistent with the zeitgeist of the time.

In retrospect, we can appreciate that what our parents and teachers were actually modeling for us was how adults in charge make **rules for children** they're in charge of. **They weren't trying to teach us how adults make rules for other adults.** Unfortunately, it left the unassailable impression that rules need to sound dictatorial to be effective.

Cultural reinforcement

In a better world, those childhood lessons would have been short-lived, and we would have had the opportunity to revise our outlook as we grew up. We might have been able to gain exposure to other, positive approaches to regulating behavior. With viable alternatives to choose from, we might have sequestered the old formulas to a mental model reserved for parenting, and moved on.

Alas, it was not to be for most people. As we moved into adulthood we encountered the same approach in the workplace. The *de facto* standard for communications from upper management to rank-and-file employees echoed and reinforced that Parent–Child dynamic.

That standard is not incidental. For centuries, the strict, authoritarian tone of voice used when addressing employees was perfectly suited to command-and-control organizational structures. Up until the most immediately recent decades, issuing direct commands was considered the most effective way to get underlings to do one's bidding. In addition, it had the benefit of preserving the established pecking order in the office. Those in charge spoke that way and they wrote that way to their subordinates. Even when bosses lost their cool and let forth a torrent of abuse, it drew no official or legal sanctions of any kind.

You may be wondering why the unfortunate individual on the receiving end didn't fight back? Regrettably, it was simply not an option at the time. Silently enduring that abuse was understood to be one of the downsides of having to work for a living. If you're curious and would like to hear some more examples of that situation, just ask anyone in your office who's been working for 20 years or more.

The good news is that today things are different. Progressive managers have learned to communicate more courteously to employees. The modern-day workplace is not the command-and-control autocracy of days past. The contemporary business atmosphere is a collaborative, consensus-building, diversity-respecting, egalitarian, and non-discriminatory environment, where employers strive to create and maintain a culture of respect. For the most part, in this millennium, it is rare that employers subject others to verbal abuse and condescending language. Today, in the majority of cases, no rule maker talks that way and gets away with it.

But many of them still write that way.

The written language, as always, is lagging behind the mores of the times. If our aim is to maximize engagement, then that gap needs to close.

Aligning Our Messaging

The irony in this situation is that many of the organizations producing rules with this aggressive language pride themselves on promoting *respect for others* as a core value.

Clearly, many organizations genuinely do respect their employees. They might even have taken steps to demonstrate it: building a nice staff lunchroom, or providing comfortable chairs or top-of-the-line technology. A few companies go so far as to take the time and effort to choose the right paint color for the walls, to create a specific atmosphere.

But some of these same organizations don't look carefully at how their administrative and operational policies are worded. As a result, any negative subtext conveyed along with that wording goes unchecked. It's a sure bet that when the rules documents sound disrespectful to employees, the poor wording packs a lot more punch than having the wrong color on the walls.

The status quo makes no sense, given the wave of initiatives aimed at improving corporate culture. The HR team puts resources into creating a positive employee experience and to build employee's trust in management. Managers and supervisors work hard to develop a culture of collaboration and create good working relationships. The Marketing and Communications team spends countless hours developing the corporate brand, not merely setting colors and fonts, but trying to convey how much you and your organization care about your customers.

When poorly-worded rules send out negative messages, all that good work is undermined.

Organizations have the ability to speak with a consistent voice enterprise-wide, and policies and related communications are every bit as much a part of an organization's presence as its other initiatives. No established corporate principle exempts rule-making from all these other efforts.

In the next chapter we're going to look at a variety of factors that merit consideration when choosing the appropriate tone for rules going forward.

Notes

2. Evolving Trends

Executive Summary

The effectiveness of traditional policy approaches is re-evaluated in light of contemporary business trends, specifically: changes in technology, management styles, and generational expectations. Adapting policies to align with modern information consumption habits and leveraging technological advancements improves both the efficiency and the effectiveness of the final product. Responding to the needs of a diverse and changing workforce allows the organization to continue attracting skilled talent, sustaining their competitive edge in a dynamic environment.

Psychological Reactance

What the traditional approach doesn't take into account is the effect of *psychological reactance*. A well-documented phenomenon, it can be summarized as the "unpleasant motivational reaction to offers, persons, rules, or regulations that threaten or eliminate specific behavioral freedoms."[2] It is an instinctive reaction for an adult who perceives that an external agent is intent on restricting their freedom of choice.

Compliance with rules is dependent upon people's cooperation. But we can't claim success if that "cooperation" is based solely on threats. If our goal is to move people up the *Ladder of Engagement*, we can't antagonize them.

If we want our employees to buy into our initiatives and be on our side when we make changes, they need to **want** to

---

[2] https://en.wikipedia.org/wiki/Reactance_(psychology), April 2024

support us. Employees who feel they're being spoken to disrespectfully respond poorly, which shows up in the form of poor compliance, attitude issues and high staff turnover.

The reaction is even more pronounced with customers, who react by heading elsewhere and not returning. At the end of the day, both employee turnover and customer dissatisfaction affect the bottom line: they drive costs up and revenues down. A similar reaction will cause a non-for-profit organization's fundraising sources to dry up, leaving it struggling to make friends again.

Not surprisingly, **the more aggressive our rules sound, the more resistance they generate.** Conversely, the less psychological reactance they generate, the more engaged people will be.

Re-evaluating the Traditional Approach

Rules that include phrases like *you must do this* and *we don't tolerate that* cannot help but suggest a mental image of a parent wagging a finger while reprimanding a child.

As mentioned in the last chapter, I'm prepared to proceed on the assumption that the traditional approach to rules was 100% appropriate for the times. We can't know for sure, of course, because we're always prone to evaluate the past through the prism of a present-day lens. A full objective analysis is well beyond the scope of this book, and while the conclusions arrived at might be academically interesting, they don't help us choose a direction going forward.

I've labelled the authoritarian approach *traditional*, but that may not be technically accurate. Many activities can be characterized as long-standing, but that qualification alone is insufficient to earn the label. A *tradition* has the peculiar characteristic that its continuation is justified by its own existence; in other words, the mere fact that something is a tradition is accepted as sufficient reason to perpetuate it.

The authoritarian approach to rule making was the de facto standard for many years. By calling it a traditional approach, I don't mean to suggest that its longevity was based solely on a desire to prolong it for its own sake. No doubt, over the years countless experts were able to justify sustaining that approach by pointing to the functional results it produced. For that reason, it was much more than a tradition; it was a proven strategy backed by evidence.

Fast forward to today. In the face of the many changes to be discussed in this chapter, the justification for retaining the authoritarian approach weakens considerably. Nevertheless, some people want to keep it alive today solely because they resist change and want to continue doing things the way they've always done them. So although it may be technically imprecise to call the approach traditional, that description is apt under the circumstances.

Trends

The pivotal question is whether the traditional approach is appropriate for today. To assess that, we need to look at the significance of some of the changes that have occurred in the last fifty years. In fact, the past two decades alone have seen developments that have a direct impact on determining how we structure and disseminate rules.

A trend can be analogized to a journey where people are characterized as either *leaders*, *followers*, *stragglers*, or *outliers*. Despite the relative sizes of those different groups, or the number of travelers overall, the journey remains the same. It's important for this discussion, therefore, to avoid being sidetracked by the inevitable exceptions to these trends, even when they stand out. For example, if I were to suggest that management today is more diligent around safety issues than in the past, I'm sure you can quickly point to instances where that assertion doesn't ring true. But even in the face of exceptions, we can still acknowledge a trend towards increased diligence around safety and conclude that organizations lagging behind are stragglers or outliers.

Some of the observations made here may seem to be overly broad and optimistic. Recognize that participation rates for new trends vary geographically, as some regions of the globe — and even of each country — adopt change more readily than others. If you're interested in this topic and reading this book, you're likely in one of those more progressive regions, and these trends won't come as a surprise.

We'll look specifically at three major areas: management style, policy consumption habits, and digital information structures. All three have implications to consider when assessing what makes a final product effective and efficient.

1. Management Style

Major changes have taken place in management science over the past few decades. The relationship between leaders and employees has been altered on a number of axes, as companies have moved away from the older command-and-control management approach. These changes centre around leadership and corporate structure on one side, and social and environmental factors on the other.

Corporate structure

Many organizations have modified their corporate structures in an effort to empower multiple teams of employees. By decentralizing decision-making and giving mid-level managers more autonomy and authority, the company can encourage innovation and support more accurate decision-making. Imparting a sense of ownership among employees has led to increased employee engagement — and job satisfaction along with it.

To support a decentralized decision-making structure, policies need to be crafted more **flexibly**. They need to be able to offer clear direction to decision-makers while allowing them to maintain their autonomy.

Flattening the hierarchy

In an attempt to level the playing field in a world where — to borrow the words of George Orwell — "some people are more equal than others," social hierarchies in the past century have been undergoing a gradual change. In the corporate world, one indicator of this change is the growth of matrix organizations, where employees may report to multiple managers and work on various projects across different teams. This structure enhances collaboration and cross-functional production, but it also requires a more nuanced approach to team dynamics.

Where an individual's immediate supervisor is no longer directing their work, policy enforcement mechanisms may require some compensatory changes.

Leadership style

At the same time, corporate leaders increasingly take on a coaching role rather than a commanding one. They focus more on guiding others to find solutions, develop their skills, and achieve their career goals. Leaders in that position cultivate open dialog, a supportive and developmental environment, and they encourage continuous learning and growth.

The traditional approach to policy wording is almost directly antithetical to that coaching style. Its continued presence at an organization has the potential to undermine the improved relationship achieved through coaching.

Accommodation

When it comes to social issues, corporations are aware of and commonly responsive to the direction of public sentiment. Today's workplaces tend to be more flexible than those in years past, valuing the need to accommodate individual employee circumstances. This flexibility shows up in various ways, such as offering remote work options, being open to alternative schedules, and an overall heightened consideration of personal needs.

This more accommodating approach can build a more inclusive and supportive workplace culture. As a result, organizations may need to reconsider their approaches to handling requests for exceptions to rules.

Recognizing diversity

Consistent with the efforts to accommodate unforeseeable circumstances, modern management is more keenly aware of the need to recognize individual differences and embrace diversity. Recognition in these circumstances includes supporting an environment where disparate perspectives, backgrounds, and working styles are valued.

This trend heightens the awareness of the importance of inclusive language in written and oral communications, and of addressing bias. It is now commonplace for rules and their associated communications to be respectful of gender, race, sexual orientation, and physiological characteristics, including both physical and neurological diversity.

Efforts to foster inclusion target an environment where every employee feels a sense of belonging and respect, confident that their needs are considered in decision-making. That aim can be achieved only by earning it. Where an organization's written rules come across as divisive or confrontational, it will have an uphill battle establishing that *respect for others* ranks as one of its priorities.

Changing demographic

Finally, before leaving this topic, I would be remiss if I didn't acknowledge the enormous influence exerted by the newest generations moving into the workforce. They bring with them the values that motivate them as well as their expectations around behaviors. Preferring consultation over authoritative decision-making, this generation has the potential to be enormously resourceful but also to be disruptive to the status quo. Generational differences pose new challenges for both recruitment and retention.

The jury is still out on the degree to which the expectations of the younger workforce will affect management style; however, one thing is clear: **the heavy-handed language traditionally used in policy drafting does not resonate with them**. They didn't hear it growing up and they don't want to hear it now. Many of them find the authoritarian approach not merely assertive but antagonizing. Unlike previous generations — who still often tolerate negative language as a necessary evil — younger workers are more likely to act out their displeasure through resistance or departure.

2. Policy Consumption Habits

Changing social and corporate dynamics are important, but they tell only part of the story. They might influence which words we choose to put into our rules statements, but they're not particularly significant in a discussion of the best way to organize those statements. The transformative factor in that area actually sits on a whole different plane.

Since microcomputers have been around for a few decades now, I don't need to expound generally on how technology has revolutionized the way we produce and consume information. Let's focus instead on a few specific aspects.

For one thing, modern readers, inundated with information, have a marked preference for conciseness in reading material. (In an effort to be tactful, I'm going to avoid the question of whether people's attention spans are actually getting shorter.)

Whatever the cause, the days when the typical reader spent hours on lengthy, text-heavy documents are gone, if they ever really were there in the first place. People are busy. They want clear, concise information that gets straight to the point. The more streamlined a policy can be, focusing on essential information without unnecessary elaboration, the more likely people will spend the time going through it.

The other side of that coin is a diminished level of patience when searching for information. There's an increasing demand for the ability to navigate quickly to highly targeted information. Users want to see only what's directly relevant to their specific situation or query, and are less likely to pore through an entire policy to find the right paragraphs. Responding to this demand calls for a more tailored approach that can focus on defined audience segments.

While we're on the topic of diminished patience, I might mention that the tolerance for outdated information in rules documents has also fallen. Unlike traditional print media, where a degree of lag in updating information might be forgiven, digital platforms invite increased expectations around accuracy and currency. The instant and dynamic nature of content delivery has led people to expect that all information — from contact details to hyperlinks — is consistently up-to-date.

The technology boost

On the writing side, technology has boosted our communications capacity and reduced the amount of effort required to reproduce information in a variety of formats. Once digitized, policy can be segmented, manipulated and repurposed to meet the demands of diverse consumers.

On the **reading** side, the wide variety of digital devices continuously challenges us to keep policies accessible and readable across a range of platforms. From desktops to smartphones, we try to keep up with presentation formats that are responsive to different screen sizes and user interfaces, ensuring that policies are effectively communicated regardless of how they are accessed.

In short, in our role as policy developers today we commit our rules to writing in new ways, and in our role as consumers we use new techniques to browse, search for, read, and repurpose them.

We continue to use the **physical** world, of course, since we still have a need to post rules on a sign in a conspicuous location. Fortunately, sign structure has not changed much.

The **digital** world has.

3. Digital Information Structures

The trends discussed in this chapter have had a profound influence on how we flow information from source to target. In a corporate environment, we consume policies today in a radically different way from how we used to before the turn of the century. We no longer physically reach for an office shelf full of binders.

Truth be told, **we don't have to reach for a virtual shelf full of binders**, either, although many organizations have merely transferred the document-policy-binder model to electronic format. To be able to plan for the future, however, we need to reevaluate our approach to structure in light of some key technical concepts.

Paper-based techniques

Today we can break free of the printed world and the restrictions that it imposes. Leveraging the power of digital navigation can release us from the confines of older approaches to information organization and presentation. To achieve that goal, however, we need to **rethink** completely the fundamentals of designing policy instruments.

With paper, the standard conceptual unit is a *document*, comprising one or more connected pages. In the policy world of yesterday, as a rule, we would typically put each policy into its own document, assemble them all and then sequence them in a 3-ring binder. Finally, we would line up the binders on a shelf.

The drafting techniques used in the paper world made sense, given the limitations. For example, when one wanted to explain the meaning of a word for the benefit of people unfamiliar with it, it was common to put that explanation directly into the text of the policy. Since paper-based documents don't have the ability to hyperlink to paragraphs or pages in other places, the most straight-forward way to provide access to information found elsewhere was through **text duplication**.

In the days before hyperlinks, policy drafters had to assemble all related information manually. To make the final product as useful and convenient as possible for the reader, it was a common practice to bring related information into the main document so it would be *all in one place*. That attempt to combine utility and convenience was a sound strategy, and their efforts were appreciated. **In a paper-based environment,** *all in one place* **essentially means that everything is located in the same document.**

Restructuring for digital

Combining utility and convenience remains an effective strategy today, but the tools have evolved. We can achieve the same goals by moving away from the physical consolidation of information and focusing our attention on navigation and discoverability. Today's consumers still want to find information easily, but **they don't have to know where it is stored to do that. They can gain access to everything they need through a well-designed Web site.** By leveraging a set of landing pages, hyperlinks, and floating boxes, we can bring any text we choose to a reader's attention at any time.

We still want all the information to appear in one place, because that's most convenient. **Today, however, information is found** *all in one place* **when it is accessible from the same screen.** The paragraphs on a specific topic that we want the reader to see no longer all have to be stored in the same document; they simply need to be displayed in proximity on the screen.

Separate front and back ends

A Web page viewed through a browser is not limited to displaying the text of a single document, but instead can display text from multiple sources. At the same time, parts of the page can act as entry points to text in other pages. That capability means that we have the freedom to arrange content in different front-end and back-end views.

In case you're not familiar with the distinction, let's look at an example to see how it works. Take a moment to browse to your favorite news Web site. Once there, survey the variety of information appearing on the home page. Do you think that all that information is saved in one document on a storage drive? Not at all! What you're seeing is a page that is actually being assembled from a series of source feeds. If you had the ability to look directly at those sources, you'd see that many of them don't look anything like the way they appear on the news page.

Now pick a news article and bring that page up to the screen. Even there, what you're seeing is the result of a compilation of material from any number of sources.

When we keep information in electronic format, we have the technical capability to show readers *curated content*. That **content can be laid out on the screen in a completely different way from its appearance in the underlying original documents**. Identical content, but with a more reader-centric presentation.

When it comes to drafting and communicating policies, this capability enables a paradigm shift — and I don't use that overworked term lightly. We can now bring excerpts from different electronic sources **together on the screen** at **the same time**, whether they are pulled from the same source document or from documents stored miles apart.

Our policies, standards, procedures, and other rules documents can now be presented to the user on a single page, even if the text is retrieved from multiple sources: different documents, different databases, even different Web sites. Readers don't care whether the material is drawn from a single server or spread over dozens of servers; what matters to readers is whether the page presents that information in a *reader-centric* manner.

In the paper world, there's no difference between the policy document that we submit for approval and the policy document that people will read the next day. One document serves both functions.

In the digital world, we can take advantage of using multiple views: one view of the rules to be submitted to the decision-maker for approval, and a different view for the presentation of the approved content.

What does that mean in practical terms? Say we have only a single policy statement that needs to be approved, for example, a statement specifying a change in office hours. The draft policy we submit for approval can be one page long and propose only that one single statement. Once approved, that statement can then be extracted and visually incorporated into the Web page displaying the general policy on office administration. It can even appear on multiple pages if we want it to, and in multiple contexts.

The end user doesn't care whether different paragraphs were combined into one document or spread among several documents at the time they were submitted for approval. How documents were structured at the time of

approval **is of no interest to them;** all they want to see is a reader-centric view of the information.

The upshot is that when we design our policy suite, we're now looking at **designing both a user view (front end) and a management view (back end)**. They work together but look entirely different.

If this model is not completely clear to you yet, don't worry. In Part II, we'll take another look at this split.

In the meantime, let's move on. Now that we've seen all the changes that have taken place in the last few decades, it's time to start building a picture of what things can look like going forward.

Notes

3. The Basics

Executive Summary

All rules made by management are binding on employees. Codifying rules in policy effectively operationalizes them. Written policy implicitly asserts authority and jurisdiction over subject matter; where either of those is lacking, the policy is ineffective. Policies are distinguishable from Standards and Procedures. Respecting those divisions helps us increase engagement, because buy-in always happens first at the policy level.

Let's start back at the beginning and work from a clean slate.

A *rule*, for the purposes of this book, is a decision made by one person or group intended to regulate the behavior of others.

Obviously, I'm not against rules in principle or in practice; indeed, I make my living based on their existence. I recognize the need in many cases for strict rules and sometimes even for extremely strict rules.

While some people resent them, rules are and will continue to be a fact of life. We need them to maintain a civil society. Without them, we would be constantly bumping into one another, both literally — on the highways — and figuratively — when we all try to speak at once in a business meeting.

Sources of Rules

Rules originate from multiple sources. We receive them from our caretakers, from government authorities, and from our religious beliefs, just to name a few. Every formal and informal organization we interact with has its own rules, so it would be impossible to produce an exhaustive inventory of the rules imposed on our lives even if we wanted to.

As we grow up, we may choose to follow various rules to a greater or lesser degree, depending on our character and our personal values. This need to choose is especially true when the rules coming from different sources conflict with one another. In those cases we have to make value judgments to support our choices.

Most of us genuinely want to do the right thing, at work, at play, and otherwise. It's more than simply wanting to keep our jobs by pleasing our bosses or staying out of trouble with the law. We try to serve our customers well, to support our colleagues, and to treat other people with kindness and respect, while at the same time being productive, effective, and efficient.

Drawing a Line

Rules are valuable when they help us distinguish acceptable from unacceptable actions. Effectively, they draw a line in the sand and tell us that one side is good and the other is bad. If the decision lands that the right side is good and the left side is bad, then we want to see people moving to the right side and staying there.

No question, it's often critical to draw this line in the sand. Any time we want to discipline or fire an employee, kick someone out of a club, fine a tenant for breach of the rules, deny a service or benefit to a member of the public, and so on, the line between right and wrong has to be clear for all to see.

We can word the rule in a variety of ways, as illustrated by the examples in panel 4. They are listed in order from most respectful to most aggressive.

Panel 4

- The right side is good and the left side is bad.
- In our office we stay on the right side.
- Please do us a favor and stay on the right side.
- Keep to the right side.
- Stay off the left side.
- People must never go to the left side.
- The left side is forbidden.
- We do not tolerate people on the left side.
- People found on the left side will be imprisoned/ dismissed/disciplined, etc.

Obviously, this list is not exhaustive of all the possibilities.

The Requirement for Writing

Some rules are formed by habit or culture and exist as part of our normal social interaction as human beings. These rules can remain unwritten so long as we want to preserve the status quo. But unwritten rules tend to be insufficient when the goal is to change people's behavior. In those circumstances, we need to formalize the rule, record it, and communicate it before we will see it take effect.

Unwritten rules create an evidentiary problem. With nothing but our memories to rely on, each of us would "know" only our own version of each rule. We'd lack reliable proof of the rule's wording at the time of approval or during subsequent communication. Moreover, the claim that a certain rule is in force but unwritten can raise suspicion and decrease people's trust in the system overall.

For those reasons, unwritten rules are problematic on a number of levels. Especially when it comes to changing the status quo, an unwritten rule — forgive my contorting an old expression — isn't worth the paper it isn't written on.

Records of decision

At their core, written Policies, Standards, and Procedures are transactional business records. They attest to one or more specific decisions being made on a specific day by a specific approver.

In that capacity, their regulatory value is negated when they don't meet basic recordkeeping requirements for the industry and jurisdiction they are created in.

In addition to their evidentiary value, the record of decision supplies two critical elements: *certainty* and *authority*.

1. Certainty

We need a common songbook if we're all going to sing together. As we each point to the governing paragraph, all fingers should be pointing to the same spot.

We need to know exactly what words the statements contain, in what order, and with what punctuation. If we're all going to be on the same page, that page needs to be clearly identifiable and accurately reproducible.

Along with that certainty we get **consistency**, **durability**, **permanence**, and all the other benefits of recordkeeping.

2. Authority

The act of approving a rule implicitly alleges two critical pieces of information: *provenance* and *jurisdiction*.

A) Provenance

Provenance traces the authority of a rule back to its origin.

The person or body approving the statement self-identifies and takes responsibility for the decision. A note at the top along the lines of *Approved by the Board of Directors* is sufficient for that identification. If we are unhappy with the rule and want it to change or go away, we know who needs to be convinced.

By approving a written policy statement, an approver explicitly asserts authority over the topic. To put it colloquially, the approver is proclaiming, *The buck stops here. We have the power to make this decision and it need go no higher.*

B) Jurisdiction

The converse claim is also inherent in that approval, namely, that the object of the policy statement falls within the scope of that approver's authority. Again, to put it colloquially, it proclaims to the world, *This issue is ours to make rules on.*

An individual or body acquires the authority to approve a rule — that is, to make both those proclamations — from one of several sources:

- It may be born of an enabling document, such as a charter, statute, or license

- It may be declared in a management document, such as corporate by-laws or an internal governance framework

- It may result from a delegation, which is the formal assignment by a higher power of the right to make a decision, or

- It may arise simply through one's ownership or sponsorship. We're allowed to make decisions over things that are ours.

The approval of a policy functions as an assertion that the subject matter is — to invoke the legal term — within the *competence* of the approver. *Competence* used in this sense is not about skills but rather about jurisdiction.

It follows that **the authority to make decisions is limited to areas within an approver's competence.**

One might think the previous sentence states the obvious, but the evidence indicates otherwise. Many, many policy documents contain statements that are technically outside the competence of the approver, yet someone insists on including those statements nonetheless. That inclusion is costly: since decisions made over areas outside the approvers' competence are ineffective, drafting them and submitting them for approval would seem to be a waste of time and resources for everyone involved.

We will examine this issue in more detail in chapter 7 when we look at policy governance.

Formal Policy

Having decided to put the rule in writing, the next question is, *Does the rule have to be part of a formal policy?* An office can obligate its customers to leave their boots at the front door simply by posting a sign. The power of that rule is not based on a consultation and approval process. More-over, the sign works even without displaying the title *Policy on Boots in the Office*. It doesn't need to identify the ap-prover or the date the rule went into effect. So why ever bother with all those formalities?

Consider a case where a supervisor directs an employee by e-mail to submit a status report every Friday afternoon. Policy or not, the employee is compelled to comply. Failure to fol-low a direct instruction without valid reason can technically be considered insubordination meriting disciplinary measures, regardless of whether the instruction traces back to a corpo-rate policy or to a direct request. So why bother making formal rules when we can just tell someone what to do?

Furthermore, that situation doesn't change when the re-quest applies to all employees. *"Status report please, everyone. In my Inbox by close of business every Friday afternoon starting this week."*

It's a plain, direct instruction. Granted, poorly communicat-ing it could negatively affect the response, so simply posting a sign outside the elevator is probably insufficient. But from a disciplinary standpoint, if the rule is appropriately communicated, then the medium recording that rule — formal Policy, paper memo, or enterprise-wide e-mail message — does not determine its legitimacy.

That being the case, when the boss wants to set a rule that everyone will submit a report every Friday, the rule can be set in one of two ways: (1) formalized in policy, or (2) disseminated by memorandum. Since both options are available, how do we decide when we need to go to the trouble of running a rule through the formal policy development and approval process? After all, that process costs time and resources, and we're best not to invoke it lightly.

One might be tempted to think that decision is based on the number of people affected by the rule, theorizing that the more people affected, the more formal the process needs to be.

That might sound intuitively right, but counter-examples to that theory are easy to find. We have formal policies about specific but extremely infrequent occurrences, for example, how to handle a situation when parental leave coincides with a planned vacation and then is unexpectedly interrupted by a bereavement. Rules of that nature are often found in formal policies despite the limited need to resort to them or the small number of people likely to be affected.

Instead of factors related to the rule's projected audience, the test for whether formal policy is required is **whether the rule is intended to outlast the rule maker.** A rule that needs to stay in place beyond the tenure of the current leadership calls for formal documentation, to assure its continuation into the new regime. Written policy remains in effect until formally amended; whereas, rules created solely by direct instruction can easily be countermanded by new instruction.

Another way of looking at the situation is that **formalizing a rule in policy is a way of** *operationalizing* it. By codifying a practice, it becomes part of the DNA of the organization. This approach both discourages policies from being impromptu and promotes rule-making processes designed to support the organization's ongoing growth and adaptation.

Policy vs Standard vs Procedure

We'll look at the differentiating characteristics of *policies*, *standards*, and *procedures* in comprehensive detail in Part II. However, I cannot hold off using those terms until then; so for the moment, this over-simplified model will suffice:

A *policy* is a decision of an organization, the same way a law is a decision of a legislative body.

A *standard* is set of specifications.

A *procedure* is a sequence of steps, with a defined beginning and end.

It's actually a really easy distinction to get one's head around, although perhaps an analogy would help. Some decades ago a recipe book was published called *The Elegance With Ease Cookbook*. The first dozen pages were filled with explanatory material where the author shared her criteria for inclusion of a recipe: it had to require less than 20 minutes' preparation time, use only typical household ingredients, and look elegant when served. Those criteria are *policy* decisions.

After the front section, we find the descriptions of the individual dishes. For each dish, the left hand page lists the specific ingredients and the quantities required. That list is a *standard*.

On the right hand page is a set of instructions for each dish's preparation, cooking, and serving. That set of instructions is a *procedure*.

Engagement Starts with the Policy

The distinction among those three instrument types is relevant to the topic of engagement: people are unlikely to support a standard or procedure if they don't first support the policy behind it.

In the cookbook I described, the criteria for recipe inclusion are at the *policy* level, and that's where the buy-in happens. Readers are unlikely to spend any time going through the recipes unless they buy into that policy, that is, unless they find value in elegant dishes that are quick and easy to prepare. The cookbook author knows that, and engages people first by reviewing the principles governing the decisions before setting out the ingredients and instructions.

This division of *policy*, *standard*, and *procedure* is intuitive to us in this situation. If I asked you where the statement *Add a cup of sugar* should go, you'd easily recognize it as a procedural step rather than a policy decision, and tell me to put it inside the recipe that it applies to rather than the introductory material.

Let's look at how this works in a corporate setting, taking an example from the real world. I've taken the statement appearing in panel 5 from a *Policy on Social Media* posted online by a branch of government.

Panel 5

It is prohibited for anyone to use an office social media account without the approval of the Director of Corporate Communications (DCC).

Will a requirement like this one get a lot of buy-in? The number of rogue social media accounts at the organization suggests not. It's easy to see why: statements of prohibition engender resistance. (For clarity, I'm not excusing the non-compliance, I'm merely accounting for it.)

To be able to fix this statement, we first need to determine whether, at its core, it is a statement of policy, a specification for a standard, or a step in a procedure. You can take a look at it again and see what you think.

My take is that getting approval from the DCC in each case is merely a **step in a procedure** — a mandatory step, perhaps, but a step nonetheless. Few people are motivated to support a procedural step on its own, especially one worded like the statement in panel 5, which exudes a particularly strong *we don't trust you* subtext.

If the organization is having trouble getting cooperation for this procedural step, it's because the policy decision behind it is opaque. It wasn't found anywhere else in that document.

The DCC, when asked to explain the reason for the requirement, replied that the organization doesn't trust people to use social media accounts properly unless they have been properly trained. That explanation sounds eminently reasonable; not only does it resonate as a sound media strategy, but it also explains the *we don't trust you* subtext.

Now that we understand the thinking behind the decision, we're in a position to **reframe** the statement to showcase the policy. One possible wording is shown in panel 6.

Panel 6

Individuals who have undergone the prescribed training are eligible to use an office social media account.

That statement represents the management decision about who gets to use the accounts, and that statement can garner buy-in from the rest of the organization much more easily than the original. Getting the approval from the DCC is merely an implementation step, supporting that policy.

Of course, we'll need to do some more drafting to create the right procedure for applying for a training account. That procedure will include a step mandating the approval of the DCC, but it will have a totally different impact. What we've done is separate *policy* from *procedure*, identify the policy decision behind the procedure, and then drafted it in a way that eliminates the confrontational attitude of the original.

We will look at other examples of how to reframe rules to increase engagement in Part III. What's important to remember, though, is that buy-in techniques apply primarily to policies, where the buy-in first takes place.

In the next chapter, we'll look at the interplay between policy and corporate culture.

4. CORPORATE CULTURE

Executive Summary

Cultural approaches to rule-making have an influence on the level of engagement. Policy wording reflects both the content of a rule and the writers' attitudes. Disseminating those two in parallel, a policy can unintentionally convey negative messaging, damaging the relationship between the parties. Organizations striving to create a culture of empowerment, trust, and accommodation can word their policies in a way that reinforces that culture; in contrast, poorly chosen wording erodes it.

Policy Reflects Corporate Culture

Workplace folklore tells of an organization whose management was frustrated by the toxic environment at their workplace. To counter it, they circulated a memo that said, "Despite our efforts to combat it, the overly negative attitude among employees has become intolerable. As a result, the beatings will continue until morale improves."

Corporate culture is a huge topic, and I don't have space in this book to do it justice. If an organization truly wants to improve its corporate culture, I highly recommend it find a specialist to help, such as Carol Ring, who wrote the Preface to this book. I would even recommend that organizations work on the corporate culture **before** undertaking an overhaul of their policy suite. It's to their benefit to have everyone rowing in the same direction before starting to making major changes to key documentation.

Our focus here is specifically on an organization's **rule-making** culture. Do the rules create a confrontational environment or do they encourage cooperation? Is there an us-against-them attitude among the rule makers vis-à-vis the rest of the organization, creating a social divide? How would you describe what getting people to follow the rules feels like: Running a prison? Leading a cause? Babysitting? Herding cats? Coaching a team? Fighting the enemy?

Along with their overt, intended content, rules convey messages and subtext. In this chapter, we'll start by looking at how to read between the lines to uncover the underlying messages transmitted by the words chosen. From there, we'll look at different approaches to setting rules, specifically along three axes:

- Do the rules reveal a culture of distrust or do they promote a culture of trust?
- Do the rules stifle decision-making or do they empower employees?
- Do the rules reflect black-and-white thinking or are they open to accommodation?

Once an organization has made some deliberate decisions around its target rule-making culture, it is then in a position to compare what they want to what they have.

Parallel Messaging

The problem with how it's "always been done" is that it puts us not merely in a break-even position, but in a deficit state. Too many current rules come across dripping with negative messages and laden with undesirable undertones.

Let's bring back panel 2 as panel 7.

Panel 7

Visitors are prohibited from entering the service area.

Returns are strictly forbidden. Customers must check all merchandise carefully before leaving the store.

Aggressiveness is not tolerated.

If you want to speak at our conference, you must submit a proposal. You must meet all our deadlines and not sell services during your presentation.

It's easy in these cases to tease out the negative messages that are woven into the fabric of the wording. They convey sentiments such as those in panel 8.

Panel 8

- We are in charge and you will do as we say.
- We are rigid and we don't care if this rule is inconvenient.
- We expect your unquestioning obedience and we are not open to discussing the issue.
- We are on the lookout for people trying to get around this rule; don't be one of them.

For most organizations, the messages in panel 8 are antithetical to the ones they'd like to be conveying, which are more along the lines of the supportive messages in panel 9.

Panel 9

- We're flexible and adaptable.

- We understand the challenges you face and can offer an accommodation if necessary.
- We value your cooperation. We appreciate that you're following the rule.
- We trust your judgment.

The wording of a policy statement cannot help but reflect both the content of the rule and the attitudes of the writer towards the people it is directed to. Those two elements are disseminated as parallel messages, and they both have an effect on the level of engagement.

Even statements that are not as brazenly dictatorial as those in panel 7 can send unintentional messages. The statement in panel 10 appeared as the first paragraph in one company's *Training Policy*. It's not a policy statement *per se*, but it introduces the policy statements that follow.

Panel 10

Under the State's Labor Code, the company is obligated to provide safety training to employees at least once a year.

The statement in panel 10 sends a terribly negative message, though that wasn't the intention. If you've detected it by this point I think you'd agree that it's not one the corporation wanted to send. If the message isn't apparent to you yet, take a moment to go back and re-read the statement before I provide an explanation.

Both corporate and personal values have an influence on how high on the Ladder of Engagement individuals are enticed to climb. The more the values behind a policy resonate with the individual, the more engaged the individual will be, and vice versa. When it comes to a training policy, I would expect to see statements more along the following lines:

- We want our employees to be safe.
- We want to help you work safely.
- We believe in the value of training.
- We want to take some responsibility for your training.

At a bare minimum, I would like to see some wording that doesn't imply the company is providing the training solely in a begrudged effort to comply with legal obligations. The absence of that language speaks volumes, sending the message that the organization views training as an added chore rather than a core activity. We will explore the relationship between policies and values more fully in part IV.

Here's another example, this time from a retail environment. The policy statement shown in panel 11 is found on the printed receipt issued by the store with each sale, as well as posted on a sign near the cash register:

Panel 11

Absolutely no returns of merchandise will be accepted without the original receipt.

As I mentioned earlier, I remain non-partisan on the merits of a policy decision. If a company wants to restrict the return of merchandise to those cases accompanied by the original receipt, I won't question the wisdom of that decision. What I will question, though, is how the decision is communicated.

Due to its heavy-handed wording, the statement in panel 11 bluntly conveys the following overt messages to the reader:

- We do take returns of merchandise.
- We have a strict process with a strict condition.
- Keep your original receipt; you'll need it should you decide to return the merchandise.

But the negative subtext is just as clear, conveying these messages:

- We don't trust you. Don't try to pull a fast one on us.
- We are not prepared to show flexibility on this policy.
- We don't really care if that works for you or not.

Later on in the book we will explore several broad wording techniques that make strict policies more palatable. For the moment, though, a number of alternative formulations are set out in panel 12.

Panel 12

We are happy to accept returns when accompanied by the original receipt.

Merchandise is returnable when accompanied by the original receipt.

We regret that we are unable to accept returns without the original receipt.

Each one of these formulations conveys all the positive messages and none of the negative ones, while retaining the level of strictness of the original.

Let's try one more example, this time with text taken from an online Web-based application. The form was pretty straightforward to complete, but this message appears at the bottom, reproduced in panel 13 with the original upper-case characters and applied boldface and underscore.

Panel 13

When you are finished you **<u>MUST</u>** select "Submit"

Wow, somebody's a grumpy-wumpy this morning. They're shouting at us. Here's some of the subtext that I can detect:

- Pay attention to what you're doing!
- We are tired of people not following our instructions.
- We have more important things to do than babysit people trying to submit applications.

True, it's only a simple procedural step, not a major policy announcement, so it's not a huge deal. On the other hand, drafting procedure in this manner does not cement an organization's relationship with its customers. My suggestions for more respectful wording are set out in panel 14.

Panel 14

Select "Submit" to continue.

The form will be processed after you select "Submit."

Complete the application by selecting "Submit."

I'm genuinely confused about why the business allows this text on their site. Are they blind to the discourtesy of the statement, or do they see it and just not care?

The subtext of a rule is a problem, of course, only if it is *unintentional*. If the organization wants to convey these messages — whatever I might think of them — then they're doing a good job. My suspicion, though, is that this issue went under the radar.

A Culture of Trust

Putting respectful language on an organization's radar entails in-depth discussion at the management level. It takes some serious introspection to identify a rule-making culture that befits the organization. Leaving it to chance means that most rules will default to the traditional style, which, unfortunately, sends some rather negative messages around trust.

Trust is a major determinant of people's willingness to follow rules. A healthy organization operates under a policy culture of *trust*, while a toxic one operates under one of *distrust*. In the last chapter I mentioned that most people are inherently motivated to do the right thing. A *culture of trust* acknowledges that fact, valuing individual contributions while supporting a collaborative approach to achieving organizational goals.

An organization's distrust of its employees or customers can manifest itself either conspicuously or with subtlety. In either case it is likely pervasive and inherently damaging. A policy culture of distrust maintained over an extended period results in the production of a large web of excessively detailed and restrictive policies. It operates under the assumption that, lacking explicit prohibitions, employees and customers will make poor choices. This defensive mindset leads to generating policies that are fear-based, focusing on preventing every possible negative scenario.

A culture of distrust is easy to spot. It is characterized by attitudes believing the worst, for example, "if our policy doesn't explicitly forbid taking office furniture home, then someone is going to do that and claim that they didn't know it wasn't allowed."

The mere possibility — however remote — that a bad action might occur is enough for management to issue a direct prohibition. **The subtext from statements worded in that way is one of suspicion and doubt in employees' judgment and integrity.**

The policies in an office operating from a culture of distrust explicitly itemize unacceptable activities. For example, in addition to a general prohibition against the inappropriate use of office computers, it spotlights specific activities, such as viewing unsuitable content, using gambling sites, and playing online games.

Conversely, a policy culture of trust is built on the foundation of mutual respect and positive assumptions about employee behavior. It imparts messages implying trust in employees ' ability to understand and adhere to professional standards, without an accompanying list of specific activities that are not office business, just to "make sure that everyone gets it." In a culture of trust, the rules would be conveyed using a policy statement like the one in panel 15.

Panel 15

Computers are provided for the purposes of corporate business.

Responsible employees know that — unless your company is in the casino business — betting at gambling sites is not a corporate activity. A policy culture of trust treats employees as responsible adults, capable of making sound decisions within defined constraints.

If a **genuine** need exists for some clarification around what *corporate purposes* are or what activities are disallowed, that information can be provided in supplementary documents in the Toolkit. Putting that kind of detail in the Toolkit sends positive messaging around being helpful; putting it into a Policy sends negative messaging around trust.

Operating within a culture of distrust can have far-reaching implications. It is one of the symptoms of a toxic workplace environment, where employees feel constantly monitored and undervalued. A distrustful atmosphere can stifle creativity, lower morale, and result in high turnover rates. At the interpersonal level, it creates an adversarial relationship between employees and management, eroding the sense of team cohesion and collaboration.

Given that complexity, transitioning from a culture of distrust to one of trust involves far more than policy rewrites; it requires a fundamental shift in the organizational mindset. As one might expect, it begins with leaders modeling trusting behavior to the rest of the organization. Moreover, it means focusing on the achievement of outcomes rather than micro-managing processes.

A Culture of Empowerment

Another aspect of corporate culture revealed by an organization's policy wording is its target management style.

In earlier chapters I talked about the legacy of the command-and-control management approach, which results in policies with precise, detailed language focusing on compliance and control. In contrast, a more participatory management style uses policy language that allows for times when we rely on individuals to exercise discretion and use their judgment.

In a command-and-control environment, hierarchical decision-making predominates, evidenced by orders flowing top-down and minimal employee autonomy. Senior management or a dedicated policy team crafts the corporate policies, often working in isolation. The primary preoccupation in this setting is on compliance and adherence to established procedures, so the policies cover a broad range of scenarios to account for all possible outcomes. They are characterized by strict limits, detailed procedures, and tight controls.

It's not unusual for employees working in organizations with a command-and-control culture to feel overly constrained and undervalued. That feeling depresses employee engagement and morale, eventually culminating in high turnover.

A culture of empowerment

The other end of the spectrum is marked by decentralized decision-making. **A culture of empowerment acknowledges that employees can be relied on to make responsible decisions and take actions that align with the organization's goals and values.**

Consistent with that approach, we often find the processes around policy development to be more collaborative. Management is open to seeking input from various levels within the organization, including those on the front lines who understand the practical implications of policies.

A culture of empowerment tends to foster accelerated decision-making, creativity, and innovation at all levels. That freedom leads to higher levels of employee satisfaction and a sense of ownership over work. Employees in such environments are likely to be more proactive, engaged, and committed to the organization's success.

Finding the right balance

Extremes at both ends of this spectrum are defensible only in rare circumstances, and what works for each industry is determined by its context. Military success relies on a firm command-and-control under-structure; in contrast, many areas of retailing have achieved enormous success by empowering salespeople to make decisions at the point of service. Emergency services like policing and law enforcement need to use **both** approaches: some situations demand a fixed protocol, while others call on the use of discretion to avoid dire consequences.

A Culture of Accommodation

Requests for exceptions to the rules are to be expected.

In my experience, a persistent uncertainty around how to handle them creates an unnecessary degree of anxiety. To avoid the anxiety, the requests are often summarily rejected, with the blunt reasoning that granting one exception necessitates granting them all. While that rationale might seem convenient, it is more tellingly a reflection of the organization's culture of inflexibility.

The "floodgates" argument is somewhat misunderstood.

The metaphor is powerful because it's easily visualized: A river flows through a little town. At times the water volume increases to a dangerously high level, threatening to overflow the banks. To control the flow, a set of floodgates was installed upstream. The closed floodgates are all that stands between a huge torrent of water pressing up against one side and the town on the other. When the floodgates are closed, practically speaking, the town water supply is completely shut off.

After one particularly prolonged season holding back the rushing river, the closed floodgates starts to take a toll. The wells run dry. The townsfolk don't know what to do. One day, a simpleton suggests that they open the gates only a wee bit, just enough to let a little water trickle into the town and replenish the wells. The town council agrees and arranges to open the floodgates just a crack.

Then the inevitable happens: the pressure behind the gates pushes them open all the way. Lesson learned.

The floodgates argument is often advanced as the justification for not permitting exceptions to policy. It asserts that even a minor change may be contra-indicated when there's the potential for the same change on a wide scale to be damaging or destructive. So far, that makes sense.

Unfortunately, it's that last condition — **the potential for damage or destruction** — that tends to get overlooked when raising the argument. Omitting that particular qualifier contorts the lesson to something more generic, more like a broad philosophy that we should never allow exceptions if we can't do the same for everyone. That interpretation is rather harsh.

Let's go back to the river. The village has a functional water tanker and making it operational would help alleviate the problem. Alleviate, but not solve. Given its capacity, the tanker can haul enough water to meet only 10% of the daily demand. Clearly that's not as good as a 100%, but it's a lot better than zero. Unfortunately, the town has a policy that *no one gets water until everyone gets water*. The rationale: they don't want to open the floodgates.

Can you see the logical fallacy? It comes from extending a perfectly good argument made for one set of circumstances to cover all other situations. We have to be prudent when applying these kinds of cautionary principles in cases where the decisions can inhibit practical solutions to a pressing problem.

Let's see what this issue looks like in a corporate context. Company A and Company B have a lot in common: all their staff want two monitors to be attached to their computers, and both companies have an insufficient number of monitors to supply everyone in the office with two. The policy at both companies states only that *each employee is equipped with a computer and a monitor.*

At that point the similarity ends, because the companies have different approaches to the role of policy and the nature of accommodation.

At Company A, no one gets two monitors. The policy is narrowly interpreted as meaning "no more than one monitor," resulting in an all-or-nothing situation. Given that approach, Company A is loath to accommodate anyone's request to be an exception until the monitor supply doubles. Like the poor thirsty townsfolk, everybody will suffer until arrangements can be made on a global scale. The employees may be unhappy, but the people doling out equipment feel secure in the knowledge that by raising the floodgates argument they can refuse requests for a second monitor without worrying about the repercussions.

At Company B, a number of people have two monitors. The company has made an accommodation several times, and hopes to grow that number over time. The people managing the equipment are happy to track as many requests for a second monitor as they can, even if most of those requests go unfulfilled for the foreseeable future.

What's going on here? The salient difference is the corporate culture around rules and exceptions. In a world without enough monitors to go around, neither company likes to say no to these requests. But the attitude is markedly different.

Company A considers any request for exception to be an imposition, so much so that they don't even want people to ask. The company prioritizes uniformity and control over flexibility and adaptability. From its point of view, each request for accommodation is an **unwelcome intrusion**. Acquiescing to it would be opening the floodgates, causing damage from which they could never recover. When faced with a request, their response is simply, *No, it's against our policy*, which shuts the requester down and creates a divide.

In contrast, Company B is open to requests for exceptions and accedes to them when it can. It values pragmatism and responsiveness to individual needs. The worst thing that can happen, it reasons, is not being able to fulfill the request and disappointing someone. Their response is more compassionate and collaborative: they have a principle to help them decide who will get priority and they give out a second monitor when they can. When they turn down a request, they say something along the lines of *We wish we were able to give you one, but we don't have enough just now. We'll put you on a waiting list for when we do.*

Weighing criteria

When a request for accommodation is based on a disability of some kind, the response of the organization tends to be more positive. Organizations committed to removing barriers for people often aim to satisfy 100% of those requests. The trap, though, is when *disability* becomes the only cases where requests for accommodation are honored. The floodgates argument is misused when it becomes the default response for every request we aren't obligated to fill.

Sure, in many cases involving requests for exception, issues of fairness may be at play. But ways to resolve issues of fairness exist that don't involve saying no to everyone. When we were children, an exasperated parent or teacher might have taken the toys away because everyone wasn't sharing them nicely. As adults, we have other ways we can deal with conflicting needs that don't involve punishing everyone involved.

Being True to Our Target

The best time to make decisions about the optimum rule-making approach for the organization is prior to drafting policies.

This relationship between management style and policy wording is not insignificant. Policy both sets the tone for organizational culture and has an impact on how employees perceive and engage with their work environment.

Rules cannot be effective when our approach to management and our approach to communicating rules are misaligned. If the written rules belie our assertions that we trust people, we lose credibility. I've seen situations where organizations produce reams of strict policy requirements, all set in a command-and-control, Parent–Child voice, but won't call them *policies* because they don't want to be perceived as dictatorial.

"People here don't like *policies*," they tell me, "so we just call them *guidelines*."

Employees are not so easily fooled. One look at those "guidelines" and they hear the dictatorial tone immediately.

I believe the appropriate analogy is "putting lipstick on a pig."

The purpose of policies is not to keep people in line; it's to help people do their jobs well. An organization will not be successful trying to convince its employees that it values *trust*, *inclusion*, *collaboration*, and *respect* if a simple reading of its rules quickly reveals that the real objective is *obedience*.

5. STAKEHOLDERS

Executive Summary

The wording of policy instruments responds to the needs of four major stakeholder groups — developers, consumers, policy managers, and approvers — the last of which are at times overlooked as a distinct group. In some circumstances, internal services like Audit, HR, Contracting, and Communications have a consultative role in the drafting process. Lawyers need to be consulted, too, while bearing in mind where policies diverge from contracts and how the drafting rules differ.

Up until now, we've been swiveling back and forth in an assumed two-party relationship: writer and reader. In practice, though, more interests are at stake than those two. For the wording of rules to be effective on an enterprise-wide level, the needs of all stakeholders warrant consideration.

These needs go beyond the standard operational underpinnings that everyone at every organization looks for: clear direction, established processes, proper supervision, functional technology and tools, appropriate training, and so on.

To produce a functional policy suite, the following groups of stakeholders have special needs to be taken into account:

1. Policy developers
2. Policy consumers
3. Policy approvers
4. Policy managers

5.   Other
- Internal Audit
- Human Resources / Contracting
- Legal
- Marketing and Communications

The first four are major stakeholders; policies are responsive when they take the needs of all four into account.

In small organizations, the individual who approves the policies may also be the developer, the policy manager, or all of the above. That's a lot of hats to wear. Moreover, since the policy presumably applies across the board, that individual also has a stake as a policy consumer.

Even in those situations, though, the activities are quite distinct: policy *development* ends the moment before approval and policy *management* and *consumption* pick up the moment after. As a result, the needs of each role are distinguishable in organizations of any size, even when a single individual represents multiple stakeholders.

The other roles are relevant only to particular aspects of the process and may go by other names in your organization. They may even be outsourced — with the exception of Internal Audit, which tends to be absent from smaller for-profit organizations.

This chapter looks at each role in turn.

1. Developers

Let's start with the rule writers. Their job, at its core, is to develop rules that meet the needs of the other stakeholders.

To do that properly, developers rely on the presence of three specific mainstays.

First, the potency of the finished product is dependent on a sound *governance framework*. The entirety of chapter 7 looks at this most critical component.

Second, to be consistent both across the organization and across time, developers need *standardized templates* to work from. As foundational pieces, these templates

- help maintain a uniformity of structure across documentation
- reduce the development time required for new instruments, and
- lower the likelihood of the unintentional omission of certain sections.

We will look at these templates more closely in chapter 17.

Third, developers need access to a set of *editorial tools*. These tools include corporate style guides, terminology management aids, and general language resources such as dictionaries, lexicons, and grammar references. We will look at this topic more closely in chapter 18.

2. Consumers

The group of stakeholders that seems to get the most attention are the eventual consumers of the policy, and by *consumers* we mean the people to whom the rules apply.

In reality, though, policy consumers are **less like a single group and more like a set of groups**, particularly in large organizations, where front-line workers have separate needs from back-office workers, and those differ again from the needs of executives.

The most important distinction to make among consumers, however, is between *SME* and *everyone else*. Those two camps may overlap, but they are distinct for one simple reason: SME **consume policies in their own areas of expertise differently from the rest of us.** HR professionals use HR policies differently from the way non-HR professionals use them, Finance professionals use Finance policies differently, and so on for all areas of specialization.

As a result, policy consumers fall into one of two categories: (1) people who are consuming policies in their own area of specialization, and (2) everybody else. We'll look at the implications of this distinction when we start organizing rule-related material in part II of the book.

3. Approvers

Policy approvers are a distinct stakeholder group, albeit one that often goes unrecognized as such.

In a small organization, where the rule developer and the approver are the same individual, the difference is academic; but whenever the approvers sit above the developers in the hierarchy, the separate needs become immediately apparent. Whether the approving body is a single individual, a group of individuals, or a group of groups, those needs have an influence on their behavior.

To prepare a proposed policy for submission to an approver, developers spend a great deal of effort on the construction of argument and support. If you've experienced this process already, you are familiar with the need to build a case. Before giving their approval, decision-makers will ask countless questions about the content of the proposed document as well as about costs, risks, and consequences. We try to anticipate them all and prepare responses for them.

What tends to get overlooked, however, is the approvers' need for material to be properly **filtered**. Approvers' time tends to be quite dear, and sometimes not made available to us as often as we might like. That delay can be frustrating for everyone else, since a proposed policy normally comes to a standstill until the approval process is complete.

As developers, however, we are in a position to show respect for the approvers' time by eliminating some of the obstacles to quick approval. When extraneous information sits in the documents under consideration, it opens the door to people spending energy discussing topics that take us down rabbit holes. We can fix that problem and speed the process up by arranging the information so that tangential details are available but don't compete for their attention.

First, we can separate product from packaging. The proposed Policy is succinct when it contains only the statements approvers need to make decisions on. Supporting material covering facts, such as the background and context, the rationale or strategy, the meaning of technical vocabulary, and other **details not actually requiring a decision** are all best relocated to separate documents. It is decidedly frustrating when approvers turn down a proposed Policy saying something like, "We don't have a problem with any of the rule statements, but we don't agree with how the context is portrayed." Best not to paint oneself into that corner.

Second, we can reduce the approvers' workload by removing from the proposed document — or at least visually separating — any statement that has already been approved elsewhere. A statement doesn't become any truer by being approved multiple times. The duplication of work costs time and effort that can be used for other things.

Finally, we can help the process move faster by removing "weeds" from high-level documents, so the approvers do not have to filter them out on their own. The methodology for organizing policy information described in chapter 9 covers how to identify these "weeds." We can move them either laterally to companion policies or down to subordinate instruments like Standards and Procedures.

The clearer the approvers' path forward when making decisions, the less time the journey will take. Conversely, the more clutter in the specific documents that need to be approved, the more obstacles for someone to trip over.

This doesn't mean that we don't show the approvers the big picture; indeed, many approvers will not focus on specifics without having the entirety of the situation in view. What it means is that we organize that picture into components reflecting the distinction between existing rules and new content on the table, and between higher-level and lower-level statements.

4. Policy Managers

The final main group of stakeholders are those individuals who will be managing the policies once approved.

Although this book doesn't look directly at the processes around policy management, we still need the rules documents to contain elements supporting them. The most visible elements are the various pieces of metadata used to track the document's lifecycle and enable operational reporting. Typically, many of those elements are captured by the templates that the developers work from.

A number of these elements are addressed in chapter 17.

5. Other Stakeholders

The first four organizational groups discussed have a stake in **every** new rules document produced. However, they are not alone.

Other groups may need to be involved in the process, for example, IT Services might be charged with supporting the technology serving up policies to consumers. But our focus here is limited to those groups whose interest is directly related to the **wording** of the documents.

Internal Audit

The Audit branch can be a valuable partner for policy drafters, especially when it comes to knowing when statements are susceptible to ambiguous interpretation. Its professionals need to be able to understand the policies when looking at the level of compliance during an audit.

Sending policy instruments through the Audit branch prior to submitting the text for approval can be a constructive mechanism to obtain feedback on the wording of rules.

Human Resources / Contracting

Here I'm talking about the parts of the organization that engage individuals to work under both contracts of employment and contracts for services. HR usually takes charge of the organization's true employees; contractors may also fall under HR, or they may be coordinated by a contracting or procurement branch, or perhaps even the legal branch. Over and above the authorities that these groups produce to govern their own corporate operations, their general consultative role in the policy development process is often neglected.

Rule statements that *impose obligations* on an employee or a contractor have the potential to be problematic, especially those that are approved post-hiring or post-engagement.

With the exception of small, loosely-structured entities, people who work in an organization typically have detailed job descriptions or contracts explicitly setting out the terms of engagement. Those terms have the potential to take precedence over rules documents, sometimes causing a conflict with activities dictated by the policies. Procedures are especially susceptible to this conflict, since they have the potential to attach specific responsibilities to individuals without regard to whether those responsibilities fall within the documented parameters of their work. A consultation with these stakeholders in select situations may alert us to potential incompatibility, giving us an early opportunity to revamp the wording accordingly.

Communications

Communications specialists bring skills to the table which can make a policy drafter's job easier in three distinct areas. Sadly, this opportunity is virtually universally missed and, as a result, three key pieces of the puzzle often lack the finesse that a professional touch can supply.

The first is terminology management. We explore that topic fully in chapter 19, but one threshold question is pivotal: *Which group at the organization is the right group to manage initiatives around terminology?*

Often, by default, the policy drafting team ends up handling them, but that may not be appropriate. Decisions around standardizing terms and resolving terminology friction have implications far beyond policy instruments, potentially compelling changes to the organization's business architecture, information architecture, and marketing schemes. Moving to gender-neutral language and unbiased wording is not exclusively a rules issue, and Communications specialists have the skills to coordinate enterprise-wide terminology management activities.

The second is branding. Our internal policies shape a significant portion of the employee experience, exactly the same way the external ones shape the customer experience. Marketing efforts in the organization can be directed by branding strategies, and these often include specifications for a number of elements that combine to create a unique corporate voice. That voice speaks in a deliberate tone, meant to reinforce the organization's values, image, and status. It makes no sense to allow that effort to be eroded by pages of rules that clearly do not conform to that voice. If it were up to me to recommend a headquarters within the organization to lead respectful language initiatives, the Communications group would be my first choice.

The third area is around the communications efforts that support whatever *change management* activities are required after new policy instruments are approved. It's not unusual for aggressively-worded policies to be introduced and implemented using aggressively-worded announcements. Again, Communications professionals are well-positioned to add some finesse to the content of those communications.

Lawyers

The final set of stakeholders to discuss is the lawyers. They are a special group of stakeholders, because they often sit in positions of power and are not afraid to exercise it. It happens too often, unfortunately, that people tell me they want to adopt the approach in this book for their policies but their company's lawyers won't permit it.

When I run workshops today, I'm generally delighted with the degree to which the respectful language approach resonates with a wide variety of professionals. Many lawyers are already promoting policy documents with a less dictatorial tone, recognizing that organizations can improve their level of compliance with regulation by making those requirements more palatable to the people working there.

Interestingly, whenever I encounter some resistance, it almost always comes from a lawyer. Some still hold onto the notion that policies should have the strict, unyielding cadence of contracts, emphasizing legal authority over collaborative guidance. One lawyer even insisted that using more respectful language would do employees a disservice, by lulling them into thinking that employment situations don't entail a dominant–subordinate dynamic.

I can understand their confusion. When I went to law school, the topic of corporate policies came up only sporadically and we learned nothing about them outside of their legal implications. Instead, we focused primarily on their relationship to employment and contract law. When I practiced law, Policies were typically treated simply as extensions to the contractual documentation.

It was not until I moved out of law and into the business world that my eyes were opened to the notion that Policies are a lot more than that. They are not merely legal instruments; they shape leadership styles, management practices, corporate culture, and workplace wellness.

Policies versus Contracts

Policies and contracts have different purposes. **A contract takes an inherently adversarial approach while a Policy takes a cooperative one.**

The goal of a contract is to establish the agreed rights and obligations of the parties. An employment contract sets out the terms of employment — in theory, to protect both the employer and the employee, although in practice it usually heavily favors the side of the employer.

The primary consideration when drafting contracts is *legal defensibility*, not interpersonal relations. We don't really care whether the people we're contracting with are positively engaged or feel warm fuzzies when reading it. In the vast majority of cases, the contract is signed and then never seen again unless a problem erupts that needs to refer to the contract text for resolution. That focus on legal precision can result in a cold and strict tone, which is perfectly acceptable in contracts.

Policies, on the other hand, are meant to help the organization function smoothly. They have the ability to encourage compliance through *engagement* rather than intimidation.

Well-written Policies set a positive tone for the organization, and contribute to the ongoing employee and customer experience long after the initial employment contract is signed and put away. Drafting a Policy as if it were a contract misses an opportunity to foster a positive corporate culture. We run the risk that, instead of improving engagement, it will engender resistance by being too impersonal and legalistic.

The lawyers and the various SME in the organization are likely on the same page when it comes to the desired outcomes, but their methodologies differ. The legal system is still primarily adversarial in approach; an organization's policy regime is collaborative. To strike the right balance, policy drafters and legal professionals need to collaborate. We don't want our Policies to be drafted exclusively by lawyers any more than we want our contracts to be drafted exclusively by policy writers.

A lawyer once explained to me what was actually happening in the exchange of documents between the business area and his legal office. His words are still with me today:

"If people just drafted policies in everyday language," he told me, "I wouldn't have an issue with them. Instead, they draft them in pseudo-legalese. That means that I have to take the document and fix it to be good legalese. I wouldn't have to use legalese at all if the original were written without it."

A telling comment, isn't it?

I recommend passing all draft corporate Policies through the legal department for a review of potential risks. Once the lawyers identify and assess those risks, management can decide if any specific policy statement entails any risk they are unwilling to accept. Ultimately, the goal is to harmonize legal soundness with the collaborative spirit that defines a well-functioning organization.

Notes

6. THE DOCUMENTATION LANDSCAPE

Executive Summary

It is important to distinguish primary sources — being those that set rules — from secondary sources, which restate or explain them. Primary sources are most functional when tailored to the vocabulary of subject matter experts, prioritizing precision. Secondary sources, in contrast, offer plain language explanations to a general audience, focusing on practicality and ease of understanding.

Policies, Standards, and Procedures all sit within a larger landscape that comprises all the documents used and maintained by the organization. It's time to pull back and survey that landscape to see how everything interacts.

External vs Internal Information

For convenience, I'm going to refer to an organization's intranet as the *office manual*, by which I mean to include all the documents, Web pages, and database screens that contain information to help people do their jobs.

Examining the contents of the office manual closely, we can identify five separate groups of documents serving as sources of information. These groups can be divided into two broad categories, based on the information's origin:

- *Internal information* — generated inside the organization (3 groups), and
- *External information* — generated outside the organization (2 groups).

Identifying the origin of the information is key to determining accountability for its validity or accuracy. To know whether we can rely on any piece of information, we need to know *who is vouching for its truth*? When we come across a statement in the manual prohibiting bringing pets into the office, we need to able to answer the question, *Whose rule is that?* Does it come from the company? The building management? The city? The penal code? Who do we check with to see if the rule has changed?

For *internal information*, the organization itself bears the responsibility for accuracy. The information is considered correct when the organization validates it as such.

In contrast, *external information* is assessed for accuracy by evaluating the credibility of its *source*. For example, when seeking a copy of the text of the US Constitution, we would likely disregard the version posted by the local school's grade five class in favor of the one posted on the government's official Web site. We accept the information from a verified source as correct when the source itself validates it.

The documentation landscape is illustrated in figure 3. We will look at each of the five groups of sources in turn.

Decisions Made Outside Your Organization

External rules are those generated *outside* the organization. They can be attributed to one of two types of origins: *External Authorities* and *Other Sources*.

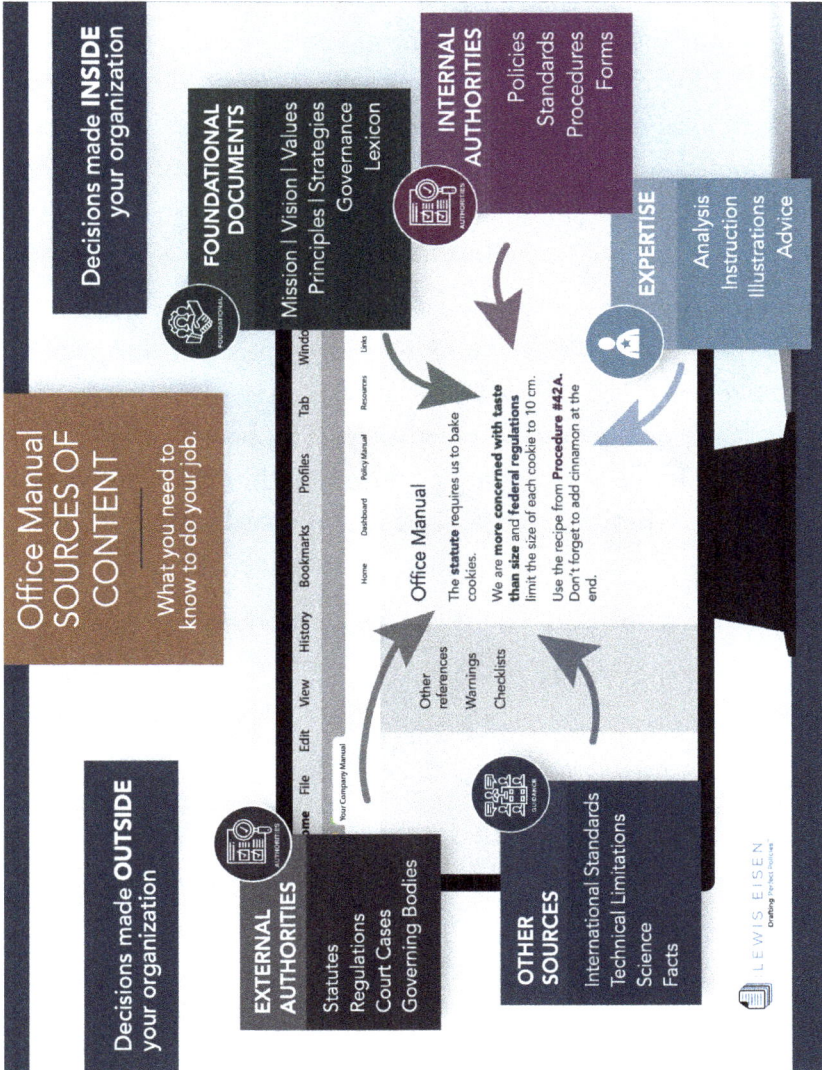

Office Manual
SOURCES OF CONTENT

What you need to know to do your job.

Decisions made **INSIDE** your organization

FOUNDATIONAL DOCUMENTS

Mission I Vision I Values
Principles I Strategies
Governance
Lexicon

INTERNAL AUTHORITIES

Policies
Standards
Procedures
Forms

EXPERTISE

Analysis
Instruction
Illustrations
Advice

Decisions made **OUTSIDE** your organization

EXTERNAL AUTHORITIES

Statutes
Regulations
Court Cases
Governing Bodies

OTHER SOURCES

International Standards
Technical Limitations
Science
Facts

Home   File   Edit   View   History   Bookmarks   Profiles   Tab   Windo

Home   Dashboard   Policy Manual   Resources   Links

Your Company Manual

Office Manual

The **statute** requires us to bake cookies.

We are **more concerned with taste than size** and **federal regulations** limit the size of each cookie to 10 cm.

Use the recipe from **Procedure #42A**. Don't forget to add cinnamon at the end.

Other references
Warnings
Checklists

LEWIS EISEN
Drafting Perfect Policies

Figure 3

Group 1: External Authorities

This group of information sources encompasses all of what we might think of as *official regulation*. It includes statutes passed by the government, as well as subordinate documents like regulations, decrees, and ordinances. Municipal by-laws belong in this group as well, along with court and tribunal judgments. In other words, this group includes any *government decisions* that have an impact on an organization's activities.

Also included in this group of sources are the regulatory requirements of *professional bodies*. Lawyers, engineers, medical practitioners, and other professionals are typically subject to oversight by some form of authoritative or licensing body. That body establishes rules that bind the professionals, and then monitors their compliance.

Statements sourced from External Authorities are operative whether or not they are "approved" inside an organizational policy.

Group 2: Other Sources

This group of sources includes *facts* and *technical information* originating externally that may constrain an organization's decisions or activities.

For example, every computer operating system has a few specific characters (such as asterisks and colons) that it cannot accommodate within a filename. That limitation constrains the document naming conventions an organization adopts. Those constraints are non-negotiable, as are all the restrictions imposed by an operating system, so from the point of view of the organization those constraints are simple *facts*. Just as is the case with External Authorities, statements of fact are true even if they're not "approved" by the organization.

Including facts inside a Policy lengthens the document — and thereby the entire development process — unnecessarily. Moreover, their presence is misleading to the approvers; they are ostensibly being asked to approve every statement in a proposed policy, although, in reality, **existing facts are not candidates for approval.**

It's common, unfortunately, to see facts drawn from many domains of knowledge being slipped into corporate policies. Here are a number of examples of statements of fact that I have come across in Policies, waiting to be "approved" along with the rest of the document. For each fact, the actual source of that information is in parentheses.

- "water freezes at 32°F/0°C" *(science)*
- "the company was founded in 2015" *(history)*
- "*Generally Accepted Accounting Principles* set depreciation at 30% in this case *(externally-developed standards)*
- "the device doesn't function under water" *(manufacturers' specifications)*
- "the boardroom table can accommodate up to 20 chairs" *(physics)*
- "the elevator can't hold more than 10 people at a time" *(licensing restrictions)*
- "the cleaning solution is caustic" *(chemistry)*

- "break-downs are difficult to fix" *(direct experience)*, and
- "if you let go of the leash, the dog may run away" *(common knowledge)*.

Facts as constraints

The items described in source groups 1 and 2 act equally as constraints on the activities of the organization. An organization can no more produce widgets that are outlawed by the penal code than it can change the caustic nature of a chemical.

The information from these external sources is still important, and may need to be conveyed to employees and customers at the same time as the Policies themselves. Fortunately, the office manual can accommodate both, and can integrate both sets of information seamlessly if that makes for the most reader-centric presentation.

The expanse of legislation

Some people ask why the External Authorities group doesn't sit as the topmost box of the entire landscape. It seems odd to them that it appears at a lower level than the Foundational Documents. "After all," they ask, "aren't an organization's mission and vision subject to the law?"

The short answer is yes, but it's more complex than that. Similarly, often an organization will claim that it is governed by only a single statute, such as a business corporations act, a hospital act, and so on, but that claim is not entirely accurate, either.

When you stop and think about it, the number of statutes that constrain an organization's activities can fall into the **hundreds**. Not only do we need to count statutes that specifically set compliance requirements for each industry, but we also have to include the laws that apply universally, coming from all three levels of government — national, state/provincial/regional, and local/municipal. These laws broadly cover multiple topics, among them:

- Penal codes
- Copyright and patent protection
- Illegal food, drugs, and contraband
- Import and export control
- Taxes
- Highway traffic and vehicle standards
- Labor codes
- Building codes
- Privacy protection
- Freedom of information / Access to information
- Security of information
- Health and safety controls

In fact, **no organization is subject to only one statute**. To specifically determine the correct positioning, however, we need to distinguish entities *created by statute* from those that are *privately formed*.

Some organizations — mostly government, but also many not-for-profit, charitable, and political ones — are creatures of statute. For them, that statute is their *enabling legislation*. Enabling legislation can establish a mandate, set operational and reporting parameters, delegate powers, and so on. A small number of organizations may actually be the product of more than one piece of enabling legislation.

In the documentation landscape, the foundational documents sit higher than everything else. Without them, operations don't get off the ground. Where enabling legislation creates a mandate, that statute can reasonably be positioned above it in the hierarchy. But **only** that statute. All the other applicable laws, regulations, court decisions, and so on, work to constrain—not drive—the activities of the organization.

For example, the *Freedom of Information Act* can be characterized as *enabling legislation* for a handful of entities that were created by it. For everybody else, it's merely *applicable legislation*, influencing the foundational documents as they are developed.

Decisions Made Inside Your Organization

Moving to the other category of information sources, we come to *decisions made inside your organization*. Statements in this category fall into three source groups:

- Foundational documents
- Internal Authorities, and
- Toolkit documents.

A hierarchical relationship exists among these three groups. Foundational documents *inform* the authorities, and those in turn inform the documents in the Toolkit. Where a statement in a lower group conflicts with one in a higher group, the higher one takes precedence.

Group 3: Foundational Documents

Long before anyone puts pen to paper to draft policies, organizations create a number of documents setting out basic decisions on how the business will function overall. Foundational documents reflect the thinking done to launch and steer the ship, so to speak. Ranging from the broad-based to specific, they can include

- a *mission* or *mandate*
- *vision* statements
- corporate *values*
- *goals* and *targets*
- *key performance indicators*
- *research* and *white papers*
- *strategies* and *plans*.

Foundational documents are amended infrequently, but it does happen. Because foundational documents inform the authorities, amendments to the former often require consequential changes to the latter.

We'll look at specific foundational documents more closely in part IV, when we look at values-based policies.

Group 4: Internal Authorities

The *Internal Authorities* group holds the Policies, Standards, Procedures, and official Forms, all of which are based on internal decisions.

In chapter 3, we talked about how to determine whether we need to issue a formal policy or simply to communicate instructions directly to one or more recipients. The test for a statement of policy, you may recall, is whether the rule is intended to outlive the rule maker. We also looked at how codifying a statement in policy makes it part of the organization's *modus operandi*.

Once we know that a rule belongs in a policy instrument, we need to do more than slap the title Policy at the top of the page. *Formal authorities* are so designated because they undergo the systematic approval process the organization undertakes for those kinds of rules documents. It's the rigor of that process — however extensive or minimalistic the organization wants to make it — that turns what would otherwise be a transactional document into a formal authority.

Once approved, Internal Authorities typically signal their formality by bearing indicia exclusively allocated to authorities, for example:

- a title incorporating a *reserved document type*, such as *Policy on …*, *Standard on …*, etc.
- a formal structure, such as a standard *template* or standardized *headings*
- accessibility through a virtual or physical *space clearly marked* as leading to formal authorities, such as a designated folder, or a landing page for corporate Policies.

In the paper world, offices use tangible indicators like authorized *signatures*, official *stamps*, and designated *storage cabinets*; in the electronic world, software supplies equivalent functionality.

Official Forms

I'm sure you noted the inclusion of *Official Forms* in this source group. While beyond the scope of this book, Forms work in tandem with the three main authority types to complete the instructions around the collection of information. For example, a procedure could specify that a salesperson is to collect either

- a customer's name, address, and telephone number, or

- the information requested in *Form 17A—Customer Information.*

In this way, the Form has power matching that of a Standard or Procedure.

When Forms are not systematically coordinated with the other authorities, the possibility for conflict arises. Take the situation, for instance, where a policy specifies that the collection of customers' personal information will be restricted to what is necessary to fulfill the required transaction. In the absence of coordination, a rogue form could easily include fields requesting all sorts of unnecessary information, effectively circumventing the policy.

This book contains no chapter on Forms, so this is the only time you'll see them mentioned. For that reason, I'll make two clarifications before leaving the topic.

First, organizations typically have a variety of forms and fill-in templates in circulation, many of which are not *official Forms*. A form can exist as an independent artifact, or be embedded within a larger document. Only those forms that undergo a *formal approval process* become official and can be included in the authorities group. All the non-official forms — upper- or lower-case *f* — are part of the Toolkit.

Second, form development requires decisions along two facets: what information to collect and how to elicit it. Whether customers' names comprise one element — *first and last name* — or two elements — *first name, last name* — is a *business decision*, part of the organization's information architecture. The determination of the best way to lay out fields visually to elicit those elements is a *design decision*.

Group 5: The Toolkit

The final group, the *Toolkit*, contains all the supporting documents we want to supplement the information in the other four groups. It's in these documents that we present, explain, illustrate, and expand on all the information people need to know to be able to do their jobs.

Because these documents speak directly to those who are governed by the rules, they are most effective when they are written in *plain language* and are *easy to navigate*.

Toolkit documents may appear in several versions, tailored for different audiences. That option gives us the flexibility to direct some materials to management and others to rank-and-file employees. They may be reproduced in multiple publication formats, in various levels of granularity, and even translated into different languages.

Since Toolkit documents are informed by documents from all the other groups, the information in them is correct only so long as it doesn't contradict them. The currency and accuracy of the Toolkit can be maintained by setting up a process whereby changes to policy instruments are followed by a review of affected Toolkit documents.

Most organizations find it more expedient to permit the Toolkit documents to be approved at a level lower than the approver of the Policies and Standards. As we will see in the next chapter, the delegation to a lower level of the authority to approve support documents gives the organization the latitude to modify the Toolkit more quickly and with fewer bureaucratic stumbling blocks.

Authorities/Toolkit vs Mandatory/Optional

Some people confuse the *Authorities vs Toolkit* distinction with a *mandatory vs non-mandatory* distinction.[3] They are quite different. What separates Authorities from the Toolkit is the *process* used to approve the document, not the mandatory or optional nature of the content.

Authorities undergo a prescribed *formal process* for development, approval, and repeal, and the **statements in them set requirements that are mandatory, optional, or discretionary**. A policy, for example, can contain a statement giving employees the option to work from home.

In contrast, *Toolkit* documents can be produced any number of ways and are typically approved at a lower level. Like the Authorities, they can contain statements describing mandatory, optional, and discretionary requirements. The e-mail communication from the boss obliging everyone to

---

[3] I have replaced the word *Guidance* used in previous editions of this book with *Toolkit* because it was inadvertently reinforcing that confusion.

submit a weekly report, discussed back in chapter 3, is a *Toolkit* document with a mandatory requirement.

Signage

Signage is a document type that falls in the *Toolkit* group, but is often mistakenly considered an *Authority*. The sign in figure 4 is an example. It's being used to implement the policy, but it's **not the policy itself**.

In chapter 3 we noted that, at their core, written Policies, Standards, and Procedures are transactional business records, attesting that specific decisions were made on specific days by specific approvers.

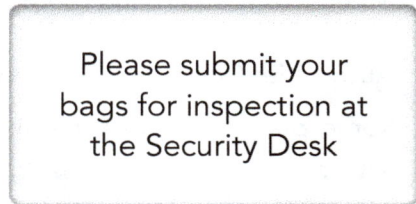

Please submit your bags for inspection at the Security Desk

Figure 4

The content of the sign conveys none of those facts. Even if it contained that information, the sign is not the transactional record of decision; it is merely a communications medium.

The original decision is found back in some policy, standard, or procedure on office security, perhaps part of a larger set of rules indicating the following:

- Security personnel maintain a security desk at the entrance to control admission.
- Security personnel have the authority to search bags of people entering the building.
- Security personnel have the authority to bar entrance to the building, based on

✦   what they find in the bag, or

✦   an individual's refusal to submit a bag for search.

And so on. These are all statements of policy. To implement them, one or more procedures have been established for initiating, conducting, and concluding a search, and one of the procedural steps is making some form of request for cooperation of individuals entering the building. For the sake of convenience, that request has been posted on a sign; but **the request itself is not a policy statement**. Like a *How To Vote in the Election* Web site, it tells people what they need to know, essentially eliminating the need to read the original policy instruments.

Now that we've surveyed the documentation landscape, we have a sense of where policies, standards, and procedures fall in the bigger picture, namely, on the *internal decisions* side of the page. The depiction of the three source groups as a vertical hierarchy in figure 3 is not haphazard; in fact, it aligns with the governance of the organization, which is the topic of the next chapter.

Notes

7. POLICY GOVERNANCE

Executive Summary

Clear governance lines are companions to the instrument hierarchy, matching approval levels to various instruments. Policy statements that exceed scope or level of approval are of no force. External Standards are incorporated by means of a statement adopting them; internal ones are incorporated by means of a statement enacting them. Setting the approval level of Standards below that of Policies, where feasible, maintains the separation between operational details and business oversight.

Governance Framework

Organizational governance is essentially about pinning down who has the authority to make various decisions and what processes are involved.

A *governance framework* provides a structured backbone to rules creation, ensuring a consistent approach to development, review, and approval across the organization. Not only does a strong framework support an organization's mission, but it also promotes accountability and transparency, both of which are essential components for building trust. Weaknesses in an organization's governance framework can have negative consequences for implementation and enforcement.

Our concern here is how governance interacts with policy writing. The documents derived from governance-related decision-making start at the highest levels — charters, by-laws, and so on — and continue down through the various decision-making bodies of the organization, covering the entire gamut of the *decisions made inside the organization* side of the documentation landscape.

Authority and Responsibility

Governance looks at both an entity's *authorities* and its *responsibilities*, and those two are not the same thing. **An authority is a power of decision; a responsibility is a statement of allocation.** You may be familiar with the saying *Responsibility without authority is a recipe for frustration.* When the manager responsible for boosting store sales is denied the authority to make decisions around marketing, stock, pricing, and other impactful elements, the job can easily become a maddening no-win situation.

We'll look at responsibilities more closely in chapter 17; for now, what's relevant is that **assigning a responsibility typically does not include an accompanying authority.** When a document means to assign both authority and responsibility to an individual or group, many organizations use the term *accountability* for that purpose. Holding someone accountable for a specific result implies

- a delegation of authority to make at least some of the decisions that lead to that result, and
- an expectation that the individual will take some degree of ownership for outcomes.

Accountability often also entails the duty to evaluate those outcomes against the responsibilities assigned and the authority granted.

Governance Principles

Governance operates under a number of principles, several of which are directly applicable to policy development. Not respecting any of these five principles puts the governance documents at risk of being dysfunctional.

1. Entities have boundaries

Every decision-making group in an organization is established with a defined scope of authority and range of responsibilities.

Clarity of scope and range is a prerequisite to effective operation. When the scope of authorities and responsibilities across the board are well-defined, every group knows exactly who does what.

Fuzzy boundaries, in contrast, produce two sets of problems. On the one hand, where the boundaries seemingly overlap, groups are liable to step on each other's toes. On the other hand, where there's a gap in coverage, we witness parts of the organization's activities for which no one takes responsibility.

2. Authority cascades downwards

The power to make policies is granted to the highest level of the organization by statute, charter, or contract. In the absence of a specific prohibition to the contrary, that power is delegatable from higher levels to lower levels.

3. Authority is valid only when documented

Anybody at an organization can purport to make any rule they like, but a rule can operate only when the rule maker has the authority to make that rule. That kind of authority cannot be "implied" or "understood"; it is valid only when supported by written evidence.

Following principle #2 above, a delegation of authority is valid only when it comes down from a level higher than the delegate; for example, Policies can authorize the approval of Standards and Procedures by a lower level. These statements of delegation are of greatest value when they are transparent and accessible to all relevant stakeholders.

The need for proper documentation cannot be overstated. **A missing link of delegation in a chain of authority has the potential to invalidate all the decisions made below that level.** The potential for invalidation of a decision raises a risk that it may not be enforced in a court of law.

4. Presence of checks and balances

Rule development processes include a system of checks and balances as safeguards to make certain that the governance of the organization is respected throughout the process. Requirements for acceptance by specific branches of the organization are established to prevent the abuse of power.

5. Restriction to areas of competence

Chapter 3 introduced the notion of decision competence as one of the determinants of rule validity. Let's look at the issue more closely.

Decision Competence

As we saw in chapter 3, by approving a rule or a set of rules in a Policy, a person or group is implicitly asserting that the decisions are within their competence. Decisions outside their competence are clearly unenforceable.

Most people recognize this issue quickly in the most clear-cut cases, but fail to spot it in more subtle cases. To see how this vitally important test has far-reaching implications, let's look at some scenarios where issues of competence validate or invalidate a rule.

Cases where competence is geographically based are ridiculously obvious, so using one of those cases as an example makes it easy to spot the flaws.

Geographic jurisdiction

Imagine that one of the state governments in the United States — say, Massachusetts — were to approve the policy in panel 16.

Panel 16

People living in Britain must wear hats at night.

It's absurd, of course. The government inside one nation obviously has no legal authority to make rules binding the individuals inside another. In the vocabulary of law-making, we would say that regulating the wearing of hats in Britain is outside the competence of a US state government.

But how did we reach that conclusion?

One way is to examine the parameters of what the state government constitution—or its equivalent—allows it to regulate. According to the *Constitution of the Commonwealth of Massachusetts*, that legislative body claims jurisdiction over matters "arising or happening within the commonwealth, or between individuals living there."[4] Since Great Britain is not within the geographic boundaries of the state, the latter's rules don't apply to the former.

Another way would be to identify the specific body that **does** have the competence to make those rules if it wanted to. We don't have to look hard for that one; that would be His Majesty's Government in London.

When we recognize that the Massachusetts Constitution doesn't claim jurisdiction over matters in Britain and the Government of the UK does, the competence issue in panel 16 becomes obvious.[5]

Subject matter authority

While geography is an easy-to-spot limitation imposed on decision-making competence, others may not be so readily apparent. Panel 17 shows a statement extracted from one organization's employment policy.

---

[4] Chapter I, Article III

[5] A few laws do exist that **reference** activities taking place on foreign soil; for example, laws may prohibit people from entering a country if they have participated in terrorist activity anywhere in the world. The activity can happen anywhere; the law itself is applicable only within the jurisdiction that passed it.

Panel 17

Employees are forbidden from using illegal drugs.

That rule is ineffective because it goes beyond the competence of the organization.

Employees are already prohibited from using illegal drugs by definition. Where government laws prohibit the use of a substance, an organization subject to those laws can't make rules overriding them. Unless the government has delegated powers down to the organization to make decisions about the legality of drugs, the organization doesn't have a say in the matter. Purporting to "approve" this statement in a policy is making a decision outside the competence of the organization.

Statements restating an existing law or truth are not policy decisions. When we want to remind people of that law or truth, we have other documents to put it in.

(Incidentally, it's not clear why the prohibition in panel 17 wasn't directed at **everyone** at the organization. Specifically picking on employees is unnecessarily divisive, and could be evidence of a culture problem at the organization.)

Delegated authority

Within an organization the same question arises: does the approver have the competence to make the decision they are purporting to make?

Let's start with a simple example: a prescribed corporate dress code. Consider a situation where the organization's Accounts Payable group proposes a rule forbidding the wearing of sandals in the office, and wants to record that rule in a Policy approved by its own senior officials. Before anyone starts to look at whether this policy is a good or bad move for the company, the threshold question of governance needs to be addressed: does the Accounts Payable group have the authority to make rules about what people wear?

If we don't ask that preliminary question, we open the organization to abuse. Can the Facilities branch issue the same policy? What about the Security branch? Surely we would have governance issues if we simply allowed every group to assign itself policy topics on a first come, first served basis.

I chose this example because its absurdity is obvious. We know that different branches are given authority over their broad operational fields, so as a practical matter we expect that their rules need to match those fields. If a rule about sandals were issued by the organization's Security branch, it would be defensible only if the approvers can establish how footwear poses a security risk. If the rule emanated from the Facilities branch, we would expect to see a risk related to building maintenance.

But not all cases are so clear-cut. Consider a company whose Marketing branch and Customer Service branch each issues its own policy on the correct greeting for customers as they enter the store. What if the two greetings conflict? The competence question is, *Who has the authority to make that rule?* In that situation, good governance documents would go a long way to resolving what could become a nasty turf war. Once it is clear which group has the authority over greetings, we will know which of the two policies is valid.

Authority for disciplinary matters

A similar problem occurs when a policy that threatens some kind of disciplinary measure in the absence of compliance is approved by a rule-maker lacking disciplinary authority.

Take, for example, the policy in panel 18.

Panel 18

Users who share their network passwords will lose account privileges.

If this policy were issued by the HR department, we probably wouldn't have a problem. But in many organizations, this policy comes from the IT branch. In those cases, for this threat to be properly actionable, the governance model has to have accorded the IT branch some kind of disciplinary authority. After all, it's one thing to remove someone's computer privileges for operational reasons; it's quite another to do so for disciplinary reasons.

Without that authority, a disciplinary statement is a hollow threat. It would be unfortunate for the organization if a grievance tribunal decided in an employee's favor on the grounds that a rule went beyond the competence of the approver. In chapter 13, when we look at breaking down internal policy silos, we will see how those two branches might collaborate to make this statement work.

Definitions beyond competence

Decision competence applies to definitions as well.

I typically come across this kind of overreach of authority in university and corporate policies against sexual harassment. Often those policies contain a definition of what constitutes sexual harassment. It's commendable that the institutions have a policy on the topic, but that definition is superfluous.

We are fortunate in most first world countries to have laws against sexual harassment. Those laws supersede any definition made by an organization. "Sexual harassment" in your jurisdiction is what the legislation and the applicable Supreme Court say it is, not what the organization's policy says it is. Where the corporation's definition differs from the courts', it will lose that contest every time.

The same is true for any concept where we are required to defer to a legal definition. Common examples cover issues like what constitutes breach of copyright, theft, disclosure of private information, and so on. Any definition the organization "approves" takes second place to the legal definition.

Incorporating Standards and Procedures

A hierarchical policy architecture means that Standards and Procedures fall below Policies, and need to be incorporated into the suite of regulatory instruments in some way.

External Standards are incorporated by means of a policy statement *adopting* them. Internal Standards are incorporated by means of a policy statement *enacting* them.

Procedures, normally bespoke to the organization, are rarely imported from external sources, but the comments here apply to Procedures as well.

An adoption or enactment statement can *mandate*, *recommend*, or *permit* the Standard or Procedure. An organization may even want the flexibility to mandate different levels of applicability to different situations and organizational units. Statements that take advantage of those options are illustrated in panel 19.

Panel 19

Standards #10 and #12 apply to Web pages published by group A.

Standards #10 and #15 apply to Web pages published by group B.

Web pages published by group C need not conform to any standard.

Adopting an external Standard

Easy as pie. All that's needed to adopt an external Standard is to say so, in either a Policy or another Standard. A simple statement of adoption might look like the example in panel 20.

Panel 20

The company adopts the W3C Web Content Accessibility Guidelines version 2.1 as the standard for corporate Web pages created on or after October 30, 2023.[6]

---

6 https://www.w3.org/TR/WCAG21/

Any approval body having the authority to set standards inherently has the authority to adopt standards.

Enacting an internal Standard

Almost as easy. Standards created internally can be enacted in one of two ways. The first is along the same lines as the previous example, adding a statement to a Policy, as in panel 21, specifically calling out the Standard by name.

Panel 21

Graphics software packages used in the office are limited to those authorized in the *Standard on Office Software*.

While that format looks straightforward, it has two disadvantages. First, it's the policy equivalent of what software developers call *hard coding*. Each existing Standard or Procedure would need to be named in a Policy somewhere. Incorporating rules documents one at a time is cumbersome and not particularly efficient. Another disadvantage of hard coding is that renaming the Standard demands a coordinate change in the Policy that enacts it.

Second, and perhaps more importantly, it means that the decision-making body approving the policy is also approving the Standards and Procedures. In an organization that's smaller or where roles overlap, that may not be an issue. In those cases, it might be expedient to put all the approval authority into one group to streamline operations. In a large organization, however, this conflation of roles becomes a problem.

Separating oversight from Weeds

Consider a larger organization with an Executive Management Board as the top governing level. Approving all Policies, Standards, and Procedures across the entire organization, it's composed of the most senior leaders. They meet once a month to review policies submitted for approval. They are the C-Suite — the CEO, COO, CFO, etc. — all high-power thinkers with the capacity to look at the organization from the 10,000 ft. view.

The day will come when we need to amend the *Standard on Office Software*, to add a new product to the list. Who should be approving that change?

That kind of amendment is not about an opportunity or obstacle at the 10,000 ft level; it's back down on the ground. In fact, it's down in the weeds. The decision to add another piece of software to a Standard is one best made in the trenches, with our sleeves rolled up and knee-deep in … well, you get the picture. When SME in a field need to evaluate technical data, and to make logistical decisions that take into account industry standards, physical and technological restrictions, the costs of purchase and maintenance, the level of training required, and so on…they need to immerse themselves in the details.

The organization is not functioning in the most cost-effective manner if decisions about weeds are made at the oversight level. To a degree, the stumbling block for some leaders is a lack of trust in leadership at the lower echelon. That reticence can be costly.

If we've engaged specialists then we need to let them make some decisions; if we can't trust them, we have issues a lot bigger than how to word policies. From this point on, I'll work from the assumption that we've hired good people, we trust them, and they are capable of making sound decisions.

Delegating authority for Approval

The more efficient way to incorporate Standards and Procedures into a policy suite is to insert a *delegation statement* into a Policy. Again, I'm following the example set by the way statutes and their regulations are handled. The statement would look something like the one in panel 22.

Panel 22

The Director of HR is authorized to approve Standards and Procedures on the following:

- Onboarding new employees
- Maintaining records of attendance
- Keeping records of disciplinary matters

    etc.

Delegation statements can also include a set of principles or criteria delineating the direction, targets, or constraints that the decision makers need to take into account.

By yielding the approval authority for Standards and Procedures to entities below those required for Policies, rules development can take place simultaneously at multiple levels.

Bipartite Approach

This bipartite approach, splitting off Standards approval from Policy approval, allows us to allocate accountability in the organization more appropriately.

Crafting a standard involves a different set of decisions from crafting the policy enacting it. Those who shape the specifications in a Standard are SME. By being the approvers of the Standard, they are accountable for ensuring that **each specification is technically defensible**. Amending a technical specification is a technical decision, not a management one.

In contrast, enacting or adopting a Standard may have business implications, and that piece is a management decision, not a technical one. By embedding the enacting statement inside a policy, the policy approver takes responsibility for decisions around the scope of its adoption.

Let's look at how that split works in practice by looking at a business operating a chain of restaurants. Its food safety experts have determined the appropriate cleaning standard, shown in panel 22, to be used when closing down at the end of each day.

Panel 22

Kitchen Shut-Down Standard

- Surfaces scrubbed with antiseptic cleaning solution.
- Refrigerators set to 4°C / 40°F.
- Heating surfaces cooled to room temperature.

- Perishables double-wrapped in plastic, then stored in glass or metal containers.

After reviewing this Standard, senior management agrees to make it mandatory for every restaurant in the chain, and enshrines that in a Policy.

What if someone in the organization were to object? Separating the approver of the Standard from the approver of the Policy helps us direct the objection to the right level.

Victor, for example, thinks double-wrapping food before putting it into a container is overkill. He argues that double-wrapping doesn't keep the rolls any fresher than single wrapping. Victor can first take his objection up with the approver of the Standard who, as a SME, is in a position to entertain technical discussions.

Sophia objects for a different reason: she claims that implementing the Standard would cost too much time and money and will dig into the profits. That objection is best dealt with by the approver of the Policy, who decides whether the Standard is mandatory, optional, or recommended.

When weighing the merits of Sophia's objection, the Policy approver may seek out the Standard approver to hear their side of the argument. At the end of the day, though, it's the policy approver who decides whether the hardship imposed on the business is more or less important than the technical consequences foreseen by the subject matter experts.

8. Enforcement

Executive Summary

Policy compliance can be a collaborative exercise, rather than a confrontational one. Enforcement techniques can modify both behaviors and environments. Excessive harsh language and hollow threats are typical signs of a dysfunctional regulatory system. To incorporate discipline measures, business lines need to work with the HR branch — typically the only one authorized to mete out punishment — to map infractions to the general disciplinary grading system.

The Big Picture

Policy compliance is an enormous topic in both breadth and depth. Extending far beyond the drafting elements, it ranges from education to feedback mechanisms and from monitoring to enforcement. Increasing the level of compliance requires the creation and nurturing of an environment where adherence is viewed as normalized behavior. That environment is sustainable when it is reinforced by social norms and peer pressure.

Some people hear the word *compliance* and immediately equate it with *enforcement*. That reaction is somewhat unfortunate, because **compliance has a collaborative aspect to it** as well. In many cases, an organization's ability to claim full compliance with a set of requirements can even be a source of pride, used both for advertising purposes and to motivate employees through the recognition of their efforts and teamwork. Initiatives around culture, incentives, and education can encourage people to head in the right direction.

Similarly, when people hear the word *enforcement*, they often immediately equate it with *discipline* and *punishment*. That's also unfortunate, because **enforcement need not be a negative experience**, whereas discipline and punishment are almost always negative.

Those associations are strong, making the road from compliance to discipline seem short, virtually eliminating the wide spectrum of activities that support various pieces of it.

Enforcement Strategies

Enforcement strategies fall into one of two lanes: modifying the environment and modifying human behavior.

Modifying the environment

Modifying the environment is a strategy that can be invoked both proactively and reactively. It looks to minimize the conditions favoring a policy breach by altering the physical, technological, or organizational context. The goal is to make compliant behavior easier and non-compliant behavior more difficult. Since our focus here is policy wording, I won't spend a lot of time on this topic, but I'd like to raise a few points.

Examples of environmental modification include everything from posting additional signage to physically locking a door. It also includes preemptive steps like configuring software to do validation checks on information before storing it, re-designing forms, and using software blocks to prevent access to certain Web sites.

Preventative measures will only take us so far. Security professionals tell countless tales about workarounds to blocking mechanisms. Some people creatively look for holes and weaknesses — not necessarily out of malice, but often merely to make things more convenient for themselves. Taking away their convenience comes at a price: being unable to skirt a roadblock makes people unhappy, and in some cases they make their unhappiness known to everyone around them.

Actions aimed at increasing compliance, whether directed toward the individual or toward the environment, are much more successful when the atmosphere is cooperative rather than confrontational. Actions that are seen as invasive spur resistance quickly, and rendering the environment inhospitable will bring us the same lack of support as antagonistically-worded policies. If our goal is maximum engagement, then the best way to achieve that is to get people to **want** to have the environment changed, making it easier for them to comply. For that reason, **modifications are best received when made in the spirit of helpfulness**.

Modifying human behavior

The ability to modify someone's behavior is based on the mutual recognition of some form of relationship between the rule maker and rule follower. That relationship can be formalized, as with an employment contract, but it can also be situational, such as between citizens and lawmakers, commercial enterprises and customers, or buildings and visitors.

We don't normally think of the enforcement actions we take in the face of a non-compliant customer or client as *discipline*. The store that won't take back a bathing suit once the package has been opened is not "disciplining" the customer, nor is the doctor when turning away a patient who, in breach of office policy, shows up repeatedly to the office without an appointment. While both situations involve the enforcement of an existing policy, the insistence on policy compliance by the store and the doctor is not done with *punitive intent*.

In an employment situation, the modification of individual behaviors includes a set of specific interventions intended to make compliance not only more likely, but more desirable. These interventions can include training, incentives, audits and inspections, re-negotiation of contract, and — yes indeed — disciplinary measures.

The disciplinary process in a corporate setting is a feature of a contractual arrangement, such as employment contracts or those between an association and its members. Values-based policy looks to strengthen the ability to modify behaviors by appealing to specific values shared by individuals and the organization. We'll cover that topic in Part IV.

Functional Regulatory Systems

In many cases, low policy compliance is often symptomatic of a *dysfunctional regulatory system*.

When running a workshop with a room full of policy drafters, I often ask how many of them also have responsibility for enforcing the policies they write. Usually about 20% raise their hands. Next, I ask how many of those who said yes have actually been given the *tools*, the *training*, and the *authority* to carry out enforcement. All but one or two hands are lowered.

This situation is but another example of *responsibility without authority*. Too many SME are ordered to *tell people what to do and then make sure they do it*; but in most circumstances, that assignment is ineffectual. Without fixing the dysfunctional system behind it, compliance levels are likely to remain unchanged.

The best way to portray why that system is dysfunctional is to contrast it with a functional one. The administration of automotive traffic laws will serve as a straightforward and easily relatable example, since it is found in virtually every legal jurisdiction.

We start from the position that the state has an overall interest in making roads safer and reducing accidents. To achieve that goal, governments implement one or more strategies aimed at regulating driving within their own borders. Inevitably, one of those strategies includes curbing the speed of traffic on public roads.

To implement that strategy, each municipality is charged with setting speed limits for its own roads. In response, the municipality employs some SME in vehicular traffic. Those experts get to decide whether the speed limit on any particular road will be set at 40, 50, 60 or whatever — in miles or kilometers per hour.

In a manner of speaking, these experts develop a series of micro-policies on vehicle speed. For each decision establishing a speed limit on a stretch of road, as a policy maker they need to able to articulate two things:

1) a *defensible rationale* for the decision, and

2) the *risks* of not setting that limit and of non-compliance.

That's it; the job stops there. Those individuals have zero involvement with enforcement. Instead, as you know, that piece of the puzzle is assigned to a totally separate group of professionals.

As the designated enforcers of speed limits, the police are provided with the three minimum elements required to do that job properly: the *tools*, the *training*, and the *authority*. Once properly equipped, they are in a position to start looking for offenders. They don't act in isolation, of course; other groups are also key players in the speed enforcement process, such as the court system and the driver licensing bureau. The speed limit enforcement process is a complex machine that involves a number of participants ... but it doesn't include the individuals who drafted the rules being enforced.

The enforcers, when they eventually come into the picture, are for the most part disinterested in the policy development history. They tend not to care **why** a road was assigned a particular maximum speed. One could try to convince the police officer, the license bureau, or the judge that the road could stand to carry a higher speed limit, but I doubt it would be a good use of one's breath. (If you end up being successful at it, do feel free to let me know.)

In a functional regulatory system, **rule writing and rule enforcement are complementary but separate processes.** The experts in rule making work on one side of the table,

the experts in enforcement on the other. Each has been giv-
en the requisite tools, training, and authority to do their jobs.

There may be cases — in areas other than road traffic safety
— when the combined responsibility for rule making and
enforcement could be assigned to the same team. That
approach is not inherently wrong, but it works only when
the assignment is accompanied by the tools, training, and
authority for both roles.

Leveraging the HR Disciplinary Process

Statements around discipline in a business line's policies are
valid when the governance documents give that business
line the authority to impose discipline.

That situation is unusual, though. To ensure the uniformity of
the disciplinary process across an organization, normally a
single business line has exclusive authority to issue warnings, initiate proceedings, and levy consequences. Typically,
that business line is the HR branch. Its disciplinary process is
applicable to breaches of rules emanating from all parts of
the organization.

The discipline process tends to be graded in severity, so
that minor offenses bring minor consequences and serious
offenses are treated more severely. Where a business line,
like IM/IT or Finance, does not have its own disciplinary
powers, it can incorporate its infractions into the corporate
grading system by working directly with the HR branch.

Let's take the Facilities group, for example, which rarely is
accorded disciplinary powers. It can work with the HR
group to incorporate infractions to its rules into the general

discipline grid: for example, putting chewing gum under the desk might be a low level 1 infraction, while taking an ax to the furniture in the lobby would be a serious level 5 infraction. Punishment would be meted out according to the normal corporate practice for infractions, by the people who have the authority to do that.

Dysfunction reflected in the wording

What's particularly germane to this book, however, are the visible signs of a dysfunctional regulatory system. Often it is revealed in the wording of the organization's policies.

In the absence of any real authority to enforce their policies, drafters compensate by reaching for the only tools in their arsenal: words. They attempt to beef up compliance by inserting harsh words into the rules, such as *always* and *never* and *no exceptions*. It's as if they're being forced to raise their voices to be heard. The policy grows longer, sounds stricter, and talks meaner.

The frustration created by being put in this position is palpable. It has an impact on employee morale and organizational stability, and serves only to increase the *us-against-them* divide that we looked at in chapter 4.

When one's only weapon is the ability to issue threats, one issues more of them. But warnings like *Failure to comply with this policy may result in consequences* sound pretty hollow in the overall scheme of things. Moreover, apart from being vague, it presents a subtext of distrust: the drafter doesn't trust that people will follow the rule in the absence of a threat.

Unenforceability Revisited

Our last stop on the topic of enforcement is to look at where it may cause a problem at the policy drafting stage.

Whenever *unenforceability* is cited as a reason for not instituting a policy, it raises some red flags for me. I respond by bringing three questions to the table:

(1) **Exactly** what aspect of the rule is alleged to be unenforceable?

(2) Is the allegation accurate? and

(3) Does unenforceability *per se* invalidate that rule?

Remember that fictional Massachusetts law in the last chapter, purporting to regulate the wearing of hats in Britain? My discussion in the last chapter focused on the lack of competence by that approving body over that topic.

Some people might characterize my concern as just a fancy way of saying that the rule is unenforceable, but that's not true; at least, I'm not sure what the enforceability issue would be. It's not as simple as saying that the US can't enforce a law in Britain, because British and US law enforcement agencies cooperate extensively when they need to.

So let's see if we can pinpoint the concern.

The "unenforceability" of a rule is not an objectively measurable state; rather, it is a conclusion reached after evaluating the circumstances. Typical observations tending to lead people to this conclusion are the following:

- Infractions are difficult to detect or prove.

- Infractions are not easily attributable to a specific source.
- Evidence of the infraction is perishable or transient.
- Enforcement mechanisms are ineffective, too costly, or unavailable.
- Enforcement happens too late in the process to avoid the damage.

Even if those observations prove true, does that mean we shouldn't approve a rule?

Take the first two observations above, related to detectability and attributability. High-tech espionage is illegal in many jurisdictions around the world, despite the inherent difficulties in detection and tracing. Yet no one advocates that those laws should come off the books until we come up with an easier way to expose spies. Even if infractions are difficult to detect today, they might not be tomorrow. Those laws stand, despite potential difficulties in enforcement.

The third observation doesn't seem to stop municipalities from passing laws forbidding noisy parties after a certain hour. The fourth observation doesn't prevent us from passing anti-pollution laws that are costly to monitor and police in sparsely-populated areas, and the fifth observation is not a bar to having a law against murder.

The notion that enforceability creates an insurmountable obstacle just doesn't hold water.

In fact, many of these observations are excuses. For decades governments resisted passing laws to control tobacco smoking in offices, restaurants, and public places, consistently tendering the excuse that those laws would be "unenforce-able." Yet today laws restricting smoking in public places exist all around the world. Why the change? It's not that we are witness to amazing advances in smoke-detection ability or law enforcement. What opened the door to advancement was solely a change in people's attitudes.

PART II — INTERNAL AUTHORITIES

Chapters in this part

Notes

9. Primary vs Secondary Sources

Executive Summary

Policies, Standards, and Procedures are primary sources for setting rules, and are fundamentally distinct from secondary sources that repeat, explain, or elaborate on the rules. Primary sources are most functional when tailored to the vocabulary of subject matter experts, prioritizing precision. Secondary sources, in contrast, offer plain language explanations to a general audience, focusing on practicality and ease of understanding.

Documentation Landscape

You may recall that many of the principles put forward in this book are based on a legislative model. A country's legislation is the primary legal source of rules intended to influence people's behaviors, so the model has a lot to teach us.

In chapter 6, we examined the documentation landscape. We saw that the fourth group of information sources, *Internal Authorities,* includes Policies, Standards, Procedures, and official Forms. Internal Authorities are informed by the Foundational Documents, and in turn they inform the documents in the Toolkit.

This chapter will look more closely at how to select content for Policies, Standards, and Procedures.

Primary vs Secondary Sources

All too often, a document with the word *Policy* in the title is really a dog's breakfast of brand new rules, existing rules, general advice, best practices, definitions, examples, and commentary. In those cases, we can't tell whether the document is intended to be a *primary* or a *secondary* source. Combining those two into a single document compromises the ability to characterize its contents correctly.

A *primary source* is an original, authentic, statement made firsthand. The words come directly — to use the vernacular — "from the horse's mouth," or from an eye-witness to an event. In the documentation landscape, **primary sources sit in Group 4: Internal Authorities.**

A *secondary source* is someone else's report of those words or those events. Created after the primary source, the information is given to us secondhand. **Secondary sources sit in Group 5: Toolkit documents.**

This distinction is not new by any means. Researchers, librarians, historians, and archeologists preserve the distinction right up front, because **conflating primary and secondary sources risks completely invalidating the results** of the research.

Lawyers make a similar distinction: primary sources — mostly official legislation and court decisions — are referred to as *law*, while the secondary sources — being the encyclopedia-style texts containing synthesized law and annotations by learned scholars — are referred to as *legal authorities* or *legal commentators*.

The distinction is fundamental: **primary sources set rules; secondary sources restate or interpret them.**

If we are the ones setting a rule, it goes into a primary source; if we're merely regurgitating someone else's rule, it goes into a secondary source.

An equally important principle is that a **document cannot be both a primary and a secondary source** at the same time. When we look at a piece of legislation — which is always a primary source — we can see that every substantive statement in it is the authoritative instance of that rule. Legislation does not, in addition, contain commentary, examples, instructional material, and so on, because that material is secondary source material.

As we sit down to draft a new document, one preliminary decision is critical: *Is this new document intended to be a primary source or is it a secondary source?* In other words, are we creating a new written authority or are we making statements attributable to an existing authority? The answer we give definitively determines the nature of the contents.

The Role of Authorities

In chapter 5, I talked about how policy consumers fall into one of two categories: (1) people who are consuming policies in their own area of specialization, and (2) everybody else. HR professionals make specific demands on HR Policies that the rest of us don't; likewise with IT professionals and IT Policies, Finance professionals and Finance Policies, and so on.

Like all good authorities, policies are written for accuracy and precision, not to be educational tools. Individuals unfamiliar with the field should not be expected to read through an authority and immediately understand it. While a large number of people may be governed by a specific Policy or Standard, a much smaller number will ever need to read it.

Traditional policy developers still insist that everyone in the organization — regardless of which group they fall into — should be able to read their policies and benefit from the wisdom within. "Everyone whom the policy governs should read it," they say. That myth is pervasive.

To see what makes it a myth, it may be helpful to look at a point of reference. What does this scenario look like in the outside world?

Authorities and guidance in the outside world

At some point in your life you may have voted in a political election. If so, let me pose the following question: *Before casting your vote, did you first read the local equivalent of the Elections Act?* No???

Perhaps you applied for a passport at some point. Did you start the process by reading through the statutes and regulations governing passports? Today, do you prepare to file your annual tax return by reviewing the applicable *Income Tax Act?*

In all those cases, the governing statutes mentioned are the *authorities*, the legislative equivalent to corporate policies. They set out the official rules dictating the way we vote, get a passport, and pay taxes, and they apply to anyone who's even just **considering** engaging in one of those activities.

I'm going to go out on a limb here and speculate that you have managed to cast a vote, travel with a passport, and experience the bureaucratic joy of tax returns, despite never having read any of the original documents setting out the official rules. Am I right?

Frankly, unless you're a specialist in one of those fields, I would be surprised if you'd ever even cracked those documents open, much less read them. In fact, despite my having impressed their fundamental importance upon you, I suspect that you're not going to add any of them to your holiday reading list. Fortunately for us, the government doesn't insist we read them before we begin pestering it with questions.

The bottom line is that our being governed by an official set of rules has never been a sufficient inducement for us to read them. Even the ones that directly apply to us are not on our radar. Moreover, that approach is entirely reasonable: we are governed by statutes numbering in the hundreds and regulations numbering in the thousands. We can't possibly read them all.

If we do read any specialized documentation in preparation for government-related activities, it's most likely to be information found on the government's Web sites or in booklets provided for that purpose, titled something like *Instructions for Voters* or *How to Apply for a Passport*. **Those sites and booklets are user manuals**, produced specifically to provide the information we need to be able to complete the task at hand. Well-written user manuals don't overload our brains by making us read any parts of the legislation we don't need to know. The contents are limited to practical, easy-to-understand explanations covering only relevant material.

Not everyone takes the time to read user manuals, of course. Still, those booklets are far more likely to be read than the original statutes.

In fact, for the majority of us, the legislation is not even a fallback position. When we come across something we don't understand in one of the little booklets, we don't seek clarification by reaching for the statutes; instead, we are most likely to seek out a specialist in the field who can answer our questions.

That self-help technique makes perfect sense; when we aren't expert in a field, we typically don't feel competent to deal with expert subject matter. We tend to believe that our own understanding of an authoritative document in someone else's field is too prone to error to base decisions on.

Other parts of our lives operate similarly. We may have played Monopoly®, but it's unlikely that we've pored through the complete official rules. Many of us have chaired a meeting without ever wading through *Roberts' Rules of Order*, and have learned to drive a car without scrutinizing any of the applicable motor vehicle legislation.

Authorities are go-to reference sources when a dispute needs be to settled, not the day-to-day reading material guiding what we do.

Most of us feel that being forced to read those authoritative documents carefully before taking action would be an onerous burden. Now imagine how other people feel about being forced to read the policies we've written.

People are far more likely to read documents written specifically to help them do their jobs. If we can supply good Toolkit documentation, telling people only what they need to know in a given situation, they will be far more receptive to reading that. Afterwards, if they still have questions, they will contact us for an explanation.

Change of mindset

Every so often, a reader gets to this point in my book and drops it in horror. They're not happy with my distinction between the needs of SME consumers and everyone else.

"If the average reader can't understand your policy," someone wrote, "that's your failure as a writer and all the guidance documents in the world cannot rehabilitate your error."

Yep, that's definitely the traditional view. It's somewhat out of step with the model of legislation demonstrated by the election, passport, and tax examples. It's also inconsistent with the importance of **maintaining** technical language in policy instruments, a point covered in the next section.

Besides — not to put too fine a point on it — the **average** reader is not the lowest one in the group, it's the one in the middle. If the average reader can understand the text, then so can the half of the group above that reader, but not the half below it. Aiming for the average still leaves a significant number of people who need support material to be able to be functional.

It's hard enough to achieve a level of clarity in our policies where all the SME in that field are in agreement about what each policy statement means. Personally, I would not add the extra burden of raising the bar to include everyone else in the office, especially if we're only going to aim for the top half of the group.

Use of Technical Language

Too often, a policy instrument is "dumbed down" because of the fear that some individual, someday, somewhere, may read the document and not understand it.

That fear pushes the SME to re-draft the text into everyday language, creating a tension between finding terminology that is appropriate to the field and using wording that speaks to the layperson.

But hold on a minute! The (incorrect) assumption underlying that language simplification effort is that **everyone** is supposed to be able to read a Policy and understand it.

If we respect the fact that authorities and Toolkit documents have **distinct purposes**, and proceed on the basis that primary sources are predominantly for use by SME and secondary sources can be prepared to service other audiences, then that tension becomes much easier to resolve.

To be useful to professionals, policies might need to contain some technical language that the layperson may not understand. There's nothing wrong with that. The situation is no different from the technical language found in the *Income Tax Act*, the *Elections Act*, or any other statute dealing with a technical subject. Same for *Robert's Rules of Order*, the *Generally Accepted Accounting Principles*, the W3C's standards for HTML 5.0 ... the list could go on and on.

Defining *clarity*

Technical language is a tool used by specialists in a field to achieve accuracy and clarity of expression, resulting in a shared understanding among professionals.

We say that we want our policies to be clear, succinct, and respectful, but if *clear* doesn't mean that **everybody** can understand it, then what does it mean?

Clarity when drafting a policy instrument means the *absence of ambiguity*.

I recommend what I call the *ten eyes test*: do five SME all agree on what the policy statements mean, what the decisions are, and where the lines are being drawn?

Let's look at an example, this time from the health care industry. A local hospital has a Policy containing the statement shown in panel 24.

Panel 24

All incoming cases presenting sub-dermal or sub-cutaneous lesions are treated as epidemiological risks.

I have no clue what that policy means. But so what? I'm not a medical specialist, so whether I understand that policy has no bearing on anything. Truth be told, even if they rewrote their policy in lay terms, I still wouldn't read it. I'm just a patient. When they want me to follow some rules, they will post a sign or hand me a pamphlet called *Information for Patients*. The rules in the pamphlet need to be in plain language so I can understand them, but the statements in the primary sources that inform the pamphlet can be as technical as they need to be.

I don't want the airline industry to dumb down its safety policies, standards, and procedures so that I can understand them. Similarly, I don't want the government to dumb down the building code, the elevator safety standards, or any other specialized document. If those professionals need to take advantage of technical jargon, then let them. I ask only that anything they want me to understand be put into simpler language in a separate document.

A reader once took me to task on this point, claiming that I held the statement in panel 24 out as a bad rule. Actually, not being a medical specialist, I have no clue whether it's a good or bad rule, so on that point I remain totally neutral. What I do feel strongly about is that its value as a policy statement should not hinge on **my** ability to interpret it, even if it applies to my situation.

What's important is that the medical specialists are all in agreement on what the policy statement means. If they don't all agree, then we have a problem that needs some attention! That problem needs to be fixed before going any further. On the other hand, if they agree on what it means, then they can explain those parts we need to know in language that everyone else can understand.

When drafting a policy, it's difficult enough to obtain agreement among the experts in that field. Far too often, when I dig a bit, I find that the SME in an organization don't all agree on what each statement means. That situation is a recipe for disaster.

If we can achieve a single, common understanding of a given wording among the experts, we have done as much as can be expected. It is onerous and unnecessary to impose the additional requirement that non-experts need to understand it. Provide the non-experts with good Toolkit documents and they won't ever need to read the original policy instruments. The Manual will tell them everything they need to know.

Keep the Policy in our back pocket

A Policy is like a wall stud rather than the wall itself. It supports the wall, but it shouldn't be visible when we walk into the room. If the Toolkit documents, as they appear in the office manual, are well written, most laypeople never have to see the original authority.

SME will reach for the Policy when they need to check it in the context of a problem. Like the dictionary, they can turn to it as required.

On rare occasions, someone will come to challenge a statement in the manual. They're upset, for example, that the office manual says they can't chew bubble gum while working at the service counter. They storm into our office shouting, *"Show me!* Show me where it says that in the Policy!"

On those occasions, we will be prepared. We calmly reach into our back pocket — figuratively speaking — and pull out the original Policy. We point to the appropriate statement and softly say, "See right here? Where it says 'no masticatory substances'? That means bubble gum."

Apart from that situation, most laypeople need never read the actual Policy, much less understand it.

From Policy to Manual

If your current policy looks like the dog's breakfast that I described earlier, don't despair. I have an easy way out for you.

Your document probably tells people everything they need to know. If it's clear and effective, it reflects a lot of work and that effort need not go to waste. To leverage everything it can offer, we're going to move that document from Group 4 to Group 5 of the Document Landscape, and then we're going to create a brand new instrument to be the Internal Authority.

Start by renaming your document, changing it from *Policy on Widgets* to something along the lines of *Understanding Our Policy on Widgets*. **Now, instead of a fractured authority, it becomes a valuable secondary source.** As a document in the Toolkit, it tells people everything they need to know about the topic.

Now go through that document and try to **identify a primary source for each statement in it**. You can credit a statement to any document type in Groups 1 to 4. It's especially collaborative when you can identify the source as one of the Policies produced by another section of the organization. Alternatively, you might determine that the statement was actually written by a subject matter expert trying to explain things. That's fine; for now, just note the source as SME.

As you go through the document, there will be some statements for which you can find no authority, but which require weight that can be provided only by an official approving body in the organization. Those kinds of statements are candidates for the replacement *Policy on Widgets*. Collect those together, and add new ones as you find them.

This approach is equivalent to writing an academic paper in college. Our paper is a secondary source. When we need to quote the origin of a specific statement we insert a footnote, pointing readers to the primary source. We don't footnote every sentence in the paper, just those that we suspect will be challenged by the professor or other readers.

By taking this approach, we're able to repurpose the original work to best advantage.

At this point, you might still find it challenging to identify the different types of source statements. In the next three chapters, we'll look at the distinguishing features of Policies, Standards, and Procedures.

Notes

10. POLICIES

Executive Summary

Consistent with the distinction between primary and secondary sources, the body of a well-written Policy is limited to statements of policy. Standards and procedures belong in separate documents, and educational material, explanations, and commentary are all appropriate for Toolkit documents in the office manual. We want our office manuals to be as comprehensive as possible; in contrast, we want to keep our Policies as succinct as possible, reducing the amount of time needed for drafting, consultation, and approval.

What goes where? tends to be the most common question I'm asked. Having come across so many dog's-breakfast–style Policies, people are understandably confused about how to organize the different kinds of rule statements.

What Belongs in a Policy?

The policy template can elicit standard elements, such as the title, date, approver name, objective, and so on. In contrast, the body of a well-written Policy contains only *statements of policy*. Period.

No standards and no procedures. No explanations, no commentary, no examples. No reminders, *nota bene* (N.B.) statements, or disclaimers. Just statements of policy. After approval, we can take all that supporting material and present it in the office manual, along with everything else people need to know to get their jobs done.

We just finished covering the distinction between primary and secondary sources in the last chapter. Statements setting original rules belong in the Authorities; everything else belongs in Toolkit documents.

Reminding readers about an existing law or fact is an educational activity, not a regulatory one. We do not write Policies to educate people; we write them to set rules that don't yet exist. The policy development process takes enough time already, without someone adding unnecessary work.

Comparing processes

Which kind of document takes longer to approve in your organization: a Policy or a piece of instructional material? In most organizations, a Policy needs to go higher up and involves more steps and check-points than most other documents.

As a practical matter, obtaining approval can be arduous and lengthy. Extraneous material chews up the time and resources of drafters, consulted stakeholders, approvers, translators (if that's part of your process), and everyone else involved in the policy development process.

Every statement in the document has the potential to serve as a stumbling block, should someone object to the way it's worded. The fewer stumbling blocks a Policy contains, the faster it can progress toward approval. Leaner documents have the ability to move through the stages of development and approval more swiftly than the bloated variety.

Save the policy work for the statements that have no choice but to go through the formal approval process, and put the other statements somewhere that involves less work.

Requests for inclusion of content

One of traps that plagues policy drafters is the incessant contribution of content from well-meaning colleagues. Everybody seems to want to add some statement to our Policy, with reasons ranging from the compelling to the fanciful.

In my experience, a large majority of these requests are motivated by a desire to achieve one of the following goals:

- education
- elaboration
- justification, or
- comprehensiveness.

Individuals tendering these statements typically justify their requests with a rationale. We can tell which of these goals actually underlies the request by listening for clues in the wording of the rationale.

Education

Requests resulting from the desire to *educate* people are punctuated with concepts around increasing knowledge:

"People need to know this information."

"We need to remind people about this."

"We need everyone to know where this rule comes from."

Fortunately, we can educate people using other types of formats: instructional material, promotional material, live training, and others from the larger Toolbox. Educational statements belong in the office manual; in a Policy, they serve only as clutter.

Elaboration

Requests that come from a wish to *elaborate* use words related to comprehension:

> *"Some people won't understand the Policy unless we expand on it more."*

> *"We need examples to help people understand."*

> *"People might be confused if we don't include some sample scenarios."*

The desire to increase comprehension is laudable, and I'm going to assume that they are correct: that extra information will be key to some people's understanding. How fortunate that all those examples, elaborations, and explanations can go into that same educational document.

Justification

People wishing to include statements of *justification* use words related more to logic and reasoning:

> *"We want everyone to appreciate why the rule is this way."*

> *"People will want to know what's driving this."*

> *"We can't just put the end point in the document; people need to see how we got here."*

No question about it, statements providing rationale and justification are useful both for the people being asked to approve the Policy and for those looking back in posterity wondering about the thought process involved. The appropriate documents to hold this type of information are strategy papers, cover sheets, and supplementary reports, all of which can accompany the Policy as it makes its way through development.

When a bill goes before an elected government body for approval, the bill itself does not contain the justification for its existence. Any background information, justification, or supporting evidence comes in a separate document accompanying the bill. Once the bill is passed into law, that supporting document is moved elsewhere for safekeeping, and the statute or by-law that's left contains only the rules.

Draft Policies are the corporate equivalent to those bills. If the justification for a rule changes, we don't want to have to amend our Policy just to update the justification! Keep those documents separate.

Comprehensiveness

Finally, people wishing to include statements for the sake of *comprehensiveness* use words related to scope and breadth:

> *"We need to cover all the angles."*
>
> *"People will want to know everything."*
>
> *"Why shouldn't it all be in the same place?"*

We've already seen that a good Policy does not have to be a compendium of everything to know on a given subject. That's the role of the office manual.

We want our office manuals to be as comprehensive as possible and our Policies to be as succinct as possible.

A good office manual provides people with all the *who*, *what*, *where*, *when*, and *how*, along with everything else they need to know to do their jobs, educating, explaining, justifying, and filling in the gaps. Adding statements to Policies that educate, explain, or justify the rules effectively turns them into an office manual.

"Policy" Redefined

Based on this discussion, I can now update the simplistic definition of *policy* put forth in the Introduction:

A policy is

- a decision
- **within the competence of the approver**
- **making something true that isn't yet true.**

All three attributes are required. If there's no decision, it will be **non-functional**. If the decision is outside the competence of the approver, it will be **impotent**. If it is about something that has already been decided, it will be **superfluous**.

Using this definition as a test for inclusion while drafting will help keep our Policies as succinct as possible.

Restatements of law

Statements that simply rehash an existing law are not statements of policy. Take the examples in panel 25.

Panel 25

Employees must handle all hazardous substances in accordance with existing laws and regulations.

All documents are subject to applicable freedom of information and privacy legislation.

All hiring must comply with the *Americans with Disabilities Act*.

In each of these examples, the statement is true whether or not it appears in a policy. It can't become any truer than that.

An organization's policy instruments lose their integrity when they make it look like others' decisions are their own. The organization didn't make the decisions in panel 25, so inserting them inside a internally-authored instrument misrepresents the true approver of those statements. Including them in a policy falsely portrays the statements as corporate decisions.

That portrayal, aside from misrepresenting the truth, sends a self-aggrandizing message. It sounds like the organization is saying, "We don't want our employees to abstain from illegal drugs at work because the government says so. We want them to do it because **we** say so. If we discipline them, it won't be because they broke the law, it will be because they **disobeyed us**."

All statements with an *Employees-must-follow-the-law–type* phrase have the same shortcoming: they are true whether or not an organization puts them into a policy.

Testing for Inclusion

Since a policy statement is not *true* until approved, the approval itself officially enacts the statement, functioning as a notional on-switch. Approval turns the statement from *not yet true* to *true from now on*.

It's easy to test whether something is outside the competence of the organization. Try sticking the word *hereby* — or a derivative phrase like *hereby confirmed*, *hereby considered*, etc. — into the statement and see if it works. If the statement is not an accurate reflection of reality, then we know that competence is lacking.

Two corporate policy statements are found in panel 26.

Panel 26

Employees are hereby forbidden from using illegal drugs.

The back storage room is hereby considered for exclusive use by the shipping branch.

Granted, in both cases the wording sounds stiff and pretentious, and we wouldn't write it that way. But the test works: inserting *hereby* accentuates the presence or absence of competence, making it easier for us to see. The first statement is inaccurate, because that rule was already approved by an authority higher than the corporation. That inaccuracy tells us that competence is lacking. The second statement sets a rule that becomes valid on the date of approval, so it is indeed a candidate for policy.

Be careful with this test, though, because it only works in one direction. If the *hereby* statement is objectionable, like the first one in panel 26, we can safely conclude an absence of competence; being unobjectionable, however, is not necessarily a guarantee of its presence.

I'm not suggesting that all issues covered by legislation are off limits. A valid policy statement can extend or supplement an existing law.

Take, for example, a municipality with a by-law limiting motor vehicle speed to 55 km/h (35 mph) on major roads. A company that makes crystal chandeliers has the policy shown in panel 27.

Panel 27

The maximum speed for company drivers on delivery runs is 40 km/h (25 mph).

This company policy neither reformulates nor contradicts the by-law; rather, it adds an **additional restriction**. The policy is valid so long as the by-law doesn't prohibit that kind of restriction. Policy approval is still represented accurately: the company is the approver of the statement containing the more restrictive speed limit.

Instrument Titles

Policy instruments need titles. Apart from the basic triptych *Policy*, *Standard*, and *Procedure*, a number of possible titles can be pressed into service, among them:

- Authority
- Catalog
- Code
- Directive
- Guide
- Guideline
- Handbook
- Instructions
- Key
- Manual
- Matrix
- Obligation
- Protocol
- Regulation
- Requirement
- Rule
- Scheme
- Specification

The nuances differentiating these types of instruments may be subtle, but that's not really a problem for most organizations because they don't need to distinguish instruments to this level of granularity.

There's no magic to these document titles. Often the name chosen is arbitrary, based on the whim of the drafter. One organization's *Regulation* could be another's *Specification*.

Personally, I like the basic three for simplicity's sake. I also recommend using the format *Policy on ...*, so we would have a *Policy on Widgets* instead of a *Widget Policy*. The latter format can be problematic, as demonstrated in the ambiguously titled *Interim Staffing Policy*. Altering the order of the words will let us clarify whether we have a *Policy on Interim Staffing* or an *Interim Policy on Staffing*.

Be careful with *Code*. In many jurisdictions, calling some-thing a Code implies that it's comprehensive and exhaustive, thereby negating the validity of any rules outside it. The best example is the *Penal Code*, but we also have a *Building Code* and a *Civil Code*, not to mention *Code of Conduct* and *Code of Ethics*, both covered in Chapter 11.

Ultimately, whether terms like *Protocol* or *Scheme* signal a primary or secondary source document in your organization is really up to you. Whichever you decide, internal consis-tency is a prerequisite to making the system functional. If the *Protocol on Contracting* is a formal Authority but the *Protocol on Hiring* is merely a set of recommendations, much confusion will ensue.

What matters is that going forward all **documents titled the same way fall into the same document source group**. When an organization officially adopts one of these supplementary titles, the affected group of sources in the Documentation Landscape need to reflect it.

Some organizations have tried to get fancy, assigning instru-ment titles to documents based on the different audiences they are written for. For example, the title *Policy* might signal an authority directed at senior management while the title Directive is aimed at front-line workers. Do what works for you, but always preserve the distinction between Authorities and Toolkit documents. That distinction is relevant to deter-mining the level of approval required in the organization based on the policy architecture.

One final note. In chapter 4, we looked at the cultural impli-cations of titling a document in a way that's inconsistent with its true purpose, for example, giving what is obviously a strict policy a title such as *Guidance* to make sure nobody's feathers get ruffled. If it were me, instead of trying to blunt the impact of the instrument by mischaracterizing it, I would work on improving the rule-making culture in the organization, so that people can receive strict rules without getting their backs up.

Standard operating procedures

A number of organizations work with a series of documents they call *standard operating procedures*, often shortened simply to *SOP*.

Based on the definitions I have used up to this point, that title might appear contradictory; indeed, some people have suggested to me that the existence of the phrase *standard operating procedure* is proof that the line separating standards and procedures is blurred or even non-existent.

Standard operating procedures are indeed procedures, and the potential for confusion is limited to the English-speaking world. In English, the word *standard* can be either a noun or an adjective. In the phrase *standard operating procedure* it acts as an adjective. *Standard* in this case means that the operating procedure either (1) has been standardized, or (2) is intended for use in standard circumstances. Contrasting phrases are *ad hoc operating procedure*, *special operating procedure*, *emergency operating procedure*, and others with qualifiers clearly indicating their applicability to non-standard circumstances.

The same confusion doesn't happen in languages where the adjective takes a different form from the noun. *Standard operating procedure* is rendered in French as *procédure opérationnelle normalisée*, clearly using the adjectival form *normalisé(e)* instead of the noun *norme*.

One Policy or Many?

Even when we limit our Policies to policy statements, we have a preliminary structural question to answer: do we want to end up with one single large Policy or a number of smaller ones? I hear this question debated a lot in the planning stages.

On the one side, some people want a single all-inclusive totally comprehensive tome containing all the relevant statements on a particular subject and are not concerned if it ends up extremely long and complex because at least it will put all the requirements relevant to a given subject in one place and spit them out in one breath, just like this sentence. (Phew.)

In contrast, some people don't. They like to break the material up. They prefer multiple documents. Each document has its own subject. Each is short. Each is easy to read.

Which approach is better? In Chapter 2 we talked about the fact that *all in one place* can be accomplished in a digital world without putting everything in the same document. That gives us some freedom to break the text up into different documents, but how do we decide how many we need?

Applicability and enforcement

Remember the goals: policy documents that are coherent, integrated, and uniformly structured; individual statements that do not conflict with one another; the elimination of duplication, and the achievement of clarity and succinctness.

Some pieces of legislation, like the *Income Tax Act*, have thousands of paragraphs and sub-paragraphs. In contrast, some statutes contain only one single substantive provision. Either extreme is a viable possibility.

When it comes to interpretation, applicability, and enforcement, the number of policies is inconsequential.

An old joke tells of a customer who walks into a bakery and orders a cherry pie. Before boxing it, the baker asks whether it should be cut into six pieces or eight pieces. The customer responds, "Six pieces, please. I couldn't possibly eat eight pieces of pie!"

Imagine that we've done an inventory and find that we have 400 unique policy statements. Whether we package those 400 statements into one, two, or 100 separate Policies doesn't change the fact that we have 400 statements. If we wanted to, we could have 400 Policies with one statement each, and we would still have exactly the same policy regime. **The number of rules documents does not affect our ability to apply or enforce the rules they contain.**

However, it does have a bearing on other aspects of the policy-drafting process.

Approval speed

The length and complexity of a policy document directly impact the amount of time required during the approval process. The longer the document, the more potential for it to contain points of contention that an approver might trip over. The more points of contention in the document, the longer it takes to get approved.

Using smaller documents can often provide some flexibility in this regard. Spreading policy statements over multiple documents means that a stumbling block in one document doesn't necessarily delay the approval of the others.

Navigation and discoverability

The ease of navigation and discoverability of a particular rule is a totally practical consideration. How easy will it be to find when we need it? With 400 statements, we will want a robust navigation system in place to pick out specific sections, regardless of the number of documents they are scattered throughout.

The primary concern should be the effectiveness of these navigational aids in providing quick access to the necessary policy information.

Notes

Executive Summary

Standards are sets of technical specifications, grouped together as a drafting shortcut. The specifications can range from precise measurements to general descriptions. Their applicability can be set at *mandatory*, *optional*, *recommended*, or *disallowed*, and in fact can be segmented so that different components of a standard have different applicability levels. Two specialized standards regulate human behavior: *Codes of Conduct* and *Codes of Ethics*.

A Set of Specifications

My old neighbor Susan started all her recipes with two medium onions and a clove of garlic sautéed in olive oil and white wine. That's her customary cooking base. If we wrote that down and named it the *standard onion base*, then it would be easy to reference going forward. Whenever we want to use it in a recipe, instead of naming all four ingredients again with instructions on how to sauté, we can say simply, *Start with the standard onion base, then add …*

A standard combines one or more *technical specifications* into a set so they can be referenced as a unit. It acts as a shortcut, freeing us from repeatedly writing out individual specifications every time we need them together.

The term *technical* in this instance draws on one of its older meanings: *marked by or characteristic of specialization.*[7]

---

[7] Merriam-Webster Dictionary

Not to be confused with *technological specifications*, the term applies broadly, beyond the digital realm. *Technical* skills, for example, include coding Web sites, database administration, and connecting cables, but they also include driving a forklift, tailoring a jacket, and bandaging a wound. They are all skills that require a degree of precision around certain elements to achieve a desired quality or consistency of the end product. **Identifying that precision for those elements sets a technical specification.**

A specification can be technically measurable — such as *2 cups of flour* — or generic — such as *a handful of oats*. It can range from the precise — *5.65425 grams* — to the broad — *almost three-quarters full*. It can describe items in their initial state, like a list of the ingredients in a muffin recipe, but it can also describe the target, such as *soft and chewy and lightly browned on top*.

An example of a simple standard is shown in panel 28.

Panel 28

Standard Workstation Technology Allocation

1 laptop computer

1 docking station

2 desktop monitors, minimum 24" diagonal

1 full-size desktop keyboard

1 webcam, minimum resolution 1080p

1 high fidelity headset

Typically, in the absence of an indication to the contrary, each individual specification is understood to be a compulsory element. However, a standard does permit the labelling of one or more elements as optional, so it's possible to let people choose whether to add raisins to the muffins. With that flexibility, a standard can serve as a checklist for all kinds of situations. It could be a list of

- components for packing a product for shipping
- acceptably-worded paragraphs for use in a contract
- risks to consider around a large financial expenditure
- people expected to attend a function

and so on.

Building a Standard

There's no deep secret here. We create our own standards simply by enumerating the desired specifications and packaging them into a set.

The number of specifications in a single standard can vary: its length can range from long and complicated to short and sweet. Some Standards extend several dozen pages or hundreds of lines on a spreadsheet, for example, an organization's *Records Retention Schedule*.[8] In contrast, a Standard can be delightfully brief, such as the one in panel 29. Being so short, this Standard took less than two minutes to review and approve, at which point it was ready to be interpolated into a page in the office manual.

---

[8] A *Records Retention Schedule* is a formal schedule listing the different types of records maintained by an organization, and specifying how long to retain instances of each type before they can be disposed of.

Panel 29

Standard on Office Printer Distribution

1 shared printer for every 3 workstations

Approved 2021-04-02 by the Vice-President, Operations
Last updated: 2023-12-18   Next review date: 2027-12-01

As you can see, once in a while we need so few specifications — in this case, only one — that the operative part of the Standard gets totally upstaged by all the administrative information supplementing it. That's perfectly acceptable, and no different from an e-mail message with a single sentence accompanied by half a dozen header fields.

The tricky part of drafting a standard is being careful to **focus on the outcome rather than the process.** In a cleaning standard, for instance, a specification like *the floor has been swept* is actually about the means; a description of the outcome would be more along the lines of *the floor is clear of debris.* **Procedures focus on the steps; standards describe outcomes or targets.**

Respectful Standards

This heading is a trick!

A Standard itself is neutral: neither respectful nor disrespectful. It is simply a list of specifications. It doesn't contain instructions, commands, or suggestions. It's not the recipe; it's just the list of ingredients. The words *must*, *must not*, *should*, and other terms of obligation are gratuitous. It's enough simply to list the items in a neutral tone.[9]

Degrees of Applicability

A Standard on its own is inert. It becomes operative in an organization only when called into service by a policy statement.

In chapter 7, we noted that incorporating a Standard into a suite of corporate regulatory instruments differs by source type: technically, **internal Standards** become operative through a statement **enacting** them, while **external ones** use a statement **adopting** them. However, as long as the Standard in question is clearly identified, the same incorporating language can work in either case.

Standards can be calibrated at one of four possible degrees of applicability: *mandatory*, *optional*, *recommended*, and *disallowed*.[10]

Let's go through them one at a time.

---

[9] The International Standards Organization, as well as a number of other large bodies, still use more traditional language, and it may be a while before they begin issuing requirements that don't embrace the Parent–Child dynamic. The respectful language issues on their radars are more focused on topics like gender-neutrality and acceptable terminology than corporate culture and engagement. This topic is discussed more extensively in chapter 16. For an example of government Standards written as I propose them here, see the *Federal Vehicle Standards* put out by the US General Services Administration
https://vehiclestd.fas.gsa.gov/CommentCollector/Home

[10] If you tripped over the notion of a standard being *optional*, just sit tight … we'll get to it.

Mandatory Standards

Panel 30 shows statements making Standards mandatory, using one external and two internal examples.

Panel 30

Internal correspondence is properly formatted when it reflects *Standard #21 — Office Correspondence.*

Travel expenses are reimbursed within 14 days of submission of receipts, up to the limits specified in the *Standard on Reimbursable Office Travel Expenses.*

Purchases for new equipment are restricted to those that are *IEC 60335 certified.*

Note the absence of a Parent–Child dynamic in the wording. The objective language used is sufficient to establish the mandatory nature of the Standard in each case; we have no need to resort to dictatorial constructions like *is mandatory* or *employees must follow.*

Let's look more closely at the first example in panel 30. Some readers might characterize the applicability as *optional* rather than mandatory on the basis that, while it authorizes one particular Standard, it doesn't overtly exclude others. That observation is technically correct, but it may not be determinative.

Whether a statement is sufficient in itself to be considered mandatory is dependent on the context in which it is written. If, practically speaking, no competing standards are in sight, then there's no ambiguity. On the other hand, if misunderstanding is a *bone fide* concern, for example, due to a new

Standard recently replacing an older one, it might be useful to emphasize the exclusionary nature of the requirement. One way to do that is to add the word *only*, as in panel 31.

Panel 31

Correspondence produced internally is properly formatted only when it reflects *Standard #21 — Office Correspondence.*

Other terms that can convey the same restrictiveness are *exclusively*, *solely*, *expressly*, and *singularly*.

In some cases, though, we may need to go further and plant a statement explicitly suppressing a specific Standard, as in panel 32.

Panel 32

Printed corporate correspondence uses Letter-size paper. The use of A4 paper is discontinued.

In this last example, it would be accurate to characterize the A4 Standard as *disallowed*.

Optional standards

A number of rule makers I worked with used to argue end-lessly over whether designating a standard as *optional* is a contradiction in terms. Some writers insisted that if we called something a *Standard*, we were essentially making it *mandatory*. They couldn't wrap their heads around how a set of specifications could accurately be called a *Standard* if people weren't forced to follow it. For them, a Standard is mandatory by definition.[11]

The disadvantage of that approach is having an overly rigid policy architecture, leaving no room to maneuver through more complex scenarios. In that regime, for example, it's difficult — if not impossible — to accommodate a situation that offers people the ability to choose either Standard A or Standard B.

The confusion arises from mistaking the *level of rigor* of a standard's specifications for its *level of applicability*. An illustration might help make this distinction clearer.

Systems of measurement

Two separate standards of measurement are used around the world: *Système international* (SI), which is the modern form of the metric system, and an older system, normally called *Imperial* in countries affiliated with the British Commonwealth and *US Customary Units* in the United States.

In practice, almost every country uses both systems to a greater or lesser degree: in the US, science and medicine are firmly steeped in the metric system; at the same time, the rest of the world continues to measure airspace in nautical miles and sell televisions and monitors diagonally in inches.

The specifications in each of those standards are obligatory. We have no latitude here: the dimensions for units of dis-

---

[11] This approach is used by the Treasury Board Secretariat at the Government of Canada. It would appear be to an outlier; I have been unable to find any other jurisdiction that uses the word *standard* so rigidly.

tance, weight, mass, etc., cannot be altered without offending the standard. In that sense, the standard is mandatory.

A separate issue is the **degree of adoption** of those standards by each nation. You may be surprised to learn that the US passed its *Metric Act* back in 1866, making it lawful to use that system for official dealings such as court proceedings and contracts. It never really caught on, and most of the country still uses US Customary Units. In the US, therefore, the metric system is *official* but *optional*.

The United Kingdom does a juggling act, fudging its mandatory adoption of SI to keep the sale of draft beer in pints and road signs in miles. Imperial measurement is mandatory for roads and public highways, but tourist areas have the option to provide additional SI signage. For UK highways, therefore, the Imperial standard is *mandatory* and the metric standard is *optional*.

Canada is positioned between the two systems — both figuratively and geographically. Food packaging is legislated to be in SI, but retailers are free to advertise prices in both. That puts Canadian groceries in the reverse position from UK highways: the metric standard is *mandatory* and the Imperial standard is *optional*.

Indicating optionality

A policy statement can indicate that a Standard is optional in one of several ways. In the examples in panel 33, the first two Standards are external and the last one is internal.

Panel 33

> In corporate advertising materials, measurements are expressed in metric units alone or in combination with Imperial units.
>
> Scientific articles submitted for publication have the option of referring to chemicals by the abbreviations assigned to them in the Periodic Table.
>
> Directors have the discretion to forego the *Standard Checklist for Readiness* when less than 8 hours have elapsed since the last inspection.

Degrees of applicability can even vary within the document itself. A Standard containing templated paragraphs for a procurement contract can designate some of its paragraphs as optional; for example, a statement about the treatment of currency conversion could be available for situations involving international contracting. This approach allows the decision around inclusion to be made by the individual preparing the contract, based on the circumstances.

We can even fine-tune the degree of applicability if needed. A standard has the ability to restrict the use of the optional paragraphs to verbatim inclusion, or it could open the door to effecting wording changes where the situation warrants.

Criteria for exercising discretion

When the use of a standard or part of it is discretionary, the policy maker can take one of two routes: they can specify the criteria to use when exercising that discretion or they can leave it open-ended. When taking the first route, the criteria can either be explicitly set out in the policy or can simply be provided as part of the training given to people who will make the decision.

Take a situation in a store that's part of a franchise, where a corporate Standard universally prescribes the number and length of breaks, as well as start times. The policy statement enacting it, and the statement offering the option, are set out in panel 34.

Panel 34

Break times are established in the *Standard on Employee Hours*.

The Store Manager on Duty has the discretion to change the start time for each break listed in the Standard, based on a set of criteria approved by the owner of that franchise.

The second statement indicates that parts of the Standard—break start times — are in fact optional, but come with mandatory requirements around exercising a decision to change them.

A *recommended standard* is simply a variation on a theme: it's nothing but an *optional standard* accompanied by a statement encouraging its use.

Using a Standard to Engage Stakeholders

Apart from their regulatory value, standards are excellent tools for increasing engagement in an organization's rules. To see how, let's start with the set of instructions shown in panel 35.

Panel 35

You must submit your travel expenses properly to obtain reimbursement.

1. Fill out Form 32A completely.
2. Attach all the receipts.
3. Have the form signed by a manager.

The wording in panel 35 is clearly dictatorial. We examine *embedded messaging* more thoroughly in Part III of this book, but for now suffice it to say that the subtext coming out in this wording is *We're here to instruct you and we demand your compliance.* This subtext is reinforced by the choice of vocabulary, the verb tenses, and the use of sequential numbering for the details.

Panel 36 shows what the same rules look like when converted to a standard.

Panel 36

A request for the reimbursement of travel expenses is ready for submission when

- Form 32A is filled out completely
- All the receipts are attached, and
- It contains a manager's signature.

The tone is now completely different. Instead of being officious, the subtext is *We're here to give you the information you need.*

Although the requirements of the example in panel 36 are not particularly demanding, many standards are much more complex and onerous. In those cases, getting engagement can be a significant challenge. Using less dictatorial wording helps lower resistance to compliance.

Consultation

Prior to submission for approval of any internal authority, we often have a consultation stage to run through. It is at this stage that the first signs of support and resistance appear.

Requirements drafted in the form of a standard make it easy for us to seek buy-in from others. We can take the standard and shop it around to different business units in the organization. The question to ask them is, *What will it take for you to meet this Standard?* Apart from learning if what we have written is clear, we will get a sense of how the proposed rules are perceived.

Some groups will tell us that the standard is easy for them to meet. They may already be compliant with it, or they project that they can adapt to it without difficulty. That's a clear win; score a point for the Drafting Team!

Other groups will tell us that the requirements are too taxing. Their objections will vary, but for one reason or another they don't project they can meet the Standard proposed.

If the requirements were set out in a Policy and became effective immediately, then upon approval a group not meeting the requirements would instantly be in *breach of policy*. This situation is not unusual. Often, due to the lack of pre-approval communication and controlled change management, an organization issues a new policy and immediately many people find themselves technically in breach. That's not a good *status quo* to be working from.

With a Standard, we can go back to the question *What will it take for you to meet this Standard?* With that question, we can now entertain an Adult–Adult discussion over the impediments seen by the business unit. The rule is no longer *us telling them what to do*; it's now about *understanding what the target state is.*

This discussion gives us the opportunity to jointly explore possible scenarios for accommodation, potential modifications of the specifications, and other forms of compromise arrangements. It also gives us the ability to set compliance targets in collaboration with the business unit, for example: *I see that having to meet this Standard immediately would impose a hardship on you. Could we set a target of 50% compliance by the end of this year and 100% by the end of next year?* Another possibility is *Could we set a target of 100% compliance for cases in Situation A, and 50% for cases in Situation B?*

This negotiation completely changes the relationship between the rule maker and the people being affected. It has become more cooperative and more constructive.

Even when we don't have the flexibility to accept less than 100% compliance, a standard lets us move away from a *you need to do what we say* approach. By dropping the language that perpetuates the Parent–Child dynamic, we can reduce some of the toxicity that often accompanies the introduction of new rules.

Standards of Behavior

While we may not think of them that way, documents setting behavioral benchmarks are a kind of Standard. Two main types are common: *codes of conduct* and *codes of ethics*. Those two document types are quite distinct from each other, as we will see, and in both cases, the drafting rules differ from those we have looked at so far.

Codes of conduct

A *code of conduct* is a standard for behavior applicable to a specific environment. It records the collective commitment of those who adopt it — specifically, a commitment to pursue a set of common values, such as professionalism, courtesy, honesty, and so on.

Stylistically, a code of conduct uses language more in common with a vision statement or declaration of principles than with the technical specifications found in general standards.

Tone of voice still matters

If using a dictatorial tone in policies results in a lack of employee engagement, the effect is doubly pronounced in a code of conduct. Instructions on how to be a good person lose their moral authority when their tone is disrespectful. Take the examples in panel 37.

Panel 37

Most people are intelligent and well-intended. However, sometimes it's necessary to spell out the behavior we support and don't support.

> The core of our approach is this: we will do whatever we believe is necessary to ensure that our organization is a safe and productive environment for everyone.
>
> Don't harass people. We do not tolerate harassment of other employees in any form.
>
> Everyone is required to conform to this code of conduct. Or else. Employees violating these rules will be asked to leave the organization.

You get the picture.

Clearly, this document speaks in a tone of voice entirely antithetical to what it hopes to achieve. The language is divisive, clearly distinguishing those making the rules from others who are "required" to follow them. No attempt is made to engage cooperation or to build the communal rapport so critical to the success of a code of conduct.

When I received this document, I felt as if the organization didn't trust me to be a decent person. Its entire approach is confrontational, and I'm not appeased by the half-hearted compliment at the beginning, which feels like false flattery.

The statement *we will do whatever we believe is necessary* is more than simply a threat. In this single eight-word clause, management dismisses our contribution to the success of this initiative as secondary to its intent to control the situation.

The third paragraph is almost farcical: a statement basically saying that *we don't tolerate intolerance*.

The fourth paragraph is particularly heavy-handed.

We can do better than this. If any policy document deserves to be written in a positive, courteous, and respectful manner, it would be a code of conduct that confirms we strive to be positive, courteous, and respectful.

"We" statements

The point of a code of conduct is to be a guide everyone can buy into. The targets are set for individuals to support the collective. Nothing is being asked of the reader that doesn't apply equally to the writer.

The most impactful style for codes of conduct, values statements, and declarations of principles are sentences written in the first person plural, as in panel 38.

Panel 38

We value trust, candor, and professionalism.

We believe all people are worthy of our respect.

We strive to give every customer our full attention.

We actively promote the organization's values in every interaction with the public and with other employees.

We disclose potential conflicts of interest as soon as we become aware of them.

Statements drafted in the simple present tense are more impactful than those in the imperative, and those in the first person plural are more unifying. They echo the spirit of a code of conduct, acting as a rallying cry rather than a set of marching orders handed down from headquarters.

Statements that begin with *we* are empowering, enhancing the shared sense of commitment within an organization. It's no accident that the *United States Declaration of Independence* uses the same approach: *We hold these truths to be self-evident…*

Panel 39 provides examples of statements for use in a code of conduct that are consistent with the values it espouses.

Panel 39

We are sensitive to the needs of others around us, use good judgment, and treat others with respect.

We comply immediately with direct requests to stop a behavior that is considered harassment. Specifically, we do not initiate or engage in the following:

Offensive verbal comments or jokes *[… etc. You can highlight specific behaviors if necessary.]*

When we are asked to leave the space of an incident based on an alleged infraction of this code, we do so immediately, quietly, and without drawing attention to the situation.

These positively worded statements in panel 39 are not only more inclusive, but also resonate with respect and understanding. They align more closely with the true intent of a code of conduct. By using *we* statements, we're building a community ethos that everyone—from the newest employee to the highest executive—can be part of.

This more inclusive approach turns a code of conduct from a document of *dos and don'ts* into a declaration of shared values and mutual respect. It's about crafting a narrative that everyone in the organization is not only willing to follow, but is proud to embody. In this way, a code of conduct becomes a living, breathing part of the corporate identity, echoing the collaborative spirit the organization is striving for.

Tough situations

Just to be clear, I recognize that sometimes we find more pits than cherries in the bowl. At times, an organization faces challenging circumstances where more direct and firm measures are necessary. In those cases, we may need to rely on written statements in an authority that provide security should we wish to take measures to deal with conflict, even if we reach for them only as a last resort.

I would never suggest than an organization doesn't need "heavy artillery" on stand-by; however, the code of conduct is not the armory. Statements around stringent measures to be taken in problem cases are more appropriately housed in a separate policy. That separation frees the code of conduct to guide and inspire, rather than to intimidate.

Codes of ethics

A *code of ethics* is a standard for making ethical decisions. For each situation, the justification compelling the prescribed course of action is the acceptance of an ethical duty. Take the common example in panel 40.

Panel 40

Board members have an ethical duty to disclose potential conflicts of interest.

That formulation sets out the ethical underpinning overtly. Typically, though, the drafter makes a preliminary stylistic decision: to repeat the four-word phrase *has an ethical duty* throughout the document, or to shorten it to *must* or *should* or something similar, as in panel 41.

Panel 41

Board members must disclose potential conflicts of interest.

The warnings given in this book around the heavy-handed nature of the word *must* (see chapter 16) don't apply in this situation. When it is made clear to the reader that *must* is to be interpreted as *has an ethical duty to*, the negative subtext disappears. This *must* is not born of a Parent–Child relationship; rather, it reflects a mindset about the role of ethics in the organization.

Some drafters prefer *should* in these cases, as in panel 42.

Panel 42

Board members should disclose potential conflicts of interest.

In these cases, *should* does not merely convey a recommendation. Similar to *must* in the previous example, it specifically denotes *has an ethical duty to*.

My only caution is around consistency. Using *must* or *should* in a code of ethics to stand in for *has an ethical duty to* works perfectly well so long as

- that interpretation is made clear at the beginning, and
- all instances of *must* and *should* in the document carry that meaning, rather than one of the many alternate meanings described in Part III.

Code of Conduct as a Foundational Document

Consider the experience shared by a participant in one of my workshops. Her organization takes the position that its code of conduct is the **cornerstone** of its policy suite. Having a strong values-driven code of conduct to fall back on allows it to forego drafting many rules that other organizations find necessary. The guiding principles — honesty, equity, professionalism — inform all their decisions and actions, making many detailed rules redundant.

This approach falls squarely on the *culture of empowerment* side of the scale. It might not suit every organization, but for those where it is a good fit, it opens a lot of doors. It invites us to think about the power of principles over prescriptive rules when regulating behavior, and raises the potential for a code of conduct to shape an organization's entire operational soul.

Notes

12. Procedures

Executive Summary

Procedures can specify minute details and steps without being seen as micro-managing. They can also contain duplication, so identical statements may appear in multiple instruction sets. What procedures can't do is change the parameters of a job description or contractual engagement. It is prudent to consult with whatever branch of the organization is responsible for the terms of engagement of the position being affected. A sample procedure is provided as a potential model.

Tone of Voice

Getting down to a procedure is an apt idiom because it reflects the notion of descent.

We start at the *policy* level looking at broad brush strokes. Once we have the buy-in at that level, we move to the level of *standards* and *procedures*, both of which implement the policies.

Policies and procedures have different tones. Statements that won't fly in a policy may sit happily in a procedure, and vice versa. Let's look at those differences.

What Procedures Can Do that Policies Can't

Micro-management

A procedure can elaborate on individual steps, provide examples, and include best practices. That same information in a Policy creates clutter, and tends to come across as micro-management. Take the example in panel 43.

Panel 43

Directors must set aside time each year to review and update their budgets.

What management wants to see at the end of the day is an up-to-date budget from each director, which is fair enough. Making it a requirement to *set aside time* is micro-management. On its face, the statement in panel 43 means that directors submitting perfectly good budgets would be in breach of policy if they produced them without *setting aside time*. Furthermore, the requirement to *review* the budget is superfluous, because it's not possible to update a budget without reviewing it.

If we're going to treat adults like adults, we don't need to enshrine how they organize their schedules in policies. To fix this statement, we'll want to focus on the outcome rather than the process. We'll look at how to do that in part III.

Step-by-step instruction

Procedures, in contrast, have a totally different vibe. When going through a procedure, the reader is prepared to be led by the hand, step-by-step through the process. Even a minutely-detailed instruction like *Set aside an hour to work without distractions* would not be out of place. A procedure can instruct, provide examples, and otherwise reach a level of specificity that would overwhelm a policy.

Depending on the procedure, all the helpful information that we want to provide — cautions, comments, reminders — may be perfectly at home. A warning like *Be careful when you open the box* would be totally out of place in a Policy, but might be appreciated by someone following a procedure.

Moreover, the need to avoid redundancy in policies is not applicable to procedures. As a policy statement, *Products are ready for sale after they pass inspection* needs to appear in one and only one primary source. As a procedural statement, *Inspect the product prior to releasing it for sale* can appear is as many procedures as it's applicable to.

What Procedures Can't Do

Procedures are not back doors for getting into a building when the policies bar entrance. They are informed by the policies, so in case of a conflict, the wording of the policy prevails. Where a policy prohibits an action, a procedure cannot override that prohibition.

Nor can a procedure contain a step requiring an approval that is inconsistent with the parameters specified by the organization's governance documents.

Finally — and this is the one that most people trip over — a procedure cannot modify someone's job description outside the parameters of the employment or service contract. If it looks like the steps have the potential to infringe on those areas, it's prudent to consult with HR, Procurement, Legal Services, or whatever branch of the organization handles the terms of engagement of the positions affected by procedure.

Procedure Structure

The flexibility offered by procedures with regard to the nature of their content applies to their structure, too. While every procedure contains steps to follow as its kernel, the range of possible supplementary sections of related material is quite broad.

Developing procedures is a skill on its own, separate from policy drafting. To achieve a useful result, the task needs to be undertaken by a SME who not only knows the material well, but knows how to sequence it properly.

Sample Procedure

From a structural point of view, some of the best-drafted Procedures I have run across are produced by **Policy Protec**, a company based in Edmonton, Canada.[12] The company has kindly granted me permission to include one of its Procedures as a example of a sophisticated structure. You'll find it on the next page.

The language is clear, succinct, and respectful. It is divided into multiple sections that are well organized and easy to navigate. Moreover, the approach is pragmatic, while still respecting the constraints on Procedures discussed in this chapter.

---

[12] https://policyprotec.com/
The original procedure has been shortened to fit within the page, so a few key steps are missing. Better not try this at home.

Procedure for Installing a Monitoring Well

Qualified Workers

Only qualified ABC Inc. lead technicians are eligible to lead this procedure.

Only qualified ABC Inc. assistant technicians are eligible to assist.

Required PPE

- Head protection
- Safety glasses
- Work gloves
- Foot protection

Safety Resources

- Environmental spill kit
- Fire extinguisher, 20 lb.
- First aid kit

Equipment and Supplies

- Specifications document
- Rotary auger
- Notepad and pen
- Down-hole screen

Procedure

Prepare

1. Read the Client Specifications document.
2. Don personal protective equipment.
3. Ensure safety resources are in place.
4. Prepare equipment and supplies for use.

Drill

5. Use the rotary auger to drill a 2-inch hole to the depth requested.

Install

6. Use the tape measure to check the water level downhole and note the measurement.
7. Use the hacksaw to cut the screen to the height of the water downhole.
8. Lower the screen down the hole by hand.
9. Use the auger to add pipe down the hole until it touches bottom.

Backfill

10. Use the utility knife to open bags of sand and bentonite.
11. Pour sand while measuring sand depth until it is 12" above the top of the downhole screen.
12. Pour bentonite until it can be seen downhole.
13. Lower pipe protector and hold it in place while the assistant pours sand to 6" below ground level.
14. Use the shovel to tap the protector to settle and tighten sand.

Now that we've looked at the three main instrument types, let's look at how different groups in the organization can combine forces to produce a more cohesive policy suite.

The next chapter looks at how to break down policy silos in an organization.

13 BREAKING DOWN SILOS

Executive Summary

A well-integrated policy suite reflects the interdependencies of various parts of an organization, not by repeating rules generated by other business units, but by producing an office manual that synthesizes the information into a coherent narrative. Changes in circumstances that cross the enterprise, such as the Covid-19 pandemic or the introduction of Artificial Intelligence, are opportunities for business areas to collaborate. Acceptable use policies falling under the IT policy are an anomaly; moving them back to the HR branch will unify policies to be technology-agnostic.

Policy Silos

Policy silos are a pervasive challenge.

Found even in environments where different services seem to operate harmoniously, for most organizations they represent a missed opportunity. Having policy groups operate autonomously can be beneficial, but having them forego collaboration and integration leads to inefficiencies. A lack of structured lateral connectivity not only hinders the organization's overall functioning, but also has a negative impact on its ability to serve its stakeholders effectively.

Policy silos can be analogized in the commercial world to a large department store with 10 separately-managed floor areas. When each area works without reference to the others, their inventories suffer from both overlap and product gaps. A well-run retail business coordinates its purchasing and stock on an enterprise-wide level, eliminating duplication and encouraging areas to work together to provide a seamless consumer experience.

In contrast, many policy suites present a total absence of that kind of coordination. The same statement can be found repeated verbatim in multiple instruments; no doubt, it was drafted, consulted on, and submitted for approval several times.

The world of government contracting and procurement may have something to teach us about how to avoid this kind of inefficiency. A common practice in contracting is to use a general document called something like *General Contracting Terms* or *Standard Terms and Conditions*. It contains all the statements that would be common to the vast majority of contracts, eliminating the need to repeat them over and over. Instead, each new contract contains a clause indicating that it incorporates the statements in the general one.

Many government legislatures — with the notable exception of those in the US — rely on a statute typically called the *Interpretation Act*. The statements it contains supplement all other statutes, and are applicable in the absence of a specific declaration to the contrary. For example, the *Interpretation Act* might clarify that, unless otherwise indicated, clock times in a statement are tied to local time. It sets out high-level rules, such as how to count days when a holiday intervenes, which financial currency is to be assumed, or how to interpret terms that have fallen out of use but might be still be found on the books. The provisions can be applied across the board, without going to the trouble of sending them for more debate.

Governments that use interpretation acts have drafted them self-declaring their validity; in other words, they're applicable even when they're not called out in a given statute. Section 3(1) of Canada's *Interpretation Act* reads as follows:

> Every provision of this Act applies, unless a contrary intention appears, to every enactment, whether enacted before or after the commencement of this Act.[13]

Remember those little user-friendly booklets and Web sites back in Chapter 9 that explain the *Income Tax Act*, the *Elections Act*, and so on? Some bits of information may actually be pulled from the *Interpretation Act*. Information pages don't necessarily quote the source statute for that information because the average reader doesn't care.

The General Policy

What does this paradigm look like in the corporate policy world?

A *general Policy* does for an organization what the *Interpretation Act* does for legislation: it aggregates identical statements found across the policy suite into a single spot.

Take the example provided in panel 44.

---

[13] https://laws.justice.gc.ca/eng/acts/i-21/page-1.html

Panel 44

> Where a manager's approval is required for an action, the manager's delegate is authorized to provide that approval in the manager's absence.

Instead of having multiple policies each containing a similar statement, consolidating the provision saves the organization time and effort that would have been spent on drafting, consulting, editing, approving, and publishing duplicates of the same information.

Any statement that pops up repeatedly is a good candidate for inclusion in a general Policy. The phrases found at the beginning of policy instruments, for example, repeating that *CFO means the Chief Financial Officer*, can be eliminated with one single statement in the general policy, such as the one shown in panel 45.

Panel 45

> The primary interpretation of abbreviations and initialisms is determined by the approved corporate glossary.

Partial rules

Statements in a general Policy are flexible enough that they can set out partial rules, leaving the remainder to be completed in other instruments. For example, a general policy might contain the provision in panel 46.

Panel 46

Rules around purchase and procurement do not cover discretionary items, as defined by the branch spending the funds.

The determination around which items are considered *discretionary* can be left to other policies.

A *presumptive* interpretation is one that applies in the absence of a statement to the contrary. Any statement in a General Policy can easily be made presumptive by opening it with the phrase *Unless otherwise indicated*.

Sharing Authorities

Policies emanating from a siloed policy drafting environment often suffer from duplicate statements, uncoordinated statements, and gaps. One of the telltale signs of siloed policy drafting is the presence of reminders inside policies of one group to "remember" that some other group's policies apply, such as the statement in panel 47, found in an organization's Facility policy.

Panel 47

The requirements of the *Policy on Security* apply to the elements in this Policy.

Of course they do, **even without that provision**. The presence of that statement, though, tells us that the Facilities and Security staff haven't coordinated their user documentation. If the information were presented in a reader-centric format, we would see only the requirements themselves, irrespective of which policy they came from.

At one organization I worked at, the Finance, Facilities, Real Property, and Security corporate services got together to produce a Policy on the management of corporate assets. They wanted to clarify the responsibility of each operational branch of the business to life-cycle its own assets, and so came up with the policy found in panel 48.

Panel 48

Policy on the Management of Corporate Assets

Interpretation

1. In this policy,

   "assets" includes furniture, equipment, real property, and supplies.

2. Each Section is charged with maintaining inventory, managing, safeguarding, and disposing of the assets in their possession.

The policy was drafted in that way showed a willingness of disparate corporate services to cooperate with one another to reach a common goal. What could have been spread out across five policy documents was consolidated into a single, cohesive set of statements. Job well done.

The organization's Information Management (IM) branch had similar needs. It wanted the operational branches to take responsibility for maintaining inventory, managing, safe-guarding, and disposing of the information assets in their possession. Instead of working with the other corporate services, though, it wanted to have its own Policy, and it spent an inordinate amount of time developing a separate document in parallel.

The simplest way for the IM branch to accomplish its goal would have been to throw its hat into the ring with everyone else. It would have taken only the simplest of changes: an amendment to the definition of *assets* to read as in panel 49.

Panel 49

In this policy,

"assets" includes furniture, equipment, real property, supplies, **and information holdings.**

That one simple change would have eliminated the work required to develop and consult on an independent policy. Moreover, it would have induced the other branches to take collective ownership of the requirement for managing information, just as they took collective ownership for managing their own assets.

As it turned out, the IM branch refused to go that route, insisting on maintaining its independence from the other branches. The reasoning was that information came under its jurisdiction, and it saw other branches as a threat to its power. In other words, it didn't want to play nice in the sandbox with the others. That attitude doesn't reflect well on the efficiency of the organization.

The **implementation** of an asset management policy might look different in the information world than it does in the physical world, but the concepts and values are the same. They all are based on a shared approach to responsible stewardship, accountability, and reporting.

Leveraging Existing Policy

Breaking down corporate policy silos eases change when brand new circumstances arise. We're going to look at two examples of policy frenzy: one that happens when cannabis is legalized, and one that happened during the pandemic of 2020.

Legalization of cannabis

Over the past few years, cannabis has been legalized in a number of jurisdictions around the world. Regardless of one's political outlook about the merits of that change, it's clear that in jurisdictions where the law changed, organizations had to satisfy themselves that their policies would cover any new situations that would arise.

Some executives simply panicked. "Our entire workforce could show up to work next week stoned out of their minds," they shivered, "and without a policy we can't do anything about it. They'll open us up to liability issues and cause irreparable damage to our reputation."

Those executives did what a lot of business leaders do in times of panic: they decided they needed a policy. I saw one organization spend thousands of dollars hiring a firm to draft a *Policy on the Use of Cannabis* that they didn't need. The firms generating those policies were delighted to be assigned the work and to charge a pretty penny for it. But was it necessary?

Where the organization already had rules in place governing employee behavior, discipline, roles and responsibilities, as well as appeal procedures, the most likely answer is no. A new policy isn't required every time circumstances change. Two facts are pertinent:

#1. Some substances are illegal.

Illegal substances include specific drugs, as well as specific weapons and contraband goods. Some of the items listed cause intoxication and some don't, but that fact is irrelevant. The operative factor is whether a particular substance is found on the *List of Illegal Stuff*, so to speak. Let's call the substances on this list *Group 1*.

Unless the organization is the legislator in that jurisdiction, it doesn't get to decide **what** goes on this list. All it needs is a set of rules about **how to handle situations** involving illegal substances, for example, some kind of investigatory process that kicks off when an infraction is suspected, and then some procedures to follow from that point on.

#2. Some legal substances cause intoxication.

This group of substances includes alcohol, prescription drugs, non-prescription drugs like anti-histamines, and sundry other substances. Let's call that group of items *Group 2*.

Exactly as in the case of illegal substances, the organization does not determine what's on that list. The best it can do is to have a process to deal with situations where someone comes to the office while their ability to work is impaired by intoxication. Those organizations that are concerned about that possibility have policies in place to handle it, and where necessary, they accommodate people taking these substances for medical reasons.

All the pieces are now in place. In most jurisdictions, cannabis sits in Group 1; in jurisdictions where it was legalized, cannabis moved from Group 1 to Group 2. **Nothing else changed.**

If the office policies are properly set up, nobody even has to blink! Existing policies covering situations dealing with Group 1 and Group 2 can handle a situation where a substance migrates from one list to another.

Remember when Facebook came into offices? Many people scrambled to write some kind of a Facebook policy. Later they saw people using Twitter (now renamed), so they created a policy for that. Then an Instagram policy. A Snapchat policy. But that game never ends. **If the principles are in place, we don't need a new policy for every new item.**

Covid-19 policies

The recent Covid-19 pandemic saw a surge of policy creation.

Just to be clear, there's nothing wrong with reviewing our rules when new circumstances arise, to check that all bases are covered. What creates an unnecessary amount of work, however, is an assumption that rules around the new concern need to be put in their own independent document.

Had they been asked, most policy experts would have told organizations in 2020 that a separate *Policy on Covid-19* was unnecessary. After all, Covid-19 is not the first communicable disease to appear on the radar, and it won't be the last. Yes, it involved a major upheaval to the processes and rules of many organizations, but it needn't have involved going outside the existing policy framework.

Instead of developing a stand-alone *Policy on Covid-19*, the more effective route is to approach every corporate branch that writes policy, to pose this question: *Are there any changes that need to be made to our current rules documents to accommodate the new realities posed by this situation?* We're interested to explore any real gaps in our current HR policies, IT Policies, and others.

It may turn out that the organization does identify a gap; for example, it may be clear that the lack of a work-at-home policy is no longer sustainable under the circumstances. The gap indicates that new rules need to be developed. But those rules are *work-at-home rules*, not Covid-19 rules. If we decided that we had a need to bring in rules around masks or other protective equipment, those are *health and safety rules*, not Covid-19 rules.

Combining all the rules for operational changes across the board into a single Policy for the sole reason that they all are driven by the same illness **simply creates a new silo**. I would analogize it to looking around the office, observing a preponderance of red items, and deciding that we have a need for a *Policy on Red Things*. Doesn't make much sense, does it?

Acceptable Use Statements

An anomaly has become entrenched in many offices: the inclusion of *acceptable use statements* in IT policies.

Acceptable use statements are intended to govern what people working in the organization can and cannot do with the technology we provide them. Many IT professionals and consultants push to have these kinds of policies in place, and countless templates are available on the Internet to use as a starting point if needed.

Rules around the acceptable use of office property make a lot of sense. They can go a long way to clarifying expectations around what is and is not considered appropriate. The anomaly, though, is their location: what are they doing in the IT policies?

Panel 50 contains a number of statements pulled from real-life examples.

Panel 50

When using corporate technology, users are expected to refrain from:

- conducting themselves in an unprofessional manner
- conducting activities related to another business
- creating, storing, or distributing racist, sexist, hateful, or otherwise objectionable content
- engaging in illegal activity
- harassing or bullying others
- committing libel or slander
- impersonating another individual

- disclosing any sensitive corporate information
- destroying corporate information without authorization
- endorsing a product or service without authorization

... and so on, with dozens of similar clauses.

Please don't misunderstand me: every single one of these prohibitions is a reasonable thing to ask of an employee. The problem is that **not one of them has anything to do with technology!** Almost every activity on that list would have been prohibited in an organization 50 years ago, long before the personal computer showed up in offices.

Granted, now that the computer is here, we handle things differently from before. Nonetheless, how do we justify separating what we prohibit when using technology from what we prohibit in day-to-day office life? After all, aren't the elements that constitute harassment in paper photographs the same elements that constitute harassment in digital images? The words in a typewritten paper memorandum that can bully a co-worker, aren't those the same words we worry about in electronic messages?

Let's take this argument further. When the Facilities office hands out ballpoint pens and paper notepads, does it make people agree to a *Pens and Paper Acceptable Use Policy* to ensure they won't doodle inappropriate images? Is there a clause in your *Policy on Office Furniture* that reminds people not to sit on their chairs for nefarious purposes? I didn't think so.

The origin of acceptable use policies

For decades, what would be considered acceptable use of the office telephone and typewriter was not dictated by the group supplying the equipment. Prior to the appearance of computer technology, the drafting of documents regulating employee activities in most offices fell to the Human Resources team. HR professionals held the pen on the rules dictating when we could play a radio, make personal telephone calls, and so on.

Things changed with the advent of computers. For some reason, the technology itself was seen to be the source of the problem. At the time, few HR professionals understood computer technology, and even fewer were in a position to know how to word behavioral policies to take technological innovation into account.

As a result, the burden of detailing how people should behave when using computers fell to the IT professionals, who accepted it gladly. It gave them a level of authority around rule-making in the office that the suppliers of pens and notepads never had.

What we have now is an historical anomaly, supporting an absurd situation. The behavior that happens in the hall is governed by one set of rules and the behavior that happens online is governed by another. From a policy management perspective, we have inherited a situation of silos, totally unnecessary and not conducive to a collaborative approach of office management. The downside—apart from the obvious potential for conflicting rules and divergent interpretation —

is the perception that poor behavior online is an IT problem, rather than a business one.

Obviously, we want our stance on bullying and harassment to be crystal clear. But rules of behavior have more longevity when they are medium-agnostic, applicable whether the communication is in person, through the telephone, virtual, or through paper.

If your organization is currently perpetuating those silos, it may be time to break them down. My recommendation would be to move *acceptable use policies* back into documents that come from the branch of the office having governance over employee behavior. This is a perfect opportunity for HR and IT professionals to collaborate on a policy; continuing the traditional culture-setting role of HR while taking the unique demands of technology into account.

Notes

PART III — DRAFTING

Chapters in this part

Notes

14. DRAFTING PRINCIPLES

Executive Summary

A number of drafting techniques can make rules sound positive, including favoring positive grammatical constructions, specifying the desired outcome, and converting directive statements to informational ones. Statements of micromanagement in policies, despite being well-intentioned, are susceptible to being perceived as control mechanisms; they are more palatable in procedures, where detailed guidance is not only expected but also appreciated.

Continuing our exploration on an ever more granular level, Part III tightens our focus to examine the specific wording of rule statements. This first chapter looks at the general principles guiding the techniques and recommendations made in the subsequent chapters.

The goal is for the completed rules documents to support three general values.

#1. Efficiency of process

We want them to be both robust and scalable, to accommodate the optimal flow of information and decision points, and to reduce duplication and waste.

#2. Effectiveness of regulation

We want them to improve the degree of buy-in and engagement at all levels of the organization, while promoting a consistent regulatory approach.

#3. Authenticity

We want them to portray accurately who we are and what we stand for.

Verb Tense

We're going to begin our exploration by choosing the right tense for the most pivotal part of any sentence: the verb. The variety of options available cause an enormous amount of debate around what's appropriate for a policy statement.

We can find proponents for all possibilities: Some drafters insist on using one of the modal verbs *must*, *may*, or *should* in every statement, for example, *Furniture must not be removed from the office.* Some like the simple future *will* — as in *Employees will not remove furniture from the office*, while others prefer its quaint variant, *shall*. Some find that a rule using the imperative form of a verb, as in *Never remove furniture from the office*, is too brusque, while others find it satisfyingly plainspoken. Some refuse to entertain the possibility of using a passive voice, as in that earlier example *Furniture must not be removed from the office*, claiming that it creates too much uncertainty around who is responsible; while others like the passive voice because it blunts the directness of a command. Finally, we always have the option of skirting the verb tense issue entirely through nominalization, such as, *No removing furniture from the office.*

So many choices. So let's start back at the beginning, looking at what's problematic about the traditional approach.

The statement in panel 51 is typical of a statement mandating specific business hours.

Panel 51

The office must be open from 8 AM to 4 PM.

The meaning is clear, but so are the dictatorial overtones. The tone reveals that management expects some people to evade the rule, and has chosen wording to address that possibility proactively. The subtext is loud: *we're telling you what to do very clearly, so you had better listen*. It sounds heavy-handed.

The power of the present tense

From my perspective, only one verb form consistently delivers a respectfully-worded policy statement: the **simple present tense**. It makes rules sound straightforward and unpretentious, as shown in panel 52.

Panel 52

The office is open from 8 AM to 4 PM.

The simple present tense produces a declarative sentence, describing the world in a neutral voice as a matter of fact. The statement informs people of *how we do things*, and echoes the wording used when the sentence begins with *Our policy is that* as in panel 53.

Panel 53

Our policy is that the office is open from 8 AM to 4 PM.

The use of the present tense sets the stage for employees to do what is necessary to put it into practice. It is predicated on the good faith of the people it is directed to and does not sound oppressive or confrontational.

In a majority of cases, simple declarative sentences make the best policy statements, as in the examples in panel 54.

Panel 54

A ten-minute grace period is offered for appointments.

Visitors are accompanied by an escort while on the premises.

Refunds for tickets are available up to five days before the performance.

Each statement is made as a present-day truth, a simple description of the way things look when they're done properly.

The Penal Code Approach

Some rule writers react with a bit of skepticism on their first exposure to this approach. The immediate reaction may be to characterize the present tense as "flimsy," and to doubt its ability to alter behaviors in their organizations. They point to their compliance problems or corporate culture as obliging strict rules to sound severe. "Unless the statement starts with all employees must," they object, "people will assume that management is not serious about enforcing it."

Healthy skepticism can be a good thing when it motivates digging deeper into the issue. You will recall that the entire approach of this book is based on the fact that drafting corporate policies shares some commonalities with drafting legislation. That being the case, it behooves us to find out what the world of legislation can teach us about this topic.

From my perspective, the strictest laws in the democracies around the world would sit in their penal legislation. You know: murder, assault, robbery … all the nasty stuff. How is the prohibition against these crimes handled there? Kidnapping, for example, is not tolerated in any of these jurisdictions, and they each have some form of law against it.

If the traditional corporate wording were used as the model, we would expect to find laws against kidnapping sounding something like the statements in panel 55.

Panel 55

People must not kidnap other people.

Kidnapping others will not be tolerated.

People are strictly forbidden from kidnapping one another. *No exceptions will be made!*

Clearly, criminal laws aren't worded that way. In fact, a large majority of jurisdictions manage to draft absolute prohibitions on all kinds of activity without ever using the terms *must*, *should*, *never*, and similar modifiers. Instead, they use a series of simple, declarative statements set in the present tense.

The Texas *Penal Code*, for example, prohibits kidnapping using the language set out in panel 56.[14]

---

[14] Sec 20.03(a)

Panel 56

A person commits an offense if he intentionally or knowingly abducts another person.

There it is: the simple present tense, used in the context of total prohibition. Panel 57 shows the law against arson in the State of South Dakota.[15]

Panel 57

Any person who starts a fire or causes an explosion with the intent to destroy any occupied structure of another is guilty of first degree arson. First degree arson is a Class 2 felony.

There it is again. The law on assault in the second degree in the *New York State Penal Code* is shown in panel 58.[16]

Panel 58

A person is guilty of assault in the second degree when:

1. With intent to cause serious physical injury to another person, he causes such injury to such person or to a third person.

A survey of the penal codes of all 50 US states reveals that **80% of them use this present-tense format.**[17] It serves this role more than adequately: the present tense is clear and straightforward, doesn't sound dictatorial or aggressive, and

---

[15] 22-33-9.1

[16] §120.05

[17] See https://lewiseisen.com/2021/10/15/state-penal-law-review-results/

doesn't work from the assumption that our primary goal is to evade the law. Some of those US penal codes actually state the crime in the present tense and put the punishment in the future tense, emphasizing the sequence.

The remaining ten states still use some older formulation for prohibition statements, such as *No one shall*. This wording sounds decidedly antiquated placed next to the simple declarative format.

The crimes prohibited by the various criminal codes vary from minor offenses like spitting in public to the most major ones, such as murder, treason, and kidnapping. Yet in the 80% majority of states, the penal laws are written in this non-threatening, matter-of-fact tone of voice.

In Canada, a single *Criminal Code* governs the entire country. An example of the wording used is set out in panel 59.[18]

Panel 59

268 (1) Every one commits an aggravated assault who wounds, maims, disfigures or endangers the life of the complainant.

(2) Every one who commits an aggravated assault is guilty of an indictable offence and liable to imprisonment for a term not exceeding fourteen years.

The use of the present tense in penal codes is by no means limited to North America. The United Kingdom uses the wording illustrated in panel 60.[19]

---

[18] Sec. 268
[19] *Theft Act*, 1968, sec. 1(1)

Panel 60

> A person is guilty of theft if he dishonestly appropriates property belonging to another with the intention of permanently depriving the other of it ...

Six of the seven Australian states use the present tense, as does the *New Zealand Crimes Act*, shown in panel 61.[20]

Panel 61

> Common Assault. Every one is liable to imprisonment for a term not exceeding 1 year who assaults any other person.

Nor is this approach limited to English language jurisdictions. Panel 62 contains a statement from France's *Code Pénal*.[21]

Panel 62

> *Le vol est puni de trois ans d'emprisonnement et de 45 000 € d'amende.*

In English that would be rendered as *Theft **is** punishable by 3 years imprisonment and a € 45,000 fine.*

Panel 63 contains the prohibition on theft in the corresponding law in Germany:[22]

---

[20] Sec. 196

[21] Art. 311-1

[22] §_242 StGB

Panel 63

(1) Wer eine fremde bewegliche Sache einem anderen in der Absicht wegnimmt, die Sache sich oder einem Dritten rechtswidrig zuzueignen, wird mit Freiheitsstrafe bis zu fünf Jahren oder mit Geldstrafe bestraft.

That law roughly translates to *Whoever* **takes** *movable property belonging to another away from another with the intention of unlawfully appropriating it for themselves or a third party* **incurs** *a penalty of imprisonment for a term not exceeding five years or a fine.*

I could go on, but I think the problem has been laid bare: we are faced with an absurd situation. In each country, **the strictest laws, for the most heinous crimes, are written in language more respectful than that in many organizations' policies.**

Ponder that for a moment. Evidently, we speak more courteously to criminals than to our colleagues and customers.

In fact, if an employee were to judge the severity of a rule based solely on its tone, it would be understandable if they come to the conclusion that murdering their boss is not half as serious an offense as using a meeting room without reserving it first.

The argument that strictness calls for dictatorially-worded statements just doesn't hold water.

Granted, in each of the jurisdictions cited here we can find statutes where the use of *must* is common. All that tells us, though, is that the left hand doesn't know what the right hand is doing. The truth is that for many people, as first mentioned in the Introduction, **courtesy is simply unfamiliar as a rule-writing style.**

It's time to change that. In Part I, we saw that the traditional approach to inducing behaviors is one of issuing orders telling people what to do or, more typically, what not to do. Today we know better: to get people's cooperation we need to engage them, not command them.

Our challenge to is make policy statements sound affirmative and inspiring, with the goal of **helping people do the right thing** rather than merely keeping them in line.

We'll spend the rest of this chapter looking at a number of techniques that we can use to reword rules in a way that garners maximum engagement. It may take a little practice, but once you get the hang of it you'll find people respond much better to being treated with respect than to the traditional marching-orders style.

General Principles

Unifying the tense across all our rules documents lets us maintain a consistent corporate voice. That consistency helps build trust, which is a required element for increased engagement.

Now that we've got the verb tense issue out of the way, we can start to look at rules statements more holistically.

Drafting values

Two values guide us as we craft the wording of our rules. The first one is *clarity*.

For rules, *clarity* is non-negotiable. When we evaluate a statement, if it doesn't pass the *clarity* test, we don't move on until it does. As mentioned in chapter 9, *clarity* in this context means the *lack of ambiguity*.

The second value is *respect*. We want the statement to sound respectful to the people we're talking to. I find the respect aspect harder to achieve because I grew up with the traditional language along with everyone else of my era. So I resort to two general principles to test whether my statements are consistent with that value.

#1. Assume positive intent

When we talked about corporate culture back in chapter 4 we concluded that, as much as possible, we want to promote a *trusting policy culture*. We want people to know that we are not coming to the table anticipating the worst from them, but instead we look forward to their best.

This principle encourages us to assume that people will generally approach a situation with a willingness to cooperate rather than a tendency for resistance. Furthermore, should we encounter a problem, let's assume that non-compliance is a result of circumstance, not of motivation.

By assuming positive intent we give others the benefit of the doubt. Instead of sounding defensive — as if we rely on our level of vigilance to ward off disobedience — we can sound supportive. To achieve this positivity, we will favor wording that informs people about the rule with the assumptions that *they want the information* and *they intend to act on it*.

#2. Avoid the Parent–Child dynamic

As we have seen, statements written with the *I'm-telling-you-what-to-do* approach are divisive rather than unifying. We've already talked about their historical origin, and what makes them inappropriate in written rules. We are looking instead to reinforce a healthy, Adult–Adult dynamic.

Using these two principles as a test has been helpful to me as I evaluate my written statements. When rules conform to both of those principles, they send the following messages as subtext:

- We trust you.
- We see you as an ally, not an adversary.
- We see you as a collaborator, not a minion.
- We know you want to do what's right.
- We know you will try to do the best job possible.

Some policy developers balk at those last messages. "Some people," they remind me, "don't want to do what's right or the best job possible."

Yes, sadly that's true. Similarly, some people want to throw a tantrum in a medical clinic, and some people want to commit assault and arson.

There will always be some people who want to flout the rules; however, that non-compliance is less a drafting problem than an attitude problem. In a healthy organization, that attitude is found in a small minority of cases. Don't we want to appeal to and engage the majority of people who want to do the right thing, rather than the minority who don't?

If, by some chance, you are unfortunately working in a toxic workplace, where the majority of people have an attitude problem, then your organization may need professional help to move forward. It's not a problem that can be resolved by clever drafting; the culture, trust, and teamwork issues need to be dealt with for your policy regulatory environment to be positive and functional. If your organization is dysfunctional and not working on solving that problem, you are fighting an uphill battle.

Context Matters

Set-up is just as important as execution. If we can set the context in a way that opens the door to engagement, then statements that might otherwise be considered heavy-handed may actually be perceived in a positive light.

Take a look at the text in panel 64.

Panel 64

To get your travel expenses reimbursed, you must do the following:

1. Fill out the correct form.

2. Attach all your receipts.

3. Obtain a manager's signature.

The underlying corporate attitude towards rule-making is easily apparent from the wording. Some of the underlying subtext includes the following:

- We know best and you need to do what we say.

- "Rules are rules."

- Our goal is to direct you.

Indeed, all three instructional statements in panel 64 come across like orders. Stepping back, though, the problem is not necessarily the statements themselves, but the context in which they appear. The opening sentence sets an *I'm in charge* tone right from the beginning, which then cascades into the instructions. Even when instructions trace their origins back to approved policy, we don't need to emphasize that fact. Instead, we can choose to approach the communication as if it were a form of signage, as shown in panel 65.

Panel 65

Get your travel expenses reimbursed in three easy steps!

1. Fill out the correct form.

2. Attach all your receipts.

3. Obtain a manager's signature.

The instructional sentences are exactly the same, but now the opening invitation changes the whole tenor of the relationship. The approach is no longer *we're here to set rules for you*, but has become something more like *we've made this easy for you*.

"Please"

What if we began all our rules with *Please* to make them sound nicer? Would that work?

Not really. Though it might make them sound nicer, it would also make them appear to be requests. We reach for *please* when we're telling people what to do in an attempt to soften the blow. Conflating the two is disorienting, because we want rules to be easily distinguishable from requests.

Remember the distinction between policy and signage? *Please* works well on signage.

Fortunately, many of the techniques we cover in the next chapter are already respectful enough that they don't need softening. We move away from telling people what to do in favor of informing them about our approach. In those cases, statements have nowhere to fit *please* even if we wanted to.

The short answer is that inserting *please* into a policy statement reduces succinctness without adding clarity. Since the whole of Part III is dedicated to making the statement respectful, adding it is redundant.

Quality Assurance

The two drafting principles presented are simple enough to understand but can be tricky to implement. Although we may work hard to produce a high caliber product, it's not always clear when we've achieved it. Getting a second opinion can help on that score.

The most reliable quality assurance check we can get is to ask someone else for feedback. While we might be able to proofread our own work for grammar and style issues with some accuracy, it is difficult to be objective when assessing the tone of our own documents. It is particularly challenging to detect our own unintended negative messages because our perspective is skewed. We are all prone to some degree of blind-spot bias, one of many biases recognized in the field of cognitive psychology.

In addition, it's prudent in every business to respect the *principle of separation of duties*, a standard quality assurance control used in many fields, including finance, information security, and risk management. That principle holds that to achieve objectivity and reliability in the outcome of production, the individuals doing the work can't also be the ones doing the quality assurance check. It makes just as much sense when applied to policy writing.

Language Models

No book published after 2023 discussing writing or composition can be complete without at least acknowledging the existence of Large Language Models (LLM) like ChatGPT and other Artificial Intelligence systems.

I realize, of course, that I'm taking a big risk here: my comments could be out of date before the ink dries on the page; nevertheless, I'd like to acknowledge that LLM can be a valuable tool for policy drafters for a number of tasks.

The key to success is the same key we need to apply to every other tool we reach for: **use it only for the purposes for which it was intended.** The tool is a Large **Language** Model, not a Thinking Model, Factual Model, Research Model … whatever. While it draws on information from multiple sources, it confesses up front that it can make mistakes and recommends that you fact-check important information. Despite continuous updating of its databanks, it is still subject to bias and hallucinations.

Precision in language is a different thing altogether, and it's here that the technology shines bright. It knows English really good, much gooder than me. Ask an LLM to explain the difference between *inclusion*, *inclusivity*, and *inclusiveness*, and it will provide a detailed response that recognizes subtle distinctions and conveys nuance in an impressive manner.

That ability makes LLM wonderful proofreaders. They'll accurately report not just on grammar and style, but on tone and subtext. They can help refine the language in policy documents, offering suggestions for clearer, more concise, and more engaging wording. They can advise when a statement is susceptible to an ambiguous reading, and can spot inconsistencies in language terminology.

However, as of this writing, I have not seen a language model replace traditionally confrontational policy wording with anything other than different confrontational policy wording. No doubt, that ability will come over time.

I frequently took advantage of ChatGPT when writing this book. It helped me smooth out rough spots, made suggestions for related issues, and more than once supplied me with the perfect word. It's a great collaborator, and in the end I always get the final say.

Notes

15. Drafting Techniques

Executive Summary

A number of simple language changes can turn authoritarian wording into a more respectful statement of policy, without sacrificing the rigidity of the rule itself. They center around transitioning from command statements focusing on the negative to informational statements emphasizing the positive.

Now that we're on the same page about the principles, we can roll up our sleeves and get to work. In this chapter we'll look at five types of techniques for wording rules in a way that maximizes engagement. They are not all usable in all situations, but often more than one technique can be applied to reword a specific statement.

While these techniques are useful for communicating rules generally, they are in fact geared particularly to drafting statements of policy. They were chosen specifically because they **lower resistance to buy-in**. Since buy-in takes place at the policy level, the need for these techniques in standards and procedures is less pressing.

The types of techniques are as follows:

1. Using positive rather than negative language
2. Indicating what we want
3. Signaling our response
4. Refraining from micro-management
5. Changing directions to information

#1. Using Positive Language

The first technique is the most basic. Too often, we instinctively formulate rules in the negative, as seen in the three examples in panel 66.

Panel 66

Individuals are not eligible to apply for this benefit unless they are 65 years of age or older.

This benefit is not available to individuals under 65 years of age.

You do not qualify for this benefit until you reach 65 years of age.

The fix is easy: simply swap out the negative form of the verb for a positive one, as seen in panel 67.

Panel 67

Individuals 65 years of age or older are eligible to apply for this benefit.

This benefit is available to individuals 65 years of age or older.

You qualify for this benefit when you reach 65 years of age.

This may seem like a simplistic adjustment, but it has powerful implications. The difference in the subtext of the two panels is striking.

The statements in panel 66 function like bouncers at a nightclub door, preventing people from coming in until eligibility for admission has been proven. They repeat the message *"Not you, not you, not you, either"* until someone shows them the right piece of personal identification. They let that individual pass, then quickly close up ranks to prevent anyone else from sneaking in.

In contrast, the statements in panel 67 act more like the people giving out free samples at the front of the store. *"Hey,"* they seem to call out, *"we have something that might interest you."* Those people are not there to keep the bad people out; they're there to bring the good people in.

Small change in grammar, huge change in attitude.

If our goal is to increase engagement, the right wording is key. The negative statements in panel 66 establish obstacles and withhold the benefit. As a result, they're harder for people to support. Nothing there establishes a rapport, so there's nothing to engage with.

The positive statements in panel 67, on the other hand, are worded in a way that offers a connection. We have reduced the potential for resistance because now, instead of sounding bossy, the rule sounds helpful.

This technique is powerful. If it is the only change suggested by this book that you decide to implement, you will still see a profound difference in the tone of your policy instruments and people's reactions to them.

Exclusionary terms

Some readers might find the statements in panel 67 to be lacking because the exclusionary aspect of the rule is not indicated. Adding it would turn them into statements like those in panel 68.

Panel 68

> Solely individuals 65 years of age or older are eligible to apply for this benefit.
>
> This benefit is available exclusively to individuals 65 years of age or older.
>
> You qualify for this benefit only when you reach 65 years of age.

My question would be *Is there really a need to emphasize the exclusion?* Some might insist that adding words like *only* clarifies the rule, but I challenge that. Context is key, remember? When we're talking about seniors' benefits, is it not clear that seniors' benefits are for seniors?

Adding the exclusionary term puts the bouncer back in front of the door, making it look like the purpose of the rule is to keep the wrong people out rather than to let the right people in. True, the statements are not as heavy-handed as the original ones in panel 66, but they sound **defensive.** There's definitely a *don't try to get around this restriction* vibe going on. Given the context of the rule, it doesn't really conform to the principle *assume positive intent.*

In contrast, some statements do raise a *bone fide* need to clarify whether a rule is exclusionary, such as the example in panel 69.

Panel 69

Supervisors are authorized to park in the back lot.

After reading the rule above, it's conceivable that people working both above and below the supervisor level might start flipping the page to find the parking statement applicable to them. If, given the context of the rule, the absence of an exclusionary term creates a real uncertainty, the addition of *only* removes that, as shown in panel 70.

Panel 70

Supervisors only are authorized to park in the back lot.

#2. Indicating What We Want

Written out in full, this technique actually reads *Indicating what we do want, not what we don't want.*

While the previous technique can, for the most part, be made through simple changes in grammar, this one takes a little more thought beyond the words already written on the page.

Let's start with an easy example, like the one in panel 71.

Panel 71

Don't leave questions unanswered on the form.

In this case, the rule tells us what they **don't want**, but not actually what they **do want**. It's not inaccurate, but it's not engaging either. Since it is opaque as to what the intonation of the writer is, it is open to interpretation both as a helpful statement or an admonishment. It's that last impression that we need to avoid, because it acts as a barrier.

Let's replace it with a statement that more clearly expresses what a positive outcome would look like. Any of the statements in panel 72 will do.

Panel 72

- Answer all questions on the form.
- Complete the form by answering all questions.
- Submit the form once all questions are complete.

Other suitable formulations are possible. **These statements encourage compliance through positive engagement rather than deterrence.** The likelihood of a statement worded in this way being taken as a rebuke is slim; it is more likely to be seen as a helping-hand than what's in panel 71.

Some would argue that the revised statement in panel 72 is actually **clearer** than the original, since it's explicit about what is expected and leaves less to the imagination. I won't disagree, but it seems to me that subtext is what makes the real difference. The subtext of the original statement is *Don't do it wrong*, while that of the revised statements is *Here's how to do it right*.

Let's move to a more complicated example, such as the statement in panel 73.

Panel 73

Wet boots are not to be brought into the office.

Again, it's pretty clear what they don't want; however, unlike the previous example, it's not at all clear what they do want. We're left to guess at what the alternatives are: leave boots at the front door? Outside the office? Put them in a bag and carry the bag around? Maybe they don't care which of those we choose so long as they don't see the boots. We're forced to speculate on what to do.

The clearer formulation is set out in panel 74.

Panel 74

Leave wet boots on the mat in the waiting room.

Both these examples are pretty benign, I grant you, so let's look at a case that would be more contentious. Take the statement in panel 75.

Panel 75

During business hours, employees must not use the customer entrance.

That statement puts up a barrier and offers nothing in return: no alternative is named, no path is cleared. When a rule contains no more than a prohibition, it lacks features that can lessen resistance. The subtext is that management thinks it more important to curtail an employee's freedom than to provide a functional work environment.

To increase buy-in to rules, when we close one door we need to open another. A more respectfully-worded rule might be the statement in panel 76.

Panel 76

The service door is the designated entrance for employees during business hours.

If we *assume positive intent*, that employees want to know the rules so they can act on them, then this statement is the only rule we need.

Wanting a negative

At times, we have a situation where we need to specify a negative. Where the number of things we want is so much greater than the number we don't want, it would be silly to name all the positives.

For example, let's say that we don't want customers taking photographs as they walk through our store, and we want to post a sign to that effect. In this situation, it would be silly to list all the activities that are acceptable in the store. How can we specify a negative without using negative terms like *is not permitted* or *is forbidden*?

In those cases, the best approach is to use a verb that means *do not*, as shown in panel 77.

Panel 77

Refrain from taking photos while in the store.

Since this is signage we're talking about, *please* or *kindly* would not be out of place. Note the shift in perspective, though, **moving the emphasis from the store's rules to a**

cooperative appeal to the customer. The approach is respectful and courteous.

Other possible verbs for this purpose are the following:

- Refrain from
- Abstain from
- Forego

- Omit
- Prevent
- Exclude.

The absence of *avoid* from this list is deliberate. Instead of imparting an unequivocal message that the activity is undesirable, *avoid* suggests a request for the use of discretion on the part of the reader. Unless that discretion is what's wanted, the verbs offered above are better suited to issuing a prohibition respectfully.

#3. Signaling Our Response

The traditional approach to organizational policies is that they are tools for keeping people in line. As such, virtually all rules were constructed as instructions given by the speaker to be followed by the listener.

What if we turn that completely around, writing a rule directed back at ourselves? What if the rule doesn't instruct other people how to behave, but instead advises them how we behave? Consider the statement in panel 78.

Panel 78

Customers must not send us orders on the weekend.

We can see instantly that this would be a ridiculous rule for an office to make. We can't control what customers do. In the language of governance introduced in part I, we would say that the policy approvers in our office lack the competence to govern people outside that office.

Some people's first impulse is to adjust the statement into the wording shown in panel 79.

Panel 79

Customer orders are not filled on the weekend.

At least we're getting closer, because now we're making a **policy about something we can control.**

The rule in panel 79 is functional as a policy statement, but it's not optimal. It may be accurate, but it sounds a little punitive. Instead of being appreciative that someone wants to place an order, it seems like it's reproaching the customer for choosing timing that is inconvenient for the company.

A more helpful wording would be the one in panel 80.

Panel 80

Customer orders received over the weekend are filled on the next business day.

From an engagement point of view, the policy in panel 79 shuts people down. Why would any customer be happy that the company is not serving them? The statement in panel 80 is much more customer-friendly, trying to establish a rapport and maintain the client relationship even through the weekend down-time.

At the end of the day, our office routine is the same, but our attitude and approach to rule writing have changed. We've gone from being prohibitory in panel 78 to being coldly reactive in panel 79, and finally to being helpful in panel 80.

The micro-lesson demonstrated in this example is that companies can't control what customers do on weekends. All they can control is how they react to an undesirable situation, in this case, by responding to the order when the weekend is over.

The macro-lesson, however, is much more profound: when making rules for adults, the reality is that **we can't control what other people do; we can only control ourselves**. We can choose how we respond to actions that we don't want. Respectful rule making takes that reality into account.

Live theatre and symphony owners figured it out long ago. They don't want us coming late to performances, but they can't control us and they know it. They can control only how they respond to what we do, so their policy forewarns us of that response on the ticket. Instead of a threat like *If you arrive late, you will wait outside the door until we can seat you*, the ticket says something along the lines of *Latecomers are seated at the first opportunity*.

The policy wording is courteous and helpful. The unpleasant consequence of waiting at the back door is not being wielded as a punishment for disobedience; rather, it is being offered as the best experience they can provide given the circumstances. Based on that information, as adults, we can decide for ourselves whether or not to be on time.

This macro-lesson is also the premise of the penal code legislation we covered earlier. The penal laws have not been able to stop crime from happening; the best we can do is to run a disciplinary process after the fact. For the most part, the penal code statements reflect that reality: none of them says *don't murder anyone*. What the penal codes say is that *if we find that you have murdered someone, we will react by throwing you in jail. Govern yourself accordingly.*

Determining our response

Our inability to physically control the actions of others has implications for all our policy statements. Adults will choose to follow our rules based on their understanding of how we plan to respond to various circumstances. A respectfully-worded rule communicates that response.

Consider a utility company that wants its on-site inspection agents to stop wearing shorts and sandals when visiting customers. It develops a policy containing the statement in panel 81.

Panel 81

On-site inspection agents must dress professionally when interacting with the public.

The statement in panel 81 is an old-style command, typical of policies attempting to control employees' actions.

Just as a side-note: don't get distracted by the fact that the policy statement doesn't specify what *professionally* means. Yes, somewhere — in some Standard or Toolkit document — the dress code may be described in more detail. Alternately, it might be purposely left undefined to reflect a more trusting policy culture. When rules like the one in panel 81 are broken, it's usually not due to a lack of understanding of the details; rather, it's a case where the individual knows full well what dressing appropriately means, but resists doing so.

The organization can't physically control the clothes people don in the morning. What it can control is its response to the situation. The statement in panel 82 sets out one possibility.

Panel 82

We send on-site inspection agents home when they come to work dressed unprofessionally. For the first occurrence, we also issue a warning. For subsequent occurrences, we deduct two hours' pay.

That policy tells us exactly what actions the organization will take in the undesirable situation. The examples in panel 83 give us other possibilities.

Panel 83

We restrict on-site inspection agents who do not dress appropriately to back office duties.

We dock a day's pay from on-site inspection agents who do not dress appropriately.

When an on-site inspection agent comes to work dressed inappropriately, we make a notation in their file.

When compared to the examples above, it's clear that the *must* statement in panel 81 serves only to emphasize the dominant–subordinate relationship: *You will do this because we say you must; that reason is sufficient.*

The organization has the right to set limits around behaviors. The challenge is to describe those limits, without adding an extra kicker like *We expect you to meet them.* Panel 84 contains an example.

Panel 84

The company considers delivery personnel to be ready and able to work when they

- **arrive by 8 o'clock in the morning**
- **are free from the influence of any intoxicating substance or medication, and**
- **are in possession of their driver's license.**

To complete the picture we will want a statement about what we steps we take when someone shows up in the morning not being *ready and able to work.*

One last point: remember the question about adding *please* to a policy as a softening agent? This technique doesn't only eliminate the need for it, it totally precludes its use. There's just nowhere to put it.

Rethinking compliance

The whole notion of *compliance* gets turned on its head when we draft rules this way. Our policies are no longer about discipline or punishment, they're about how the organization does things. If we are experiencing low compliance with this policy, we have only ourselves to reproach for it, because it means that when the situation arises **we** are not doing what we said we would. By deciding exactly how we handle undesirable situations, we are adopting a more mature attitude towards cooperation, recognizing the autonomy of individuals while still maintaining corporate standards.

In my experience, when an organization resorts to *must* in a rule statement, it's often because it hasn't actually determined what it will do when it encounters the problem. Perhaps the organization hopes to avoid deciding on the consequences until it's forced to; so, for the time being, it circumvents the issue by using *must*. This approach is essentially an avoidance technique, and *must* buys them time.

That indecision is what generates non-specific threats such as the vague *Failure to follow this policy may result in consequences*. That approach treats what happens next like a casino jackpot. *Take your chances and see what happens! Sometimes you win, sometimes you lose ... go ahead and test your luck!*[23]

#4. Avoiding Micro-Management

In chapter 12 we talked about the fact that procedures have the freedom to lead people step-by-step with minute detail.

That same detail in a policy statement looks like micro-management. I'm sure you've come across examples of policies that over-reach this way, when the drafters are so

---

[23] This threat reminds me of my grandmother when I was young and making mischief. She would wag her finger and say, "You'd better listen to me. Don't push me, because you don't know what I'm going to do when I get mad!" It didn't work then, either.

concerned about the process that they list the individual steps required.

Panel 85 repeats the example set out in panel 43.

Panel 85

Directors must set aside time each year to review and update their budgets.

Part of the policy drafter's job is to separate the essential elements of a requirement from the non-essential ones. The essential elements belong in the policy because they establish lines we're not willing to cross. This statement is really intended to achieve an outcome, not to quarterback the steps. Supporting elements like *set aside time* and *review* are in fact just good advice, and advice belongs in the Toolkit documents. It's easily fixed by removing the interim steps, as shown in panel 86.

Panel 86

Directors update their budgets annually.

But often micro-management is more subtle than that. Take a look at the statement in panel 87.

Panel 87

The Board of Directors formulates strategy at the broadest levels first and then moves to the development of more detailed strategies until the matter has been addressed to its satisfaction.

As well-intentioned as this statement might be, it doesn't belong in a Policy because it's really a set of instructions. The telltale sign of the parental tone of voice is the clause *until the matter has been addressed to its satisfaction.* (Kinda sounds like your mom telling you that you can't go out to play until you finish your homework, doesn't it?)

In panel 88, the micro-management is even more subtle.

Panel 88

Equipment is to be returned to the storage room at the end of the day.

Can you see it? The statement focuses on the procedural step rather than the outcome. The actual **policy** decision is the one set out in panel 89.

Panel 89

We keep equipment in the storage room overnight.

That's the outcome we want to see. Telling people to bring it to that room goes one step too far. You might think that one step is too trivial to matter, but it actually makes the difference between a statement conveying a Parent–Child dynamic and one that doesn't.

Sign-off statements

Take a look at the statement in panel 90.

Panel 90

Employees must read, understand, and sign this policy.

This commonly-found statement is a cover-your-butt element that someone decided the organization can't do without. But it's also another example of someone worrying about the steps rather than pursuing an objectively definable outcome. It comes across as openly aggressive and not particularly trusting.

I generally recommend against the inclusion of these statements. If we really want to know whether the employee has read and understood the document, that can be accomplished in a simple e-mail acknowledgement. Imagine how you would feel if your government sent you every new statute passed in the land and required you to sign it to show that you're read and understood it, solely for their legal protection.

If an organization insists on using a sign-off statement, it can be done in a more respectful way. To word it correctly, it's first important to pin down the result we really want. For most organizations, that might be an indication or commitment from employees of their willingness to be bound by the contents of the document. If that's the case, we can separate the policy decision of the statement from the transactional portion, and end up with two separate pieces.

The policy statement might sit in an HR policy, confirming the organization's approach, like the one in panel 91.

Panel 91

We ask employees to sign-off on each new policy.

That wording separates policy from implementation.

Obviously, before committing themselves, competent individuals would read through the document first. We can give them the opportunity to ask questions about the parts they don't understand. It may be true that common sense isn't as common as we would like it to be, but a policy statement explicitly telling employees to *read and understand before signing* is blatantly treating them like children.

Practically speaking, the *understand* portion of the statement is a fiction. Without actually testing employees on the material, we can't really know their level of understanding. Their own assessment of that level is of minimal value, because what they actually understand could be totally different from what we want them to understand. And, in my humble opinion, what's more useful than saying *I understand* would be a statement saying *When I don't understand, I will ask for clarification.*

If we truly feel that we need an attestation of some kind at the bottom of a policy, what might be of value is some evidence of the employee's **intentions**. We see similar statements when we sign a loan or credit card application, wherein we promise to make best efforts to meet our obligations. A more practical wording of the attestation statement might be the one shown in panel 92.

Panel 92

I commit to taking steps to comply with this policy.

We can, of course, adjust this wording to suit our preferences, while acknowledging that no attestation can achieve the same results as a proper training session.

Ensure

Sorry to have to break this pieces of news … I'll try to do it as gently as possible: the word *ensure* is pointless in a policy. **It's ambiguous at best and meaningless at worst.**

We use *ensure* a lot in conversation because it softens what would otherwise be a direct hit. In rules documents, we see it used in the manner shown in panel 93.

Panel 93

Tenants must ensure they pay their rent on the 1st of each month.

What **concrete action** is the word *ensure* in panel 93 adding to the obligation in panel 94?

Panel 94

Tenants must pay their rent on the 1st of each month.

Is it telling tenants to double-check the amount of the payment? To verify that the payment was received? To take extra care not to be late? Something else? It could be any or all of those things — or none of them. It seems to be asking for some kind of assurance.

If I were the landlord, I would rather receive the rent than the assurance. Technically, we want a rule to hold the tenant who's late with the rent in breach of policy, but we don't want to penalize a tenant who paid the rent but failed to **ensure** that they'd paid it—whatever that means. Put differently, a statement that *rent is due at the end of the month* is a policy statement; a statement that *tenants ensure they comply with that policy* is simply good advice.

If the goal is to achieve clarity in drafting, the wording in panel 95 might be an alternative.

Panel 95

> The rent is due on the first of each month. The responsibility for paying the rent lies with the tenant.

You may think I'm being petty here, but you don't have to believe me. Just ask someone whose job it is to translate the policy statements into another language. In Canada, for example, where official documents are often translated into French, the translators struggle to find the right words to convey the supposed meaning of *ensure*. It is rendered differently in each case, based on the translator's understanding of its intent in that statement. When we look at the wording of the translations, we see a variety of structures called into play, including:

- Tenants must *be sure* that they pay the rent.
- Tenants must *verify* that they have paid …
- Tenants must *double-check* that they have paid …
- Tenants must *take responsibility* for paying …

- Tenants must *pay attention* to paying ...
- Tenants must *assure themselves* that they have paid ...
- Tenants must pay ...

As we can see, in the last case they've given up trying to translate the word *ensure* completely.

Our statements are clearer and more succinct when we avoid *ensure* entirely. If we do use it, we need to be able to identify the **concrete action** that we expect to see as a result that word. After all, if the writer can't figure out exactly what action is expected, then what chance does the reader have?

#5. Changing Directions to Information

Avoiding the Parent–Child dynamic means working from the premise that people want to do what's needed to achieve a goal. What they lack is information, not direction.

Take the instructions in panel 96, for example, found on the home page of a Web site.

Panel 96

System Requirements

1. You must have cookies enabled
2. You must have Javascript enabled
3. You must use one of the following Web browsers ...

The list is a set of instructions, and an abrasive one at that. The presence of a formal title, the imperative tense in the verbs, and the use of numbering all combine to make this list reprimanding instead of helpful. The tone underlying it is *frustration*, intended to shift the blame in the user's direction: *if the site doesn't work, it's your fault because you didn't set it up right*. The relationship between the company — as represented by its Web site — and the customer is getting off to an adversarial start.

What if we assumed, however, that people coming to the site are happy to follow our restrictions when they know about them. By turning instructions into informational statements, as in panel 97, we can remove the Parent–Child undertones.

Panel 97

Our Web site functions properly when you

- have cookies and Javascript enabled, and
- use one of the following compatible Web browsers ...

This wording changes the entire dynamic between the company and the customer. Focusing on objective conditions rather than user obligations, the information looks like it's offered in a cooperative spirit. Dropping the hallmarks of formality found in the original helps to soften the approach and remove the accusatory tone.

These *you must* statements are found everywhere, typically because the writer is not aware of how aggressive they sound. They reach their pinnacle of ridiculousness when they are used in a truly voluntary situation, for example, this one from a Web site shown in panel 98.

Panel 98

> If you would like to be reminded of important renewal deadlines, you must sign up to receive a digital reminder.

Based on its length, the drafter of this statement must have been charging by the word. In any case, one possibility for the informational form of this statement is shown in panel 99.

Panel 99

> You have the option to sign up for a digital reminder of important renewal deadlines.

Intensifiers

We've already looked at how the need for *only* is context-dependent. Where it's needed, its presence provides clarity; where it's not, its presence sounds overly defensive.

A number of words are commonly inserted into policy statements to act as intensifiers. The effect on the tone of the statement is similar.

Take, for example, the word *all*. It often adds little or nothing to a rule's meaning. In panel 100, the B statements don't actually tell us anything more than the A statements.

Panel 100

> (A) We check visitors' identification before permitting entrance to the building.

(B) We check all visitors' identification before permitting entrance to the building.

(A) Managers have seven days to report accidents to the occupational health and safety office.

(B) Managers have seven days to report all accidents to the occupational health and safety office.

The presence of *all* has a subtext: it suggests either that there have been non-compliance issues in the past, or someone is afraid there might be some in the future. Unless we think that there would be a genuine lack of clarity, we can drop the word *all* without affecting the meaning of the rule.

Here are some other intensifiers that rarely add meaning to a rule, except the revelation of past problems:

- absolutely
- always
- at all times
- each

- every
- never
- no exceptions
- strictly.

When a statement uses one of those words, it's easy to test its dispensability: simply omit it to see if the requirement changes in any meaningful way.

It would be incongruous, for obvious reasons, if I told you **never** to use these words. So I won't say that. But I do try to avoid them.

Leading to the Modals

In this chapter we have looked at a number of techniques for wording rules in a way that lowers resistance to them. But that benefit comes at a cost: many of these techniques rely on our ability to pinpoint a source decision or isolate a statement of **exactly what we want**, which can be a real challenge. That challenge is what pushes people to fall back to using a *must*, *may* or *should* statement.

In the next chapter, we'll look at why we think those modals verbs help us, how they actually create more ambiguity than we realize, and how we go about selecting more effective alternatives.

16 Must, May, and Should

Executive Summary

The traditional modals *must*, *may*, and *should* impart a Parent–Child dynamic to rules, emphasizing the divide between rule-makers and rule followers. Their existence could be justified as convenient markers for distinguishing mandatory, optional, and recommended elements, were it not for the fact that in many cases they impart a meaning inconsistent with that pattern. We can replace the modal with a statement more directly indicating the decision the rule is predicated on. A large majority of those decisions are around authority, eligibility, entitlement, validity, characterization, pre-condition, sequence, and deadlines. Presenting that decision provides more clarity than the modal verbs, without the heavy-handedness. In other words, we want to inform people about the rules, but when we assume positive intent, we don't also have to tell them to obey them.

The Problem with Modal Verbs

If we're going to break the mold of negativity that surrounds rule making, we're going to want to make some significant changes. While the use of *must*, *may*, and *should* is well entrenched in policy, the justification for it belongs to a previous era, as discussed back in chapter 1. From a respectful language perspective, those words are authoritarian; for that reason alone I recommend we move away from them while maintaining any needed strictness.

Before delving into ways to reword those statements, let's review the two problems we're trying to avoid: heavy-handedness and ambiguity.

1. Heavy-Handedness

Must, *may*, and *should* are remnants of a Parent–Child dynamic. They all convey a subtext saying, *Remember that we are in charge.*

Must is a mandate: *You will do this because we say so.*

May is a dispensation: *We give you our permission to do this.*

Should is a concession: *Although we could make this mandatory, we're content merely to recommend it.*

All three of the terms reinforce an underlying presumption that two diverse sets of interests are involved: rule-makers and rule followers. That presumption alone is divisive and a barrier to a collaborative work environment.

Take the example in panel 101.

Panel 101

Employees must not park in the fire lane behind the building.

That statement unnecessarily segments the workforce. **No one** is permitted to park in the fire lane outside of emergency vehicles, management included. Wording the rule differently captures the strictness without being divisive, as shown in panel 102.

Panel 102

The fire lane behind the building is a no-parking zone.

Distinguishing applicability visually

The need to clearly distinguish mandatory from optional and recommended requirements is fundamental to rule-making, and the most common objection to dropping *must*, *may*, and *should* is the perceived loss of those visual markers.

Where visual identification is a *bona fide* consideration, we have a number of alternate indicators at our disposal:

- marking mandatory requirements with an asterisk
- putting mandatory requirements in a different font, size, or color
- using layout features to separate mandatory and optional requirements on the page
- beginning the document with a note that all requirements are mandatory unless otherwise indicated
- annotating each requirement with (M), (O), or (R).

Those methods are the ones that come from the top of my head; I'm sure you could think of some more if you tried. Making the distinction easy to see is a simple problem to fix.

2. Avoiding Ambiguity

The more serious problem is ambiguity.

When the line between these words blurs, we open ourselves up to the possibility of misinterpretation. In many instances, *must*, *may*, and *should* don't follow their own rules.

In theory, the system is cut and dried.

- *Must* means mandatory
- *May* means optional, and
- *Should* means recommended.

The International Standards Organization (ISO) uses a similar model, although the terms are slightly different. According to the ISO,

- *Shall* indicates a requirement.
- *Should* indicates a recommendation.
- *May* is used to indicate that something is permitted.
- *Can* is used to indicate that something is possible.[24]

Whichever set we choose, these definitions are problematic from the get-go. If the terms were always used consistently, we wouldn't have an issue. In practice, however, on too many occasions those words are unclear, misleading, or subject to multiple interpretations. Let's look at some of those cases.

No distinction in the negative

When the terms *must* and *may* appear in the negative, the mandatory–optional distinction disappears for all practical purposes.

---

[24] "Expressions in ISO International Standards And Other Normative ISO Deliverables."
https://www.iso.org/foreword-supplementary-information.html

Compare the A and B statements in panel 103.

Panel 103

(A) Documents may not be removed from the office.

(B) Documents must not be removed from the office.

What happened to the mandatory–optional distinction?

At the end of the day, these two statements produce identical results. Granted, **technically**, in the first case the action is merely *not permitted*, whereas in the second it is *expressly forbidden*, but in neither case is anyone allowed to remove documents from the office. In this context, *may* is not meant to offer an option.

Most likely the drafter used *may* to make the restriction **sound more polite** than it otherwise would. I refer to this usage as a *blunted must*, a literary device to make instructions more palatable to the reader. However, the bottom line is that in this context *may* doesn't signal an option. The requirement is simply more politely mandatory.

In negative statements, the argument that modal verbs preserve the mandatory–optional distinction is untenable. So let's set aside the negative forms as an anomaly, and restrict our analysis to positive statements. Is the argument any stronger?

The Ambiguity of *Must*

The statement in panel 104 uses the traditional policy wording, with *must* indicating a mandatory requirement.

Panel 104

Ferry passengers must wear lifejackets at all times.

In this statement *must* imposes an obligation. We can test that conclusion by seeing how the sentence reads when the notion of obligation is made explicit, as in panel 105.

Panel 105

Ferry passengers are obligated to wear lifejackets at all times.

Another phrase that can test *must* is *have no choice but*, as shown in panel 106.

Panel 106

Ferry passengers have no choice but to wear lifejackets at all times.

Panels 104, 105, and 106 all convey the same information, which confirms that *must* in panel 104 signals an **obligation**. That interpretation is the plain and simple meaning of the word, and if *must* consistently meant *is obligated to*, we'd have no problem.

But it doesn't, so we have one. Besides creating an obligation, in practice *must* is also used to

- grant an **authority**,
- set a condition of **eligibility**, or
- declare an **entitlement**.

Look at the example set out in panel 107.

Panel 107

The vice-president must approve all requests to borrow company equipment.

According to our interpretation of the statement in panel 104, it sounds like the vice-president **has no choice but to grant these requests** in all cases. I'm sure that the policy didn't mean to obligate the vice-president that way, but that's how the statement reads. The drafter tried to make something mandatory, and used the word *must* to do that. If there is a mandatory element involved somewhere, then that *must* is misplaced, and now **we** have no choice but to try to figure out what was actually intended.

Authority

One possibility is that an approval is required to borrow equipment, and that approval can come only from the vice-president. If that's what was intended by the policy, then it's not about obligation at all; it's a decision about *authority*. If we expressed that unequivocally instead of merely implying it, we would end up with a statement like one of those in panel 108.

Panel 108

The vice-president has the authority to approve requests to borrow company equipment.

The vice-president has the sole authority to approve requests to borrow company equipment.

Note how this new wording manages to retain the strictness of the original rule, but completely eliminates the need to distinguish between mandatory and optional actions.

Most likely, the intention was to obligate the people who want to borrow equipment to seek prior approval. **But that's not what the statement in panel 107 says.** Furthermore, those people aren't even alluded to, much less referenced.

Eligibility

An alternate interpretation of the example in panel 107 is that it mandates the order of events in a process. The intent is to make the vice-president's approval a pre-condition to borrowing the equipment. In that case, the decision is about *sequence* or *eligibility*. The intent is to make equipment available for someone to borrow **after** the vice-president has given approval. So let's say that more clearly, as in panel 109.

Panel 109

Company equipment is eligible to be loaned out upon the approval of the vice-president.

With this rewording, we're being helpful by opening a door, rather than being obstructive by raising an impediment.

Entitlement

Sometimes, the writer is so intent on using *must* in the rules that it gets inserted even when it makes absolutely no sense. Look at the example in panel 110.

Panel 110

> Employees must be given access to their own personnel files upon request.

If *must* here is intended to obligate someone to do something, the statement doesn't tell us who that someone is. Again, we have to try to figure out what's going on.

The intention likely wasn't to obligate employees to look at their own files. What's more likely is that *must* was meant to obligate the branch holding the files — again, unreferenced — to produce the employee's file upon request.

The intent here seems not to establish obligation; rather, it is more about *entitlement*. Employees who wish to see their files are entitled to see them. So let's say that outright, as in panel 111.

Panel 111

> Employees are entitled to have access to their own personnel files.

When the rule is worded this way, we're *assuming positive intent*. Given employees' entitlement to their own files, we're proceeding on the basis that whoever holds the files will do what is necessary to make that happen.

Synonyms

Is required to, *needs to*, **and others.**

We can't get around the Parent–Child dynamic by using synonyms, since they all suffer from the same problems:

ambiguity and condescending subtext. By declaring the *authority*, *eligibility*, or *entitlement* directly, we create the intended action or condition without giving an order.

The Ambiguity of *May*

Just like *must*, *may* often begets ambiguity around exactly which element it governs. Consider the statement in panel 112.

Panel 112

Employees may discuss flexible hours with their supervisors.

Again, the drafters of the statement would argue that they used *may* instead of *must* because they're not mandating a discussion, but rather providing an option. The problem here is that *may* is permitting the wrong action. That problem becomes obvious when we test what the opposite rule would sound like, as in panel 113.

Panel 113

Employees may not discuss flexible hours with their supervisors.

What exactly is meant to be prohibited in panel 112 but permitted in panel 113? Is it the flexible hours themselves or any discussions about them? If the original intent is to permit the use of flexible hours, that could be stated a lot more clearly, as in panel 114.

Panel 114

Employees have the option to work flexible hours.

If the intent is to permit the discussions about them … well, in that case we've just turned the clock back 50 years. Do we really need a formal policy statement to permit people to discuss something?

The statement in panel 112 defies clarification because it implies some facts but doesn't actually state anything specific. It implies that flexible hours might be allowed and that the supervisor has some role in that process, but beyond that we're in the dark. We can't know when we are or are not in compliance with this statement.

The many meanings of *may*

The traditional justification for the use of *may* is that is signals an option — the ability to make a choice between two or more alternatives. Whereas *must* blocks the ability to opt in or opt out, *may* opens that door.

Unfortunately, that's not all it does. There are at least six distinct uses of *may* in policy statements, each signaling something different. They are:

- the optional *may*
- the licensing *may*
- the mandatory *may*
- the potential *may*
- the permissive *may*
- the contingent *may*.

We'll go through them one at a time.

1. The optional *may*

The optional *may* is its typically claimed use, as seen in the statement in panel 115.

Panel 115

Senior analysts may apply for the supervisor position.

As expected, in this statement, *may* indicates that senior analysts **have the option** of applying for the position. Other formulations without *may* also work, as in panel 116.

Panel 116

The supervisor position is open to senior analysts.

Senior analysts are eligible to apply for the supervisor position.

If *may* consistently meant *has the option to*, we'd have no problem. But it doesn't, so we have one. Let's look at the other meanings.

2. The licensing *may*

Look at the use of *may* in panel 117.

Panel 117

Where operational requirements cannot be met with current staffing levels, directors may reassign other members to the team.

At first glance, this *may* resembles the optional one, but closer inspection reveals the intention to be greater than that. The statement is not merely offering directors the option to reassign people; it's going further, conferring them with the *authority* to do so. This policy is a *delegation statement*. More than having the option to reassign people, if directors are challenged on their actions, they are going to rely on this statement for proof of that authority. We can make the meaning explicit by using wording like that in panel 118.

Panel 118

Where operational requirements cannot be met with current staffing levels, directors have the authority to reassign others to the team.

---

3. The mandatory *may*

We looked earlier at how the distinction between *may* and *must* disappears in negative statements. I called that usage a *blunted must* — a mandatory requirement softened to sound less dictatorial. The statement in panel 118 shows the same *blunted must* in a positive statement.

Panel 119

Only approved training courses may be used to instruct workers in the use of safety equipment.

No matter how we look at it, *may* does not convey an option here; it's simply politely mandatory. This use of *may* as a tone-softener is all too common, weakening the argument that *must* and *may* distinguish the mandatory from the optional.

4. The potential *may*

In panel 120, *may* offers no option, confers no authority, nor blunts a mandatory statement.

Panel 120

Involvement in more than one car accident may affect driving privileges.

In this case, *may* indicates a potentiality or possibility. A clearer way to state that would be the statement in panel 121.

Panel 121

Involvement in more than one car accident has the potential to affect driving privileges.

---

5. The permissive *may*

Panel 122 showcases yet another use for the word *may*.

Panel 122

Once the client has produced valid identification, you may process the application.

In panel 122, *may* doesn't offer us an option, an authority, nor a new possibility. This *may* grants permission. It's the same *may* we find in the exchange, "**May** *I be excused from the table?*" "*Yes, you* **may**."

Of all the different meanings discussed here, this one carries the strongest Parent–Child dynamic. One way to remove that dynamic is to associate the permission with the object, as shown in panel 123.

Panel 123

Once the client has produced valid identification, the application process may continue.

Another possibility with this same formulation is to replace *may* with *can*, as shown in panel 124.

Panel 124

Once the client has produced valid identification, the application process can continue.

In both panels 123 and 124, we retain the permissive over-tone of the statement, but it's been depersonalized. The policy is written respectfully when it describes the state of affairs of the organization's activities without re-emphasizing the power structure.

The permissive *may* has a number of synonyms, including:

- is permitted
- is acceptable

- is allowed
- is authorized.

To this list we can add the negative form of each, such as *is not permitted* and *is disallowed*, as well as a few even more heavy-handed terms:

- is not tolerated
- is prohibited

- is (strictly) forbidden.

We looked at rewording the negative forms in the previous chapter, under technique #2 *Indicating What We Want*.

6. The contingent *may*

The final use of *may* is shown in panel 125.

Panel 125

Meals are provided to staff who may be required to work overtime.

In this case, *may* means *when the occasion arises*. If this *may* were actually about optionality, it would be contradictory given the stated requirement to work overtime.

In most cases, contingent *may* can be dropped completely without changing the meaning of the sentence, as shown in panel 126.

Panel 126

Meals are provided to staff who work overtime.

The translation test

If, after reading the above, you still believe that the meaning of *may* in policies is clear enough and that the distinctions made here are trivial, consider again the problems faced by translators. If *may* truly had the single, invariable meaning of *has an option to*, then translators could consistently use one or two equivalents for it in other languages.

However, the reality is different. In practice, translators constantly grapple with the context, trying to discern which use of *may* is intended. Since other languages handle these different meanings through different constructions, the translator ends up making a choice around which meaning to reflect. Often they choose correctly, but often they don't, in which case the translated version actually conflicts with the original. Such discrepancies can lead to significant misunderstandings.

That's not what clarity is about. When policies fail to convey the intended meaning clearly across languages, it underscores the need for precision and consideration in our choice of words.

The Ambiguity of *Should*

Of the three modal verbs discussed here, *should* suffers the worst identity crisis. It is the most versatile of the terms, and therefore the most ambiguous. *Should* has six distinct uses:

- the recommending *should*
- the mandatory *should*
- the ethical *should*
- the aspirational *should*
- the expectational *should*
- the hypothetical *should*

Let's go through them one at a time.

1. The recommending *should*

This is the traditionally-claimed use, when the drafter wishes to make a recommendation as opposed to a mandatory requirement. An example is shown in panel 127.

Panel 127

Employees should stay home when they're sick.

As a recommendation, it can easily be recast in one of the ways shown in panel 128.

Panel 128

It is recommended that employees stay home when they're sick.

We (strongly) recommend that sick employees stay home.

If a policy *should* consistently meant *recommended*, then we wouldn't have a problem. But it doesn't, so we have one. Two points are worth noting.

First, sometimes *should* means *is recommended* and sometimes it means *is strongly recommended*, but to know which of those is applicable in any given statement requires an understanding of the environment and consequences. When we use the wording shown in panel 128, we can make that distinction clear by adding the word *strongly*, but we can't do that with *should*. Consider the statements in panel 129.

Panel 129

Shrimp should be thawed for two hours prior to cooking.

Shrimp should be cooked thoroughly before eating.

Red ink should be used only for editorial corrections.

Does *should* really mean the same thing in all three? The first statement seems to be a **mild** or **moderate** recommendation, whereas the second one is a **strong** recommendation. But we know that only because we know the consequences of not following the recommendation. The third statement is a mystery; unless we know its rationale and consequences, we can't know how strong the recommendation is, and even then we'd be guessing. Using wording like that in panel 128 solves that problem.

The second point is related to compliance. A recommendation statement cannot form the basis for a finding of breach of policy. At its strongest, a *should* statement is a plea to do something without mandating it; at its weakest, it's a declaration of a best practice. Whichever is meant, though, failing to heed a recommendation is not the same as disobeying a rule.

Recall that the documentation framework separates Authorities from the Toolkit. **A recommendation is not a policy decision** and doesn't belong in authorities. It belongs in our guidance documents and wall posters.

2. The mandatory *should*

Another common use of *should* is shown in panel 130.

Panel 130

The fire extinguisher should be used only in emergencies.

Is that rule really intended to be recommended rather than mandatory? As a mere recommendation, the statement is really no more than advice. More likely, this statement was meant to be mandatory and *should* is being repurposed as a *blunted must*.

This use of *should* is more common than one might expect. More examples are found in panel 131.

Panel 131

Passengers should pay their fare upon boarding the bus.

Supervisors should report all injuries within 48 hours.

The application should be signed and dated at the bottom.

None of these statements is a meant as a recommendation.

As one might expect, using a mandatory *should* in policy documents is a recipe for disaster. The risk is that someone might interpret the statement as a mere recommendation, arguing that if the rule were mandatory, it would use *must*.

In fact, the statement in panel 130 is not really a mandate, but a statement of *characterization*. Better wording for it is in panel 132.

Panel 132

The fire extinguisher is for emergencies.

---

3. The ethical *should*

Another common use of *should* is to indicate an ethical or moral obligation. Take the statement in panel 133.

Panel 133

When you find a wallet on the street, you should return it to its owner.

The ethical *should* is stricter than a recommendation but not as strict as a mandatory requirement. Its ambiguities are easy to see in the example in panel 134.

Panel 134

Employees should avoid conflicts of interest.

That statement could mean any of the following (listed in descending order of strictness):

- Always avoid them.
- Avoid them whenever possible.
- Take steps to avoid them.
- Try hard to avoid them.
- Avoid them unless you have a justification not to.
- Avoid them unless there's a reason not to.
- Avoid them if you want to stay out of trouble.
- Avoid them if you're unsure about what to do.

Too many options here. In the absence of more information, we can't know exactly what *should* was intended to mean without speaking to the person who drafted the statement.

Some drafters justify *should* in these situations precisely because they want to exploit that ambiguity, opening the door to flexibility in interpretation. But that flexibility reflects a lack of clarity. If what we want is true flexibility, we can make that explicit. One such wording is in panel 135.

Panel 135

When determining whether a conflict of interest exists, each situation is assessed on its own merits.

---

4. The aspirational *should*

Look at the two examples in panel 136.

Panel 136

Information should be accessible, current, and accurate.

Skills training should be available to all employees.

Although they use the word should, these statements are not mere recommendations, blunted mandatory requirements, nor ethical imperatives. Here, *should* represents a target or aspiration.

5. The expectational *should*

Panel 137 shows two examples of this meaning.

Panel 137

We ship orders within 48 hours. Customers should receive them no later than seven days after that.

Welcome to the office! Inside your desk drawer you should find a laptop computer and a key.

The expectational *should* is similar to but stronger than the aspirational *should*. It suggests that when the target isn't met, it's because something has gone wrong somewhere. When the aspirational *should* falls short, the response is *let's do better next year*; when the expectational *should* falls short, the response is *let's fix that now*.

6. The hypothetical *should*

The final *should* expresses a possibility or eventuality, almost acting like a synonym for the word *if*, as in panel 138.

Panel 138

Should more information be required, the application form will be returned.

Should the item not be available, the customer's money will be refunded.

What to do with *should*

Evidently, *should* seems to appear where the intent is to signal a recommendation or piece of advice, a blunted re-quirement, a target or governing principle, a probability or expectation, or a possibility or eventuality. One can see how figuring out the correct interpretation could be difficult.

When *should* indicates a mandatory requirement, it is being misused. In all other cases it is potentially ambiguous.

Fortunately, all the *should* statements sampled here are appropriate for documents in the Toolkit, where we can add more words to provide help and context.

You might decide, after reading this section, that you still want your policy to contain statements of recommendation. In that case, to reduce the possibility for confusion, limit *should* to **genuine recommendations** and reword its other meanings.

Replacing *Must* and *May*

It's not easy retraining ourselves after doing things one way for years. I am just as prone as the next person to slip back into the traditional approach. I grew up with it and used it for many years until I learned that there was a better way. But its legacy has left a mark: we've become so used to giving instructions that it can be a struggle to pull back the layers to figure out what the pith of a rule really is.

As SME, we may know that we want to take the organization from point A to point B, and we have a sound rationale to support it. We also know, being the experts that we are, that the best way for someone to get from point A to point B is to go straight, then turn right, then turn left, and left again. So we write a policy that says, *You must go straight, then take a right turn followed by 2 left turns*, and we wonder why people aren't engaged.

In a policy, advising people of a rule is respectful; telling them that they have to follow it is not. The key to rewording statements that were originally drafted with *must* or *may* is to determine exactly what point the rule is clarifying.

Often, we use those authoritarian terms because they release us from having to explain ourselves any further. We might not plan to use them for that purpose, but they are often perceived that way by others. Let's look again at the first of the two statements in panel 1, reproduced for convenience in panel 139.

Panel 139

A. Employees must submit vacation requests at least one week in advance. Any request not submitted on time may be refused.

Why are they setting that rule? The statement shouts *because we said so. Our telling you is all you need to know.*

I assume positive intent on the part of HR rule-makers; that is, I assume that they all have a solid rationale for their rule and are not making decisions capriciously. The trick, then, is to find the point the rule is intended to clarify and bring it to the forefront, making it transparent.

It's not far-fetched to postulate that the HR workload is such that they can't promise a faster turn-around time and always fulfill that promise. Fair enough. They've determined that they need seven days' lead time to be sure they have enough time to process the request. Again, fair enough. So just say that, as in the statement in panel 140.

Panel 140

The lead time required to process vacation requests in a timely manner is seven days.

Panel 140 sets out the underlying decision, instead of telling people what they have to do as a result of that decision. By using this wording, we have completely eliminated the need to choose between *mandatory* and *optional*.

Let's look at another easy example, in panel 141.

Panel 141

> ### Applications for the manager position must be received by March 31st.

The rule is obviously predicated on a policy decision setting the 31st of March as the closing date for applications. That's all we need to say, and we can do it in several ways, as shown in panel 142.

Panel 142

> ### The deadline for applications is March 31st.
>
> ### Applications will be accepted up until March 31st.
>
> ### The competition closes March 31st.

The decision **behind** the instruction in panel 141 is the selection of a closing date. That decision has a natural consequence: anyone wanting to submit an application must act before then.

The rule maker might truly believe that some individuals won't make the leap from understanding the statement about the deadline to reasoning out, *If I want to apply I must do it by that date.* But the failure to make that leap is not a policy problem, it's an implementation problem. We can always provide supplementary information if we need to make that connection clearer, but it's not a policy statement.

Let's look at an example using *may*, like the statement in panel 143.

Panel 143

Supervisors may rearrange staff schedules as required.

In the previous chapter we saw how this use of *may* offers more than a simple option; it goes further and grants an authority. That grant is the underlying policy decision, so let's just bring that out into the open, as in panel 144.

Panel 144

Supervisors have the authority to rearrange staff schedules as required.

The decision to go from point A to point B could be characterized as a policy decision, as can the decision to get there by taking the most effective or risk-free route we can find. But determining the details of the route is an implementation step, as is telling people to follow the directions we settle on. Where a rule is actually implementing steps following logically from a policy decision, our challenge is to isolate that policy decision.

The points being clarified

Identifying these points can be tricky.

A statement that says *The homeowner may vote in the next referendum* could mean any number of things. Even if we're given a context, for example, that the homeowner did not vote in the last referendum, it's not enough. To determine what clarification is intended, we need to have the big picture. Being *entitled* to vote is different from being *eligible* to vote, being *qualified* to vote, having the *option* to vote, or even having the *option not* to vote.

A large majority of policy statements containing *must* or *may* tend to reflect decisions about these topics:

- authority
- eligibility
- entitlement
- validity

- characterization
- pre-condition
- sequence
- deadline

I can offer alternative wordings for some of these topics. Each alternative expresses a particular nuance not shared by the others, so we'll want to choose the one appropriate to the decision. However, all of these alternatives provide more clarity than *may* alone.

Authority

Panel 145 contains another example of *may* being used to grant an authority.

Panel 145

Directors may exceed their annual budget by no more than 10%.

Typically, when someone is given the *authority* to do something, they are being trusted to use their *discretion* to exercise that authority properly. Possible replacements are

- have the authority to

- are authorized to
- have the discretion to

Examples are shown in panel 146.

Panel 146

Directors have the authority to exceed their annual budget by up to 10%.

Directors are authorized to exceed their annual budget by up to 10%.

Directors have the discretion to exceed their annual budget by up to 10%.

Eligibility

Many decisions revolve around what makes an individual or object *eligible* for some activity or status. Take, for example, the statements in panel 147.

Panel 147

Employees must complete social media training prior to getting an account.

Employees may apply for a social media account after receiving training.

Some of these statements use *must* and some use *may*, but the point being clarified is really about *eligibility* rather than obligation or option. When revising these statements, the focus can be on either the **recipient** of the eligibility or the **thing** they are eligible for. Possible wording in the first case:

The individual (or entity or subject)

- is eligible for
- qualifies for/as
- is entitled to

- is a candidate for
- has the option to
- has the ability to

Examples rewording *eligibility* by focusing on the individual are shown in panel 148.

Panel 148

Employees are eligible for a social media account once they have completed training.

Employees who have completed training qualify for a social media account.

Employees have the option to get a social media account after completing training.

Possible wording in the second case:

The object

- is offered to
- is open to
- is available to
- is for

- is reserved for
- is used with
- is limited to

Examples of rewording *eligibility* by focusing on the object are shown in panel 149.

Panel 149

Social media accounts are available to employees who have had training.

Social media accounts are offered to employees once they are trained.

Social media accounts are reserved for trained employees.

Validity or characterization

Some statements using *must* are around validity or equivalence. Take, for example, the statement in panel 150.

Panel 150

Requests for reimbursement must be signed by a director.

Possible replacement wording:

The object

- is
- is valid when
- is ready when
- is treated as

- are considered
- is complete when
- is accepted when
- meets the minimum standard when

Examples of rewording *eligibility* by focusing on the object are shown in panel 151.

Panel 151

Requests for reimbursement are valid when signed by a director.

> Requests for reimbursement are accepted when signed by a director.

Panel 152 contains an example that is really about making a *characterization*.

Panel 152

> Financial applications must be treated as critical systems.

In this case, I would simplify the statement to any of the alternatives in panel 153.

Panel 153

> Financial applications are treated as critical systems.
>
> Financial applications are considered critical systems.
>
> Financial applications are critical systems.

Pre-condition or sequence

Often we can reframe both *must* and *may* statements by designating a sequence rather than mandating an activity. The statement in panel 154 is a good example.

Panel 154

> Employees must complete training prior to getting a social media account.

When we want to clarify that eligibility, authority, availability, or other grant is contingent on another event happening first, we can mandate the sequence. Some possibilities for wording are:

- is valid upon/once/after
- is ready upon/once/after
- is complete upon/once/after
- is available upon/once/after
- is eligible upon/once/after

Examples of rewording by focusing on the sequence are shown in panel 155.

Panel 155

Social media accounts are available to employees upon completing training.

Employees are eligible to be assigned social media accounts after they complete training.

Deadline

We saw one example of a deadline back in panel 140, when we looked at the rule around submitting an application by March 31st. Panel 156 contains another.

Panel 156

Taxpayers must file their tax forms by April 15th of the following year.

To reword these cases, I would focus on the time element. Here are some phrases that do that:

- The object is due by

- The object is valid when
- The deadline is

Examples of rewording using these phrases are shown in panel 157.

Panel 157

Tax forms are due by April 15th of the following year.

The deadline for submission of tax forms is April 15th of the following year.

When removing the modals, sometimes the statements are easy to reword, and other times not so much. It might take a few tries before I settle on something that more clearly reflects the decision being made. But the reworded statement is so more engaging that it's worth the time spent.

Okay, okay, enough about that topic. You must be tired of it already. (Gee, another meaning of *must*!) Let's look at how we word the other components in a policy.

17. PACKAGING

Executive Summary

Apart from the core statements, Policies contain various pieces of metadata for recordkeeping, navigation, and management purposes. These include fields capturing the title, the approver, critical dates, the objective and scope, roles and responsibilities, other versions, and enquiries. To eliminate ambiguity in the future, best practices are associated with each piece.

While policy statements form the core of our policy instruments, they still need to be packaged properly.

As a group, the documents can be more easily navigated and digested when the information preceding and following the core is standardized across the organization. Structured packaging also helps avoid the omission of critical management details. Standardizing the structure of these components prior to any major policy writing or renewal initiative will save time in the long run.

Chapter 2 explained how we eliminate duplication by planning the content of rules documents from two perspectives:

- the *back-end* (that is, what gets sent to the approvers, recorded in the official instrument, and is the source material for the manual), and
- the *front-end* (that is, what the end user needs to read to do their work).

Some of the components covered here need not necessarily appear in both views. For example, an original policy document is an incomplete record if the identity of its approver is missing. But for those reading the explanation of the policy in the office manual, that identity may not be of as much value as knowing where to direct inquiries. Similarly, the identity of the unit handling inquiries may not be a policy decision at all, but simply a feature of the organization's structure, in which case statements about the destination for inquiries can be shown to readers without having to be submitted for approval in the original policy instrument.

1. Cataloging information

Also known by the macabre label *tombstone information*, this section holds the markers that we use to identify the document. The information we're looking for is

- title
- instrument type,
- optionally, a topic or grouping, such as Administration, Operation, Finance … etc., and
- optionally, a unique identifier.

Combining title and instrument type

While short and sweet is normally the better way to go, I recommend that the instrument type — *policy*, *standard*, and so on — not only be included in the title, but that it appear universally as the first word. This practice would result in titles like *Policy on Security* and *Standard on Allowable Travel Expenses*.

Prepending the instrument type achieves two goals. First, it avoids our coming across potentially confusing document titles such as *Writing Policy*, which could reasonably be interpreted as either an official *Policy on Writing* or simply an instructional piece about policy-writing. In addition, it disambiguates titles like *Interim Service Standard*, forcing a clarification of whether we're looking at an interim *Standard on Service* or a *Standard on Interim Service*.

One enhancement to the naming convention that may be effective for some organizations is to append the year of approval to the title. This format makes it easy to distinguish the *Procedure on Reporting Safety Incidents, 2023* from the *Procedure on Reporting Safety Incidents, 2011*. This naming convention is used by some legislation to distinguish statutes that are identically-named, for example, the United Kingdom's *Copyright Act of 1956* is easily distinguishable from its *Copyright Act of 1911* and its *Copyright Act of 1842*.

Unique identifier

The unique identifier is typically an instrument number attached to the document. It can be of any length; I've seen numbering systems as a simple as *P1, P2, P3 …* etc., and as complex as *Instrument #F-2023-49-M12*.

For some organizations, developing an instrument numbering system may be an unnecessary piece of bureaucracy. Sometimes, its sole purpose is to make the policy suite appear methodical rather than haphazard, but if that's its only purpose, it may be more trouble than it's worth.

Some organizations use the unique identifier as a visible indicator of inclusion in the official policy collection, but the same indicator value can be achieved by using dedicated instrument titles, as explained back in chapter 6. On the principle that *simpler is better*, I would think some organizations could easily dispense with this artifact of systematization. If we don't need it, why give ourselves more work?

The exception to that recommendation is **multilingual environments**, where unique identifiers can be enormously helpful. Because the words in an instrument's title change to conform to the language of its contents, it can be hard to track down the equivalent policy in another language. A *shared identifier* is a common element that straddles both worlds. Even a non-speaker of Spanish would be able to recognize that *P45 Política de Compra de Computadoras* is the counterpart for *P45 Policy on Computer Purchases*.

One final suggestion: you can avoid gaps in the sequence caused by rejected submissions when you wait until after approval before assigning a permanent identifier.

2. Identification of the Approver

If it were up to me, the identity of the approver would always be the first piece of information to appear below the instrument title, because the legitimacy of every statement after that point is predicated on that approver having the competence to make the decisions that follow. (As indicated a few paragraphs back, though, that information may or may not be of value to the end user.)

Even when all the policies in an organization have the same approver, it is still good practice to identify that approver at the top of each policy. At some point in the future we might see a change of the approver's title — be that an individual, a committee, or a delegated entity—and we will want to be able to identify with certainty whether the instrument was approved by the new or the old entity.

3. Dates

A number of different dates can be tracked in an instrument. The most useful ones are the following:

- approval date
- last-updated date
- last-amended date
- last-reviewed date
- due-for-review date, and
- effective date.

Two points before we begin:

First, all these dates are dependent on **manual entry** for accuracy. You may have noticed the absence of the *last-modified date*. That's because the last-modified date is generated by the operating system, so it is only marginally reliable. As you no doubt are aware, changes to that date can be triggered by irrelevant technical events like *move* and *copy*. Relying on the system date alone, without being able to adjust it, increases the difficulty of true date tracking.

Second, some of these dates are determined by the way events play out in real life; only the last two on the list are actually the result of a conscious decision.

All dates can be isolated and stored as metadata elements. On the face of the instrument, they tend to appear before or after the core text.

Approval date

As a key piece of data for evidentiary purposes, the *date of approval* appears on the document pursuant to record-keeping requirements. Recording the identity of the approver along with the date of approval is the policy equivalent of signing and dating a piece of correspondence.

Last-amended date, Last-updated date

I'm going to deal with these dates together, because most offices don't distinguish them. We'll start with the drafting issue.

A *substantive update* to a document is different from a *clerical update*. Since the advent of personal computers, however, most people have relied on the network operating system to handle the date-stamping and, as a result, today the distinction is blurred. Due to that blurring, both types of updates often get the same white-glove treatment.

A *substantive update* changes the **meaning** of the text. Whether we're adding five new paragraphs, reversing a rule, or changing a significant word, if the meaning changes then the revised document needs a **formal** approval. The revision process might be long or short, depending on how the organization manages it, but the discussion around the changes focuses on their merits.

The new document becomes an *amended* version, and the clearest way to indicate that is by notating the date the amendment was approved as the *last-amended date*.

In contrast, a *clerical update* is a change to the text that doesn't alter the meaning. It could be a formatting or layout change, a spelling change, the updating of a URL, a position name or office address ... it includes any change that affects the **usability** of the document rather than its meaning.

The new document becomes an *updated* version, and that fact can be reflected by notating the date of the most recent fix as the *last-updated date* in the document.

The value in this distinction is its ability to speed up the bureaucracy around policy changes. When all content changes have to "go back to the committee" before being accepted, updates take longer. The backlog of requests grows, and the system gets bogged down.

However, if clerical changes can be approved at a lower level without having to go through the hoops that amendments need, they can be made more quickly. Too many policies contain broken URLs, outdated office names, and obsolete references because this distinction is being overlooked. Fortunately, once we correct the situation by setting up a system of rapid approval for clerical updates, changes can be made fairly quickly from that point on.

And what of *last-modified date*? Once we have captured the other two dates, we may not need it at all.

Last-reviewed date

When policies are amended after a review, they get tagged with a last-amended date. But what if the reviewers are happy with the *status quo*? It can't be tagged *amended* if no changes are made. The date that helps clarify that situation is the *last-reviewed date*.

After the review is complete, the date of the review is noted, along with the next *due-for-review date*.

Due-for-review date

The last date we'll look at is the *due-for-review date*, also known as the *date of next review*. It's the equivalent of the "best before" stamp found on a jar of pickles. The pickles may still be safe after that date, but we know to inspect the jar a little more carefully before sampling the contents.

A *due-for-review date* is less risky than an **expiry** date, because it doesn't leave us without a valid policy if we don't renew it in time. The policy will still be in force and users will be alert to exercise caution. After the review, or after the amendments if any are proposed, a new due-for-review date can be set.

A lot of people ask for my recommendation on the best duration for the period between reviews. They plan to set up a formal schedule to control the review cycles of Policies, Standards, and Procedures in their organization.

To be candid, I discourage that approach. Every instrument is different. Are we projecting a bedrock piece of broad brush-strokes for the next decade, or are we just trying to anticipate where the pandemic is going over the next six months? **The approvers of each instrument are best positioned to know how long before it is likely to stale-date, based on their discussions at the time.** They might be approving five different instruments related to work-at-home arrangements, each one with a forecast lifespan different from the others.

My recommendation is, instead of spending time assembling a schema for review of instruments, some of which haven't even been conceived-of yet, give the task of selecting the next review date to the approvers in each case.

Effective date

The final date we'll look at is the date the instrument goes into effect. Setting that date is a decision, as important as any other statement in the policy. For that reason, the effective date is more properly classified as a policy statement than as packaging, but its location is discretionary. By convention, in legal documents the *effective date* normally appears as either the first or the last statement in the document. That's not a bad approach for policy instruments, either.

We can forego the need for an effective date by having the approval date do double duty. If we put a statement in the *General Policy* that all instruments go into effect on the date they are approved, the need to keep independent track of the effective date disappears.

4. Objective

A clear policy objective guides the scope and nature of the contents of the document.

A well-articulated policy objective has two attributes: (1) it is a single, succinct statement, and (2) it names an objective.

Succinctness has value. Lengthy policy instrument preambles are outdated. Sticking with the older practice — that is, beginning with a series of *whereas* paragraphs — announces to the world that you have not kept up with the times.

Here's a fine but important distinction: **the policy objective is not the same as the subject objective.** A *policy objective* declares the *purpose of the document*. It details the specific achievements of the policy as a written instrument, such as *standardizing rules* or *clarifying practices*.

Those achievements are not the same as the purpose of the broader strategy or program goals that the policy supports. Stated differently, **the objective is what approving the policy achieves**, not what policy compliance achieves.

Consider the grandiose policy objectives such as those in panel 158.

Panel 158

This policy ensures the continued trust and confidence of the public in our organization.

This standard protects consumers by supporting the company's commitment to customer service and corporate integrity.

These rules ensure the safety, security, and welfare of our employees.

Yes, these goals are all noble, but they're not policy objectives. Even if the results of the rules and the projected compliance level are predictable, they are not a foregone conclusion. We will not truly know whether we have *protected consumers* or *maintained the public's trust* until some date in the future when we collect some relevant data.

The drawback to calling them policy objectives is a strategic one. In the absence of a fully fleshed-out strategy, too often the problem being attacked is considered resolved by enacting a written Policy. I like to avoid the impression that the mere act of approving the Policy is sufficient to achieve its objectives. In reality, that approval may be a milestone in the implementation of the solution, but it almost never marks the end point.

Instead, we want to focus the objective on the purpose of the document, like the examples in panel 159.

Panel 159

> This Policy consolidates the rules on reimbursement of travel expenses.
>
> This Policy updates and harmonizes hiring practices across all our corporate offices.
>
> This Standard establishes the specifications for the delivery of service to customers.

In each of these cases, we know instantly by looking at the contents of the document whether we have achieved our objective, and no one will mistake that objective for the broader results being sought.

Not *ensuring*

You may have noted that none of the statements in panel 159 uses the word *ensure* as its main verb. That choice is deliberate. Objectives formulated with *ensure* tend to look like the one in panel 160.

Panel 160

> This Policy ensures that the organization's finances are managed responsibly, prudently, and correctly.

Apart from the generic ambiguity of *ensure* discussed back in chapter 15, using that word inside an objective has two additional drawbacks.

First, it aims the spotlight poorly. **Rules themselves don't ensure anything**; rules provide direction and then **people ensure** they are followed.

You might think that last comment is quibbling, but the point is profound. Wording like that in panel 160 betrays an underlying management approach where policy approval is seen as an end rather than a means to an end. The expectation is that the problem is solved simply by approving the policy, so management is now free to turn its attention to other matters.

Second, and more significantly, the use of *ensure* in this statement represents a **logical fallacy**. It presupposes that managing finances "responsibly, prudently, and correctly" is a characterization that is objectively validated. In fact, the argument is circular: the activities prescribed are not inherently responsible, prudent, or correct; rather, **they inherit that characterization only because they are being prescribed.**

The objective in panel 160 can be reworded to be more accurate in one of the ways shown in panel 161.

Panel 161

This Policy establishes practices for the management of the organization's finances that we consider to be responsible, prudent, and correct.

This Policy prescribes what we consider to be responsible, prudent, and correct practices for the management of the organization's finances.

This Policy sets responsible, prudent, and correct practices for the management of the organization's finances.

Background information

The objective is not the place to set out background information. Almost invariably, background information stale-dates long before the policy itself.

In previous chapters we noted that we can justify our rules using other documents, such as strategy papers, reports, and cover sheets. The explanation for why we're doing what we're doing belongs in a companion document, along with other pieces of background information.

5. Scope

In some cases, it can be useful for a policy to contain a statement defining the *scope* of its application.

The trap to watch for here, though, is that *scope* **is not about the people we are addressing; instead, it's about the world we are regulating.**

Take the scope statement in panel 162, typical of what is commonly used.

Panel 162

This security policy is applicable to the management, employees, and contractors of the organization.

Again, the world of legislation is a good point of comparison. If government prefaced its laws in that style, we would see non-sensical statements like those in panel 163.

Panel 163

The requirements in this food safety legislation apply to citizens, permanent residents, landed immigrants, visitors on a work visa, and students.

That scope is absurd, because the law applies to **everyone preparing food** in the jurisdiction, irrespective of their residency status. It's far more likely that the law would scope itself relative to the object it applies to, as shown in panel 164.

Panel 164

The requirements in this food safety legislation apply to all food prepared on or imported into premises located in the jurisdiction.

Other examples of well-worded scope statements are shown in panel 165.

Panel 165

This security policy is applicable to all permanent and temporary premises where corporate activities take place.

This security policy is applicable to all corporate technology owned or operated by the organization.

This security policy is applicable to all information created or managed by the organization.

Using objectively-based criteria, we can focus on describing the situations where the rules are applicable, rather than trying to list all the people we expect to obey them.

6. Roles and Responsibilities

The words *roles and responsibilities* are often said in the same breath, as if they were one of those doublets I caution against in the next chapter. In this case, however, we aren't working with a doublet because *roles* and *responsibilities* are completely separate —albeit related—concepts.

To illustrate the distinction, I'm going to separate the pieces starting from the bottom.

Responsibilities

The basic work unit is a *task*. Tasks can be characterized by a number of attributes, such as action, status, skill required, duration, priority, and so on.

We combine tasks into groups we call *activities*, which can range from being large and multifaceted, such as serving customers, to being simple, such as locking the front door.

We dole out activities through various kinds of *assignments*. When we assign an activity to one or more individuals, we say that that activity becomes their *responsibility*.

One possibility is to assign a single responsibility to a named individual, as in panel 166.

Panel 166

Olaf guards the key that locks the safe.

Indira establishes the work rotation schedule.

Because individuals eventually leave organizations, responsibilities typically get assigned to positions, as in panel 167.

Panel 167

The manager guards the key that locks the safe.

The team lead establishes the work rotation schedule.

Now consider a project with hundreds of activities. Assigning each one separately would be rather cumbersome; so instead, we streamline the process by creating *roles*.

Roles

A *role* is a function played by an individual or group in a given situation. Instead of referring to them as *role #1*, *role #2*, and so on, to keep track of them we give them names like *chairperson* and *secretary*.

Roles are situation-specific, and one of their characteristics is that they can move from person to person: Philippe might act as *secretary* this week, while next week it falls to

Monique. Other roles in an organization could be *officer-in-charge*, *emergency contact*, *manager on duty*, and *floor safety warden*. Roles can be permanent or temporary, and assignments to an individual can be indeterminate or time-bound.

For flexibility, we can assign activities to a role, then separately assign that role to an individual or group. When we do that, we say that the *role is responsible for those activities*.

To illustrate, responsibility for the following activities might be attached to the role of *chairperson*:

- setting the agenda
- officially opening and closing the meeting, and
- moderating the discussion.

Since a role can be assigned multiple bundles of responsibilities, things run smoothly when everyone's clear on what each bundle contains.

The *assignment of activities to roles* can be exclusive or non-exclusive. Activities like *holding the company checkbook* are best assigned to one role at a time, whereas *arranging the chairs for the meeting* could easily be assigned to multiple roles without causing a problem.

Likewise, the *assignment of roles to individuals or groups* can be exclusive or non-exclusive. Roles like *orchestra leader* are exclusive, best assigned to only one person at each concert, whereas roles like *cashier* can be assigned to many people at once.

In short, to understand who is accountable for any task, we need to know

- the *activity* the task belongs to
- the *role* that activity has been assigned to, and
- the *individual(s)* responsible for that role.

As an example, *the task of locking the door* at the end of the day belongs to the *daily shut-down activity*. That activity has been *assigned to the night supervisor*, and tonight that supervisor is *Juanita*.

Assigning authority

As we *assign* a role to a named individual, position, or group, where expedient, we can also assign that role specific *rights* and *authorities*. An example of an assignment statement appears in panel 168.

Panel 168

The project lead has the authority to spend project funds.

Or, instead of assigning an authority to a role, we could assign it to an individual, a job position, or a group, as shown in panel 169.

Panel 169

- Indira Khan has the authority to spend funds. *(assigned to an individual)*
- The Office Manager has the authority to spend funds. *(assigned to a job position)*
- The Membership Sub-committee has the authority to spend funds. *(assigned to a group)*

Now that we've clarified what the terms mean, let's look at how they fit into policy drafting.

Statements on roles and responsibilities

Activities, roles, and responsibilities can be policy decisions, and as such belong somewhere in a policy document. But they can also be the product of a job description, a contract, a governance document, committee terms of reference, and so on.

The decisions to make locking the door part of the daily shut-down activity, to assign that activity to the night supervisor, and to choose Juanita to supervise tonight, need to be made **only once** to be valid. They do not have to be restated in a policy if they have already been approved elsewhere.

Take the statement in panel 170.

Panel 170

> The finance branch is responsible for monitoring expenditures related to this policy.

If, pursuant to an existing policy instrument, charter, delegation, contract, or whatever else the organization uses, the finance branch is **already** responsible for monitoring expenditures, then the statement is superfluous. Leave it out.

On the other hand, if the statement creates a **brand new responsibility for the finance branch**, then it represents a new decision and would be valid as a policy statement.

Is responsible for

The phrase *is responsible for* is often misused. True, it assigns responsibility for an activity to a role or individual, but that assignment does not necessarily mandate the activity itself.

Take the statement in panel 171.

Panel 171

Managers are responsible for daily reports.

That statement says that the responsibility for daily reports lies with the managers; that much we know for sure. But does it also **obligate** the managers to produce those reports? Consider the three statements in panel 172.

Panel 172

Passengers are responsible for bringing their own food.

Shoppers are responsible for supplying their own bags.

Homeowners are responsible for planting trees on their own property.

The first statement doesn't obligate passengers to bring food; it just lets them know that the carrier isn't going to provide it for them. Likewise, shoppers in the second statement can't rely on the retailer for bags. As for homeowners and their trees, it's not clear whether the third statement was meant to convey a *mandate* or merely an *authorization* to begin planting; all we know for sure is that the city isn't going to do it.

The statement assigning responsibility in panel 171 could be interpreted in any of the following ways:

- Managers are required to submit the reports created by people under them.

- Managers do not submit the reports but are responsible for verifying the accuracy of their content.

- Managers are required to submit every report and to chase down any that go missing.

- Managers are expected to create the reports themselves.

- Managers don't have to do anything for the reports, but if the organization runs into problems, managers are the people we're going to yell at.

Clarity in policy drafting is paramount, and ambiguity in requirements creates opportunities for loopholes. We can eliminate that ambiguity by separating statements mandating an activity from those assigning the responsibility for it — if it isn't already assigned.

7. Other Versions

Where policy instruments are available in different formats or languages, a note to that effect on the instrument can be helpful as a usability aid. For clarity, those translations and formats need to indicate whether they are *authoritative* or *derivative* versions of the original.

A number of legislatures in Canada, for example, produce laws and policies in separate English and French versions. In some cases, they declare both versions to be *authoritative*, meaning that we have two originals, each approved as a separate document, neither outranking the other.

In contrast, any versions not declared authoritative are by definition *derivative*. The derivative version has not been approved as a separate document, and always defers to the original document as the authoritative text.

8. Inquiries

A good policy instrument indicates clearly to whom people can turn when they have questions. It's helpful when a statement like the one in panel 173 finishes the document.

Panel 173

Inquiries about this policy are handled by …

Typically, the sentence is completed with the name of a position or office rather than an individual, so that the document doesn't need to be amended when the individual moves somewhere else.

18. Terminology Management

Executive Summary

Clarity of meaning relies on the consistent use of terminology, not only within a document but across the entire policy suite. Standardized terms can be captured in a common **glossary** for the benefit of the reader, and in a shared **lexicon** to guide drafters. The "Interpretation" section of an instrument reflects drafting decisions only; business decisions around the meaning of a term or phrase properly sit in the core section.

When *employee* means one thing in an HR policy and something else in an IT policy, we've got the makings of a problem somewhere down the line. Terminology management is a powerful strategy for reducing interpretational ambiguity.

The HR branch at one organization I worked at circulated a memo one day reminding everyone in the strongest of terms **not** to refer to *consultants* who worked under contract as *employees*. Understandably, the prohibition was required so the organization wouldn't unknowingly incur obligations around benefit plans, job security, and so on, putting it at huge financial risk. As a consultant contracted to that organization, it made good sense to me. No issue.

Until the following week, when the same branch proudly circulated its brand new anti-harassment policy. This one set out a list of unacceptable behaviors, describing what actions would constitute **one employee harassing another**. Taken at face value, the new policy didn't apply to me! When I went to advise them of the terminology conflict, they responded, "Oh, well. People know what we mean."

I'm not so sure the legal team would have been as cavalier.

An organization can avoid this kind of problem through active terminology management, on an enterprise-wide basis if at all possible. Coordinating vocabulary can also help drafters select the best terms in a world of culturally appropriate and inclusive language that changes often. Careful choice of words promotes both clarity of meaning and a respectful workplace.

1. Avoiding Synonyms

You may have been taught that good composition style in English demands that you take advantage of the language's enormous vocabulary. Varying the wording throughout the text helps to maintain novelty and interest.

That style does not apply to policy instruments, since they are not intended to be literature. In rules, synonyms cause confusion. Using multiple terms in a policy instrument to describe the same element — even when those words are universally used as synonyms — is as confusing as referring to one individual by different names in the same conversation.

Panel 174 contains an example. It's confusing because it's poorly drafted, so don't spend a lot of time trying to figure it out.

Panel 174

> Each time a staff member views someone's personnel files, the employee logs the date and the name of the individual.

Apart from the grammatical shortcoming that the sentence contains unclear antecedents, we have a terminological issue: four different words are being used to refer to what seems to be fewer than four individuals. The last thing we want is to have readers struggling to figure out whether we're talking about one thing, two things, or three things.

Referencing a concept using one selected term throughout a document is the easiest way to achieve clarity. I'm not sure what the original drafter of the statement in panel 174 was trying to say, but one possible interpretation can be achieved by using the wording in panel 175.

Panel 175

> When a staff member views an individual's personnel files, the staff member logs the date and the name of the individual.

2. Standardizing Business Concepts

The inconsistent use of terms might flag a problem, but we don't start fixing it by defining words. Instead, we first need to **identify the business concepts** that require terms to describe them. All the terms that get thrown around interchangeably need to be narrowed down to **one term per concept**.

For example, we might need a standardized collective term to refer to *everyone who works at our organization*, irrespective of whether they're employed, on contract, on co-op, or any other form of engagement. The typical collective terms are *staff*, *members*, *associates*, *workers* ... and others. Is one word used consistently on an enterprise-wide basis, or does everyone choose their own? I think you can figure out which of those alternatives makes for clearer policies.

Along the same lines, we might want a single term to cover *everyone in the world who doesn't work at our office*. The public? Outsiders? Residents?

We may have a term for *people we provide service to* — clients, patrons, customers — but does that term **exclude** or **include** *potential clients*? What about people we've stopped providing service to? Perhaps the business doesn't make any of these distinctions; if a concept has no business application, then we don't need a special term for it.

There's no one correct answer to these questions, but whichever terms we choose should be *officially prescribed* for everyone across the organization. We'll come back to this notion in a few moments.

3. Terminology Aids

Terminology issues tend to be contentious because people have strong feelings about the use of language.

Policy drafters work with a number of terminology tools, among them *dictionaries*, *glossaries*, and *lexicons*. Though those labels are often thrown around interchangeably, in fact they refer to three completely different types of documents.

Dictionaries and glossaries are primarily tools for readers; a lexicon is a writer's tool.

Dictionaries

Dictionaries contain *definitions*. A statement can qualify as a definition only when it fulfills some basic requirements:

- It indicates which part of speech the term belongs to, such as noun, verb, and so on

- It provides some indication of scope, often by setting out a generic description followed by some limiting characteristics, and

- It is not circular; that is, the definition does not contain the term being defined.

To my mind, we make it harder for ourselves when we call our explanations *definitions*, because it sets the bar far too high. Good definitions are hard to write, and often provoke arguments unnecessarily. Personally, I would leave the writing of definitions to the dictionaries.

I prefer the label *interpretation*, and I'm not alone. A number of governments favor the section heading *Interpretation* over *Definitions* in their statutes as a matter of course. An *interpretation* has some distinct advantages:

- It doesn't need to meet the basic requirements of a definition

- It reduces readers' expectations around the sophistication of the explanation about the term, and

- It has a lower justification threshold.

That third advantage is not insignificant. As a writer, to justify a *definition* we have to be able to defend its *accuracy*. In contrast, to justify an *interpretation* we have only to defend its *reasonableness*.

Let's look at an example to see how this distinction plays out. Assume that, prior to approval, we are circulating a draft Policy for stakeholder feedback, and it contains the text in panel 176.

Panel 176

In this policy,

"furniture" means tables and chairs

If the statement in panel 176 is found under the heading *Definitions*, the statement is clearly lacking: it's **not** a definition — and even if it were, it's not a good definition. The feedback we will receive from stakeholders would most likely focus on how inaccurate the definition is.

In contrast, if the section heading is *Interpretation*, we have more leeway. Since it's reasonable for *furniture* to be used as an umbrella term to refer to *tables and chairs*, it less likely to draw criticism.

Candidate terms for the *Interpretation* section in a policy are those that need clarification for the purposes of **disambiguation**. Simply wanting to provide additional detail is not sufficient because, as we've seen, **policies are not training manuals**. If we have a need to teach, explain, or give others some information to bring them up to speed on the topic so they can understand the policy, we can supply it in instructional documents as part of the Toolkit.

The interpretive phrase *means tables and chairs* is what linguists call a *gloss*. A gloss has none of the technical requirements of a definition; it can contain as much or as little information as we wish.

You can see where this is going, no doubt. A tool prepared for the benefit of readers is a *glossary*. It can contain terms found in both policy and non-policy instruments.

Glossaries

Every time a tricky term is used in any document, a handy hyperlink can jump people to the right gloss instantly, and then let them pick up where they left off.

Imagine how much time could be saved in the overall policy development process if the gloss for a term like *senior management* were decided just **once** and then was ready for general use. Fancy programming could even display it as a tooltip window, accessed by hovering. Moreover, if it ever needed to be amended, a single change in the glossary entry would do the trick.

The optimal situation is to have a single common glossary applicable across the organization. Practically, though, it may not be feasible to bring different business lines together due to conflicts in terminology firmly established in various industries. The meaning of *asset* in a Finance context, for example, is unlikely ever to match its meaning when used by Facilities, IM/IT, or HR SME.

Multiple entries in the glossary, or even multiple glossaries, can help keep these differences straight. What's most important is that each business line is internally consistent with its own preferred use of terminology.

Which brings us full circle: to help us be consistent, we can use *prescribed terms* and take advantage of a *lexicon*.

Lexicons

A *lexicon* is a list of words belonging to a particular group, topic, or activity.

Once we've chosen which of *sections*, *units*, *departments*, and *branches* is going to be our official term to describe the different divisions in the organization, we need to communicate that decision to others in the office who draft policies. A *lexicon* of *prescribed terms* does just that. It acts as a reference tool for writers, setting out the prescribed terms for different situations.

In a mature organization, it's common to have some kind of *editorial guide* for policy drafters, formalizing grammatical and stylistic preferences. The information it contains can be used to unify the tone of the instruments across the organization. That guide may also prescribe punctuation, orthographic, and typographical conventions, or point to approved external authorities prescribing those conventions. The *lexicon* is an important piece of that guide.

Using glossaries and lexicons

The lexicon and the glossary may share some common entries, but are essentially different documents.

The lexicon contains only terms that writers need to be careful about, and the glossary contains only those terms that genuinely warrant an explanation. An example might make this point clearer.

Assume the following terminology decisions are applicable to the organization's policy instruments going forward:

1. We restrict the use of *employee* to true employment situations, and use *staff* to refer collectively to everyone working in the office.

2. We have settled on the use of the term *Headquarters* over competing terms like *Head Office* and *Main Office*.

3. We use the term *Data Protection Officer*, as prescribed by the applicable legislation.

The first decision would show up in both the lexicon and the glossary. The lexicon would explain to writers which words to use and which to avoid for different circumstances. The glossary would explain the terms *employee* and *staff*.

The second decision would show up in the lexicon, to tell writers which term to use. It needn't show up in the glossary unless people genuinely don't know what *Headquarters* is.

The third decision would show up in the glossary, since the term is likely unfamiliar to many. It needn't show up in the lexicon, unless it's not the only term people are using for that purpose.

4. Interpretation versus Policy

An *Interpretation* section near the front of a Policy can be beneficial, since it consolidates the statements "defining" terms together in one location. But be careful with what you put there. A subtle but critical difference separates a statement set out as an aid to interpretation and one set out as a policy decision.

An interpretation statement reflects a *decision about terminology*; a policy statement reflects a *business decision*. Panel 177 contains examples of statements appropriate for the Interpretation section.

Panel 177

In this document,

- "the company" means ACME Corporation and includes all its subsidiaries
- "holidays" includes national and regional holidays, but not religious holidays
- "vegetables" includes tomatoes and avocados.

These statements are all interpretive aids. The first one is not a declaration that ACME Corp and its subsidiaries are a single company for legal purposes. All it's doing is bundling those entities together for the purpose of the document and labeling that bundle *the company*.

Similarly, the second statement is not a decision about whether religious holidays are or are not "true" holidays; it's simply saying that in the policy the term *holiday* will be used in a restricted sense.

Likewise, the third statement is not an assertion about the accuracy of classifying *tomatoes* and *avocados* as vegetables (technically, both are fruit botanically, but vegetables nutritionally). The statement is simply a **terminological asser-tion for convenience in the document**: instead of repeatedly writing the cumbersome *vegetables, tomatoes, and avoca-dos*, the collective term *vegetables* will be used to cover them all.

In other words, all three statements reflect decisions made by the drafter around the **use of vocabulary**. We would not expect to see statements in the Interpretation section where the scope of the gloss is contentious.

In contrast, a statement setting out a **business decision** around what a term does and does not include is actually a statement of policy, and it belongs in the main body of the instrument. Examples of business decisions related to termi-nology are shown in panel 178.

Panel 178

> Texting while driving includes pushing buttons to select alphabetic characters on a cell phone, but does not including pushing a single button to activate a speech-to-text dictation system.
>
> Employees are considered long-term employees once they have been with the head company or its subsidiaries for 15 years or longer.
>
> Working at home does not include time spent reading on the bus.

Those statements represent actual decisions made by the policy approver. The absence of italics around the defined term is deliberate and meaningful in this situation. In the first statement, for example, we're not merely clarifying the term *texting while driving*; rather, we're clarifying the **concept of texting while one is driving.**

Statements reflecting a business decision around what is included in a concept belong in the core section of the Policy, not the interpretation section.

Potential for confusion

We might think we're being helpful by explaining a term for non-experts inside the policy statement itself, but that explanation has the potential to create ambiguities.

Take the phrase *including meals* in panel 179.

Panel 179

We reimburse claims for travel expenses, including meals, when accompanied by original receipts.

What does that statement mean? Two different situations are possible:

- Meals while traveling are **considered part of the concept** of travel expenses.
- Meals while traveling are **not considered part of the concept** of travel expenses, but reimbursement is handled the same way.

Unfortunately, the statement in panel 179 is unclear in both of those situations.

If the first situation is true, such that meals while traveling are considered to be merely one component part of the overall category of travel expense, then *including meals* is a redundant phrase. We'd be treating travel expenses as a single concept, so the correct statement is found in panel 180.

Panel 180

> We reimburse claims for travel expenses when accompanied by original receipts.

In this situation, the SME either all have a clear common understanding of what the concept *travel expenses* entails, or they don't. If they do, then the office manual can explain it to everyone else. If they don't, they'd best decide that first! Then the ambiguity can be eliminated by adding an interpretation note to either the statement itself or to a dedicated Interpretation section.

In contrast, if the second situation is true, then we're talking about two separate concepts: (1) travel expenses, and (2) meals. In that case, the word *including* is inaccurate. A clearer formulation would be one of those in panel 181.

Panel 181

> We reimburse travel expenses and meals when accompanied by original receipts.
>
> We reimburse meals in the same way as travel expenses.

Both of these formulations make it clear that two separate concepts are involved and are not being conflated.

5. Miscellaneous Drafting Traps

We'll finish off this section by looking at two common drafting problems: *doublets* and *and/or*.

Doublets

Panel 182 provides a good illustration of how formal English retains reminders of the centuries-old habit of using legal *doublets*.

Panel 182

Applicants who plan to update, change, or modify their application forms should send or forward the updated information, changes, and modifications no later than March 31st.

While *update*, *change*, and *modify* are technically not themselves true doublets, the unnecessary repetition used in the statement is an attempt to emulate that format. More than simply being cumbersome, they directly create ambiguity.

Doublets, also called *word pairs*, are an historical vestige of the English language. Whether they still belong in legal documents is a question for another forum, but the time has definitely come to retire them permanently from policy instruments.

To understand why we have so many doublets and doublet-like structures, we have to look at where they came from. The story starts in the year 1066, when the language of government and ceremony in England was the dialect of French spoken in Normandy at the time of the Conquest. For centuries thereafter, French dominated the speech of the educated class, even though the common people continued to use one of the many Germanic and Norse dialects that had established themselves before the Conquest.

By the Middle Ages, all English juridical matters were conducted in a distinct, documented dialect called Legal French and—as one might suspect—French terms were the norm.

Things changed as English began to gain status as a language in the 14th and 15th centuries. While French remained the language of the learned and upper class for a long time, eventually it became socially unacceptable to alienate individuals who could speak only English.

Lawyers and legal practice change slowly, however, and the old Legal French terms refused to leave quietly. Over time, a custom developed in formal documents of pairing words, to provide the Anglo (Germanic) term alongside the original French or Latinate word. Scores of these pairings still exist in the language today, such as:

- will and testament
- to have and to hold
- free and clear
- null and void
- goods and chattels
- lewd and lascivious
- give and bequeath.

The terms were identical in meaning, but were used in pairs in formal situations in deference to speakers of both languages. After a while, the practice spilled into situations where it wasn't needed: writers began using doublets even when both terms came from the same language origins. Examples of these include:

- terms and conditions
- heirs and assigns
- agree and covenant
- over and above
- due and payable.

Using two terms together was thought to make a formal statement twice as clear. The upshot is that doublets eventually became the mark of English formality and officialdom. Even today, some writers still use doublets to make text sound more authoritative.

Newsflash: it doesn't work.

In fact, a doublet makes text more difficult to interpret because it's impossible to know when the two terms are meant to represent two different concepts and when they are meant to represent the same concept. In the phrase *update, change, or modify*, it's unclear whether each term is meant to convey an action distinct from the others or if they are interchangeable.

As you come across these *x and y* statements in the policies you review, make a determination that will meet the goal of language clarity and succinctness. If the phrase is in fact a doublet representing a single concept, choose one precise term to convey the meaning.

Panel 182 is much more easily understood when the duplication is stripped out and it's reworded as in panel 183.

Panel 183

Applicants can update their application forms by providing new information no later than March 31st.

And and/or *or*

A discussion of word pairs would be incomplete without spending some time lamenting over the all-too-common use of the self-contradictory conjunction *and/or*. It even appears more and more frequently in legal documents — where the drafter should know better.

And/or is the poster child for ambiguous writing. Born from an indecision around which one of those conjunctions is the correct one to use in which circumstances, it creeps into documents as a catch-all, a last-ditch compromise between alternatives. Attempting to straddle two **opposing** concepts — inclusivity and exclusivity — it suggests both without committing to either.

The use of *and/or* creates more confusion than it resolves, leaving the reader unsure about whether the statement is declaring that both requirements are to be met, or that one alone is sufficient. If you're unsure how to choose between *and* and *or* in a given situation, I recommend turning to any of a number of reliable style guides on the Internet for help.

Notes

PART IV — VALUES-BASED POLICY

Executive Summary

Revisiting the Ladder of Engagement presented in the Introduction, we look at how core values play a crucial role in improving engagement. Non-compliance with organizational rules can often be the product of a misalignment between one or more values: those underlying the policies and those held by an individual or group. We can depict how policies and other Internal Authorities trace back to the foundational documents by using the Documentation Landscape presented in chapter 6. This connection gives us a new narrative within which to discuss issues around engagement and non-compliance.

In Part I of this book we looked at the cultural aspects of policy drafting, and we saw that engagement is not a binary condition. The *Ladder of Engagement* appearing in the Introduction (page 7) presented a scale ranging from total disengagement at the bottom, through passive awareness, continuing all the way up to active advocacy. The two highest rungs are *Commitment* at number two and *Champion* at the top. I used a recipe book analogy in chapter 3 to illustrate how people don't buy into standards and procedures unless they buy into the policies behind them.

Part II looked at ways to organize different types of rules into separate documents, and Part III went into detail on various wording techniques.

We're now going to synthesize the information in all three parts to create scenarios to garner the maximum engagement possible. At a minimum, we can bring people from the ladder's lower rungs up to its *active engagement* section. We know that we're succeeding when we're able to elicit a response such as *Great policy! Every organization should have that policy!*

When we hear *Great policy!*, it tells us that we've brought people up to the *Commitment* level. If they add the tagline *Every organization should have that policy!*, then we know we've created a *Champion*.

The techniques covered in Part III can help us reword our rules statements to avoid generating resistance. Realistically, though, in many cases, this approach alone brings people up only to the level of Commitment. If we want to move higher up the ladder, we need to appeal to people's *values*.

Values are key. They represent concepts that we consider fundamental to our identity and purpose, and therefore guide our behaviors, decisions, and interactions within and outside the organization.

In this part, we'll explore how connecting an organization's values to an individual's values can evoke a personal connection, one that shows up as a higher level of engagement.

The Traditional Approach: Negative Values

To counter low policy compliance, management's traditional approach is to employ a number of tactics, including

- citing legal or political factors, such as the importance of meeting regulatory requirements

- describing the damage to reputation that accompanies being called out by public watchdog or consumer protection agencies
- invoking scare tactics, such as circulating horror stories around high profile incidents that caused major embarrassment to other organizations, and
- emphasizing disciplinary consequences for individuals who fail to follow policies.

Each of these tactics aims to evoke some emotion or value, such as fear or doubt. Unfortunately, the emotions targeted tend to be negative ones to move away from, rather than positive ones to move toward.

Stirring up negative emotions has a number of disadvantages. One is that their presence tends to erode trust and morale. In a corporate setting, people on the defensive are unlikely to respond to statements promoting fear and doubt with an outpouring of love and kindness.

A second problem is that those emotions become closely associated in people's minds with the organization. That result is not helpful. Increasing engagement relies on creating mental associations with positive emotions.

The final disadvantage — probably coming as no surprise — is that their effectiveness is fickle. We saw a case of ineffectiveness in the Introduction when we looked at the threats on the sign in the medical clinic.

Here's where values can help us. We get more desirable results when we appeal to emotions that are positive and motivating. **We can increase support for our policies by clearly** linking them with positive values, thereby harnessing the power of engagement that values can bring.

Foundational Documents

Values, of course, do not exist in a vacuum. To see how they interact with policies, we need to look at the context in which they operate.

In Chapter 6 we covered the *Documentation Landscape* (page 99). On the right side it shows a hierarchy of documents holding decisions made inside the organization, split into three source groups: Foundational Documents, Internal Authorities, and Toolkit documents. The order of influence is represented visually; each group informs the contents of the documents in the group below it.

Until now, I have been working from the assumption that all the foundational documents are properly in place, so that we can focus on the Internal Authorities. At this point, however, we're going to move to the highest level of the hierarchy and examine those foundational documents, starting at the top. If we're missing any, policy update time provides a good opportunity to point that out to the powers that be, to see if they're willing to fill the gap.

To see how the elements interact, let's postulate a fictional government-created hospital, established under the relevant legislation to serve a particular geographic area.

We'll start by looking at its mission.

Mission and mandate

An organization's *mission* is its primary purpose and goal, clearly and succinctly explaining why it does what it does. Typically, a mission would change only if it needs to adapt to major evolution, such as a change in focus, shifting social norms, or environmental limitations.

When an organization's purpose is established by another entity — most often the one that created it — it is called a *mandate*. In rare occasions an organization is constituted by one body but receives its mandate from another.

The mandate of our fictional hospital, handed to it at inception, is *To provide medical services to the people living in Springfield*.

Conflict of mission and mandate

Once given a mandate, an organization doesn't require a separate mission statement. When the mandate points to the north but the mission is to go west, we have a conflict. Whenever an organization has been given a mandate, the most straight-forward mission it can undertake is to fulfill that mandate to the best of its ability.

Inconsistent mission and mandate statements are problematic because they can be used to justify conflicting actions. Unchecked, they pose a risk that someone might resolve a conflict between the two in favor of the one that was meant to be subordinate to the other.

If the hospital were to articulate a separate mission, we would expect it to be something like *To uphold the highest medical standards when delivering healthcare services.* In fact, our hospital has decided to anchor itself on its mandate alone, and forego drafting a separate mission.

Vision

Below the mission, we find the *vision*.

A vision is a depiction of what the world will look like when the organization achieves its mission. While mandates and missions are normally conveyed in one or two sentences, a vision can provide as detailed a picture as it needs to.

A well-articulated vision can serve to inspire and mobilize stakeholders towards a common goal. Having everyone working to achieve the same target both unifies the work-force and helps direct decision-making as issues arise.

Note the key distinction between a mission and a vision: a mission focuses inward at who we are and what we do; a vision focuses outward on the world around us and what it will become.

Directly informed by its mandate, the hospital's vision might read something like this:

"Our vision is a community where all patients receive affordable medical care promptly, our professional staff have ample opportunities for growth and education, and everyone feels welcome and valued."

Leader's prerogative

Establishing the vision is a role for the topmost leadership. A captain first announces the ship's destination, and only then invites those who want to be part of that journey to come along. The **wrong** sequence would be to bring all the passengers aboard before the destination is set, pull anchor and leave port and then, while sailing, ask for a collective decision on where the boat should be headed. That approach might work for reality television because its absurdity makes for good spectacle, but it's rarely successful in the real world.

At one organization I worked at, management invited over 5,000 employees to help craft the vision statement over a four-month period. It's not hard to imagine how discordant the results were, but what did they expect from a 5,000-member committee? A more useful exercise might have been to hold discussions helping people understand the mandate, mission, and vision, as the leaders see them.

Once an organization's mission and vision are solid, it can move down to the *values*.

Values

Values guide our behaviors, decisions, and interactions by acting as criteria and directional arrows, helping determine our choices whenever we arrive at the proverbial fork in the road.

Both organizations and individuals can hold a large number of values, the most fundamental of which are called *core values*. That designation is not to be thrown around lightly; it is reserved for values that take precedence over all other considerations. *Safety* is a good example of a core value held by many organizations and individuals, as it is non-negotiable.

In practice, espousing more than two or three core values is unrealistic, because situations inevitably occur when different values point to different paths forward. In those cases, someone will have to make a decision about which core value takes precedence over the others.

Our hospital has declared its core values to be *compassion*, *safety*, and *inclusiveness*.

Strategies

The final pieces of the hierarchy to identify before we bring everything together are the *strategies*.

Strategies are broad approaches to making the vision a reality. Instead of continually making course corrections on the spur of the moment, the organization creates forward-looking strategies — both long-term and short-term — and uses them as roadmaps to move its agenda forward.

To support the part of the vision that foresees an environment where *everyone feels welcome and valued*, and consistent with its value of *inclusiveness*, our hospital has developed three broad strategies:

- a diversity strategy in Human Resources
- an accessibility strategy for the physical layout, and
- a training and awareness strategy.

Cascading Influence

Now we can examine the pieces in the Documentation Landscape as a system to see how foundational documents cascade down to the others.

Foundational documents start with *conceptual components:*

- We begin with a mandate or a mission.

- We then develop a vision, informed by the mission.

- To guide our journey to the vision, we identify some core values.

Then, we add the *practical components:*

- With our values in place, we aim towards the vision by devising a number of strategies.

- To support those strategies, we create pillars in the way of governance, infrastructure, budgets … and *policies*.

- To flesh out the details around the implementation of the policies, we develop *standards* and *procedures*.

Let's go back to Springfield to see the system in action. So far, our fictional hospital has the following documents:

Mandate (drafted by the body that created it)

To provide medical services to the people living in Springfield.

Vision (informed by the mission, setting a target)

A community where all patients receive affordable medical care promptly, our professional staff have ample opportunities for growth and education, and everyone feels welcome and valued.

Core Values (those we do not compromise on)

Safety, compassion, inclusiveness

Strategies (supporting the *everyone feels welcome and valued* part of the vision and consistent with the value of inclusiveness)

- a diversity strategy in Human Resources
- an accessibility strategy for the physical layout, and
- a training and awareness strategy.

Now we can develop *policies* to support those strategies.

Policies

In support of the diversity strategy, the hospital has approved the following authorities:

Policy on Diversity in Hiring

Policy on Diversity in Contracting

Policy on Equity and Inclusion

Policy on Respectful Workplace.

The *Policy on Diversity in Hiring* covers a number of topics around accommodating religious practices, disabilities, and neurodivergence.

Because no one will buy into the standards and procedures if they don't first buy into the policies, the hospital took pains to craft policy statements that will engender the maximum engagement. The *Policy on Diversity in Hiring* contains the following statement:

> The Chief Human Resources Officer (CHRO) has the authority to set standards and procedures around the recruitment and hiring of staff that support our commitment to be transparent, objective, and culturally sensitive.

That statement, delegating the decision-making around the technical details to the most capable SME, was drafted carefully. The wording is clear, concise, and respectful, and has the potential to bring people up to the active engagement levels on the ladder.

The CHRO stepped up to the plate, and produced a series of instruments, including:

> **Procedures on Structured Interviews**
>
> Standard on Inclusive Job Descriptions
>
> Standard on Recruitment Practices, and
>
> Procedures for Onboarding and Integration.

That first instrument establishes a number of procedures around conducting interviews in a way that's transparent, objective, and culturally aware.

Our policy suite is ready to go to work.

Changing the Discussion

Let's suppose that a problem comes to our attention: Gene, a member of the hospital's HR staff, has been interviewing prospective employees in a way that is inconsistent with the steps set out in the *Procedures on Structured Interviews*. Assume that the facts are not disputed; Gene readily admits to conducting interviews his own way.

By understanding how policies and other Internal Authorities trace back to the foundational documents, we have a fresh narrative within which to discuss both levels of engagement and situations of non-compliance.

Investigating the misalignment

We want to understand why Gene's actions diverge from our approved practice. Something somewhere is misaligned. We invite Gene to engage in a discussion.

Our goal is to find out where the misalignment is so we can target it directly. To do that, some detective work on our part is in order, starting up at the *values* level.

The procedure in question traces its origin up to the value of *inclusiveness*, so we start our investigation there and work our way down. I have mapped the hierarchy in figure 5.

Although it's highly unlikely, Gene might tell us that he doesn't believe in *inclusiveness*. That attitude is not beyond the realm of possibilities. If Gene does take that position, an appropriate response might be something like, *"That's unfortunate. You might want to consider getting a job in an organization whose values more closely align with yours."*

FOUNDATIONAL	Mandate	To provide medical services to the people living in Springfield
	Vision	A community where all patients receive affordable medical …
	Values	**Inclusiveness**
	Strategies	**Diversity Strategy in Human Resources**
INTERNAL AUTHORITIES	Policy	**Policy on Diversity in Hiring** "procedures around recruitment … that support our commitment to be transparent, objective, and culturally sensitive."
	Standards	
	Procedures	**Procedures on Structured Interviews**

Figure 5

After all, where inclusiveness is a core value, anyone who does not support it is not an asset to the organization. In practice, that situation would be rare: when an individual's core values clearly clash with an organization's values, that individual is less likely to seek or take a job there.

Let's proceed on the basis that we have the more typical situation: Gene is onside, believes in inclusiveness, and wants to work with us. That's a great common starting point, when we are all in agreement on the operative *value*.

We can then move down one level. Despite his commitment to inclusiveness, Gene might think that the HR *strategy* supporting it — in this case, the **diversity strategy** — takes us in the wrong direction. If that's Gene's position, we can now engage him in an Adult–Adult discussion about the strategy.

If the strategy is not the sticking point, we continue the investigation down one level. Perhaps Gene supports the **diversity strategy** managed by HR but doesn't think that the *Policy on Diversity in Hiring* is the right pillar to sustain it. In that case, we can entertain an Adult–Adult discussion around the *Policy*.

Finally, if it turns out that Gene supports the strategy and the Policy, but finds the prescribed *procedures* for the structured interviews to be too time-consuming or ineffective, we can have an Adult–Adult discussion about that, too.

Without this narrative as a backdrop, our discussion might be very different. It would focus on the fact that the policy says employees must conduct interviews a certain way and Gene is in breach of policy. Bad Gene. Discipline time.

By starting with common ground — values — we have a definitive starting point for our investigation. Instead of having to resort to a Parent–Child approach to rule making, we are able to conduct a mutually-beneficial discussion along the lines of *Is this the best way for us to support this value?*

When Values are Opaque

When the value underlying a policy is transparent, it's relatively easy to get people engaged. In contrast, when that value is not apparent, people end up having to guess what it is, and in many cases they guess wrong. When that happens, their failure to follow the policy is based on the rejection of the incorrectly perceived value.

Let's look at an example of a rule statement where the underlying value is opaque. I often come across a "policy" that looks something like the statement in panel 184.

Panel 184

> Dates in metadata and data fields must be entered in YYYY-MM-DD format.

Regardless of whether the document containing it has *Policy* in the title, the statement in Panel 184 is not in itself a policy statement. When we look at it closely, we can see that it is essentially a combination of two components. The first component sets a technical standard: YYYY-MM-DD. The second component seems to be a step in one or more procedures, but we don't have enough information to understand the context. Until we know more, I'm going to refer to it simply as the *date format rule*.

That rule offers little to engage people. It contains no overt clues to the underlying policy, so we have no way to understand what's driving it.

In some cases, when I ask about the driver for that rule, I've been told that the computer program in question doesn't offer a choice of date format. If that's true, then we're talking about an **external constraint**; and, as we know full well by now, an external constraint is not a policy decision and does not need internal approval.

But if the rule is not externally imposed, what's driving it? Superficially, it looks like a haphazard decision by one branch of the organization trying to control what other branches do. Or it could simply be someone's personal preference that they're now imposing on everyone else just to prove that they're in charge. What's wrong with the date format we've always used? This looks like just one more decision from some part of the organization that has no clue how our section works.

Did you see what just happened in the previous paragraph? I made all kinds of assumptions, and then I reacted negatively to those assumptions. When we guess, we often do not paint a pretty picture.

In that light, it's easy to understand how resistance to a rule builds. People follow policies when they support the values that they **perceive** are behind them. In the absence of evidence, my mind jumped immediately to the conclusion that the driving value was *control*. That conclusion put me on the defensive because, like many people, I do not like being controlled.

So how do we fix this? To replace the rule as written with a policy statement that has the potential to engage people, we follow two steps: first, **identify a positive value**, and then use it to **generate a better policy statement**.

Uncovering the value

I start all these investigations with the same question: *what is the value behind this rule?*

Determining the precise value typically requires some serious introspection by the rule makers. In my experience, they're often not really sure themselves. Had this question been posed at the time the rule was drafted, the value might have been identified and made explicit, so there would be no guesswork about it. Since that didn't happen, we have no choice but to try to reverse-engineer the thinking. So we're now trying to figure out *What positive value might have contributed to the decision to adopt this rule?*

The challenge in this exercise is to arrive at an answer that is in fact a genuine *value*. Often, the people behind a rule will cite a "value" that actually doesn't hold water. They're not trying to mislead anyone; they're simply not consciously aware of what's really driving the rule at its core.

This is one of those cases. When I ask people to name the value behind the rule in panel 184, the response offered is typically either *standardization* or *consistency*.

Values vs methodologies

Both *standardization* and *consistency* are good approaches for an organization to take. The problem is that these are **not** *core values*, at least as far as most organizations are concerned. They both are merely *methodologies* or *strategies* used to achieve the core values.

This distinction is critical. *Standardization* as a core value, for example, looks strikingly different. Consider Adrian Monk, the fictional detective in a US-based television series that originally aired about twenty years back. Detective Monk suffers from obsessive-compulsive disorder and a number of phobias. In the weekly stories, it is exactly that neurodivergent approach to crime scenes that supports his unusual ability to solve cases.

For Detective Monk, *standardization* may actually be a core value. If five glasses of water are set on a table, they all need to be filled to exactly the same level. It's irrelevant to him whether that level is good or bad, right or wrong, useful or useless; what's important is that the level of all five glasses be consistent. Any instances of deviation from a standard disturb him. In his case, *standardization* is truly not a means but an end.

If *standardization* itself were really a core value for organizations, they would be loath to compromise on it. They would standardize every aspect of their operations, from furniture and dress codes to activities and conversations. They would proudly declare: *We do not compromise on standardization.*

Most organizations don't operate that way. They don't adopt *standardization* for its own sake; instead, they turn to it when they project that it will bring them another benefit. For example, an organization might standardize computer hardware to achieve *interoperability*, or perhaps to benefit from an *economy* of scale for purchase or maintenance. On a different plane, it might standardize hiring practices to achieve procedural *fairness*, or fix correspondence templates to achieve a uniformity of *branding*. In those cases the real values driving the rules are related to interoperability, economy, fairness, or branding. Although it might be a visible manifestation of the core value, *standardization* per se is simply a strategy for most organizations.

Back to our date format rule. It doesn't fit in any of the situations just described. Standardizing the date format does not promote interoperability, economy, fairness, or branding.

So what's driving it?

Digging deeper

In this case, standardizing the date format was likely intended to improve the *accuracy* of information. The organization has several strategies to support *accuracy*, and one of them revolves around information standards.

That explanation is defensible. It's not unreasonable to think that an organization would set accuracy as a core value, especially if the integrity of information is vital to the success of their business.

We can **test the validity of a claim that something is a core value** by asking whether there are any occasions when the organization is prepared to compromise on accuracy. Being resolute to a position is a feature of a core value. The answer in this case is that a hospital is unlikely to compromise on *accuracy* when it comes to information. In contrast, *standardization* would seem to be context-specific. The hospital is unlikely to insist on standardizing something that negatively affects the accuracy of information.

Our answer is bolstered when we look at how individuals treat that value. If an organization claims *accuracy* as a core value but doesn't take care to ensure that dates are accurately recorded, its credibility is tarnished. Deliberately keeping inaccurate information feels dishonest, so employees are likely to leave. That personal commitment to *accuracy* tells us that it is a core value.

That kind of commitment is unlikely to occur based on *standardization*. If the organization professes *standardization* as a core value but in fact doesn't standardize the date format, will people be motivated to leave? Unlikely. They might grumble and be unhappy, but *standardization* just isn't revered enough by most people — apart from Detective Monk—to justify leaving an organization.

Connecting core values

Now we have a challenge: although it seems to be the core value motivating the *date format rule*, *accuracy* is not on the menu. The hospital's core values are *safety*, *compassion*, and *inclusiveness*. To complete this chain, we need to connect *accuracy* with one of those values.

The most obvious choice is *safety*. It's reasonable to think that an organization would commit never to compromise on safety. When an organization professes to be safe but in reality isn't, people will leave. *Safety* passes all the core value tests. In addition, associating *accuracy* with *safety* is not a far stretch: it's relatively easy to see how emphasizing the accuracy of information can support safety efforts in a hospital setting.

Crafting the policy

Now that we have identified the core values — *safety*, supported by *accuracy*, and the governing strategy — *standardization*, we are in a position to craft a policy statement to address the date format. We're looking to formulate a policy that people can positively cooperate with, commit to, and perhaps even champion. **The policy statement serves as a bridge connecting the imposition of a standard with the foundational pieces above it.**

One possibility is the simple statement in panel 185.

Panel 185

> We use a standard format for all dates across the organization.

We can now trace a direct line from the YYYY-MM-DD requirement in the Standard up through this policy, through the strategy, all the way up to the core value at the top. By making this connection, we can leverage people's buy-in to the value as a tool to increase engagement in the policy.

Reframing Non-compliance

Resistance to a policy can be a sign that an individual is favoring their own values over those of the rule maker.

The non-compliant employee has core values, too, and they are just as valid. Values like *excellence*, *peace of mind*, *enjoyment*, and similar self-preserving values help us get through the day in one piece.

Moreover, the value that underlies psychological reactance is just as powerful a motivator as values like *safety* and *compassion*. Wanting to *do it my way* is an expression of the value of *independence* — a perfectly solid value that can produce many positive outcomes in people's lives.

An individual or group's non-compliance with organizational rules can often be traced to a conflict between their own values and those of the organization.

The "why"

I've often heard it said that employees will not comply with a policy unless they understand the *why* behind it. That statement may be true, but it doesn't tell us which *why* they're looking for.

Some people interpret *why* to mean *Where does that rule come from?* or *What happens if I don't follow the rule?* That interpretation is a possibility, but often when someone insists on hearing the *why* behind a rule, they're not necessarily asking about the source or the punishment or the risks of non-compliance.

In many cases, *why* is actually posing a deeper question, along the lines of *Why should I be guided by your value instead of my value?*

The answer to this question is one that can make or break compliance. An ineffective answer is something like *Because I said so*. A better answer would be along the lines that the value behind the policy supports the *mission* and *vision*, whereas the individual's personal values don't necessarily do that. We're basically showing that the rule is consistent with a larger view, and connected to the big picture.

That argument can be sound, though, only if the core values claimed by the organization actually support its mission and vision. If the values are disconnected from the highest foundational documents of the organization, they can't help us increase engagement.

Lead with the Values

Because values have the power to engage and motivate, they are excellent tools to use for priming people to change. By starting off with common values, we establish parameters for what comes next.

Priming

Priming is a technique to support persuasion.[25]

A study undertaken in a supermarket illustrates the point well: In part 1 of the study, someone stood holding a cheese tray and stopped passersby to ask if they'd like to try a sample. The majority of people declined.

In part 2, the same person holding the same tray of cheese first asked passersby whether they considered themselves to be adventurous. To that question, the majority of people answered yes, and only then were they offered the cheese. There were far more takers this time than in part 1.

---

[25] The notion of priming comes from Robert B. Cialdini's book *Pre-suasion: A Revolutionary Way to Influence and Persuade.*

No one likes having to make a decision without warning, or to feel rushed. If we want the approval process to be smooth, it helps to lay the foundation early: shop around goals, concepts, values, and principles supporting the statements we plan to put before them in the policy. Once those waves have made their splash and then died down, we can expect smoother sailing.

A practical example

This book, for one, is a good practical example.

In part III of the book, I present a variety of drafting techniques for your consideration. To prepare you for those techniques, I needed to do a bit of priming.

I realize that I'm introducing concepts and approaches that are completely at odds with what many people believe. Had I presented those techniques up front, they might have landed with a heavy thud. To avoid that, I needed to bring us all together first, helping people to be receptive to new material.

Two values underlie the approach of this book: *clarity* and *respect*. I started talking about clear and respectful rules as far back as the Introduction, and I reinforced those values as the text progressed. If you stayed with the book, it's because those values resonate with you. That resonance is possibly what has kept you reading the other chapters.

By establishing common ground through shared values, we open the door to collaboration.

Priming the approvers

Values are also useful tools to reach for when preparing policies for submission for approval.

For a long time I witnessed the frustration of policy drafters who spent countless hours preparing a submission for approval, only to have it turned away for some reason. Not necessarily rejected — just sent back for revision. Somebody didn't like some statement or understand some issue, and so approval was delayed.

The approach to document organization and to drafting statements covered in parts II and III of this book can help the approval process run more smoothly. Those techniques eliminate a number of common stumbling blocks that tend to hold up policy approval. But another tool can be used to grease the process: priming.

Instead of giving the policy approvers a set of documents to discuss, start with the values. A few months before we expect to have our draft ready, go to the approvers and ask for approval on the values that underlie that policy we're going to be proposing.

If the approvers don't like those values, we'll know up front, before we put too much work into the document. Before making the pitch again, we'll need to find values that are acceptable to the approvers.

Once the approvers agree that we're working with the correct values, we've crossed a major hurdle. When we return later with the proposed policy, we can lead off by recapping the discussion around the values — which have already been approved. Once the values are confirmed, the approver is primed, much more open to tasting whatever we're offering on the tray.

Obviously, I can't promise that every policy we propose will be approved. But I can promise that we'll always have a common ground for collaborative discussion.

Postscript

Change is constant.

Rapidly evolving workforce demographics adds another layer of complexity. The reaction of the generation of Millennials, known for valuing respect and open communication, is markedly different in comparison to previous generations. Their influence necessitates major adaptations in our approach to employee and customer engagement, which will inevitably be reflected in our policies.

Language, too, is in a constant state of evolution. Wording once considered polite can become quaint and stiff before we realize it. Choosing good wording is even harder when trying to find the right balance between formal and casual language, since those factors vary by industry and geography as well as by culture and generation.

Clearly, our policies both reflect and influence our organizational culture. A culture that values open communication, respect, and collaboration will naturally foster policies that embody these principles. As we look toward the future, it's essential for policy makers to remain open to change, to listen actively, and to approach policy development with a balance of firmness and understanding.

This book, too, will age. When that happens, I encourage future readers to take the advice given bearing in mind the context of the times when it was written, tailoring the application of the principles to the evolving landscape of their organizations.

Some things come and go, while others are less transient. We know of at least one truth that's timeless: **courtesy and respect will never go out of style.**

Examples of Statements for a
GENERAL POLICY

The following provisions apply to statements contained in Policies, Standards, and Procedures in the absence of a specific indication to the contrary.

1. The primary interpretation of abbreviations is determined by the official corporate List of Abbreviations.

2. Incidents of non-compliance with policy requirements are handled as disciplinary matters, following the Procedures established by the Human Resources Branch.

3. An individual's direct supervisor is the initial point of inquiry around interpretation on a statement in a policy instrument.

4. Holidays includes statutory and indigenous holidays recognized in the region where the office is located.

5. When a time period is measured in days, the end date is calculated using business, not calendar, days. When a time period is measured in weeks, months, or years, the end date is calculated using calendar weeks, months or years.

6. References to furniture and equipment denote corporately-owned assets. References to bank accounts, computer accounts, and online services denote accounts opened in the name of the organization.

CLEAN DESK POLICY (SAMPLE)

Approved by: Vice-President, Corporate Affairs
on March 1, 2020
Next review date: March 2028

This policy clarifies the requirements around office tidiness and security.

Interpretation

In this policy,

> "employees" includes contractors and students, and

> "supervisor" includes the main point of contact for a contractor.

Requirements

1. Employees are entitled to leave work for the day once their work areas conform to the *Clean Desk Standard*.

2. The responsibility for explaining that Standard to employees rests with their supervisors.

3. The Director of Security has the authority to grant exemptions to this policy for a period of up to one week.

4. The General Facilities Committee is authorized to amend the Standard as it deems appropriate. Amendments take effect 10 business days following their publication.

5. (a) After an employee has left for the day, Security Officers have the authority to collect any documents from the employee's workspace that they find left out in the open.

(b) The Director of Security is authorized to establish a procedure for the retrieval of those documents by the employee entitled to them.

6. This policy is effective immediately.

Inquiries

Inquiries arising out of this policy are handled by the Security Office.

Ce document est disponible en français sous le titre
« Politique en matière de rangement du bureau ».

Last updated February 24, 2024
Intranet/policies/cleandesk.html

OTHER PUBLICATIONS BY THE AUTHOR

Unlocking the Golden Handcuffs: Leaving the Public Service for Work You Really Love

These Words Go Together, a reference guide to well-formed phrases in contemporary business English, 4th Edition

The Canadian Lawyer's Internet Guide, 4th Edition

Technology in Practice, A guide to managing computers in the law office, 2nd Edition

ABOUT THE AUTHOR

Through workshops and speaking engagements, Lewis helps organizations take the pain out of policy drafting.

He brings a unique set of skills to this discipline. After obtaining an Honours BA in Linguistics, Lewis graduated from University of Toronto Law School and practiced law for a few years.

In 1986 he moved into the area of law office technology management, a field still in its infancy at the time. He worked with a variety of for-profit and not-for-profit organizations, gaining extensive experience in the corporate support function.

He worked for 17 years in the Government of Canada, spending the last several years specializing in developing administrative policies, mostly for the Information Management and Web Content Management support functions. He has written several books and dozens of articles for journals and newspapers, and speaks frequently at venues around the world.

He is an avid fitness enthusiast and gardener, currently based in Ottawa, Canada.

www.ingramcontent.com/pod-product-compliance
Lightning Source LLC
Chambersburg PA
CBHW071317210326
41597CB00015B/1252